# THE NEW LEADERSHIP

# *MANAGING PARTICIPATION IN ORGANIZATIONS*

**Victor H. Vroom**   YALE UNIVERSITY

**Arthur G. Jago**   UNIVERSITY OF HOUSTON

Prentice Hall, *Englewood Cliffs, New Jersey 07632*

LIBRARY OF CONGRESS
*Library of Congress Cataloging-in-Publication Data*

VROOM, VICTOR HAROLD, 1932
  The new leadership: Managing participation in organizations
Victor H. Vroom and Arthur G. Jago
    p. cm.
  Bibliography: p.
  Includes index.
  ISBN 0-13-615030-6
  1. Management—Employee participation. 2. Decision making, Group.
I. Jago, Arthur G., 1949.  II. Title.
HD5650.V76 1988        658.3'152—dc 19        87-28092

Editorial/production supervision and
interior design: Carole Brown
Jacket design: Ben Santora
Manufacturing buyer: Raymond Keating

**The following are trademarks employed in this work: IBM
and IBM PC are trademarks of International Business
Machines Corporation. COMPAQ is a registered trademark
of COMPAQ Computer Corporation. Apple is a registered
trademark of Apple Computer, Inc. Managing Participation
in Organizations and MPO are trademarks of Leadership
Software, Inc.**

Printed in the United States of America
10  9  8  7  6  5  4  3

ISBN 0-13-615030-6    01

Prentice-Hall International (UK) Limited, *London*
Prentice-Hall of Australia Pty. Limited, *Sydney*
Prentice-Hall Canada Inc., *Toronto*
Prentice-Hall Hispanoamericana, S.A., *Mexico*
Prentice-Hall of India Private Limited, *New Delhi*
Prentice-Hall of Japan, Inc., *Tokyo*
Simon & Schuster Asia Pte. Ltd., *Singapore*
Editora Prentice-Hall do Brasil, Ltda., *Rio de Janeiro*

# CONTENTS

*CHAPTER TEN*

# MOTIVATIONAL OUTCOMES IN DECISION MAKING:
*Subordinate Commitment* **136**

*CHAPTER ELEVEN*

# PARTICIPATION and HUMAN CAPITAL　**146**

*CHAPTER TWELVE*

# APPLYING the NEW MODEL:
*Putting It All Together* **160**

*CHAPTER THIRTEEN*

## USING the MODELS in DEVELOPING MANAGERS and ORGANIZATIONS    189

# FOREWORD

Leadership. Surely here is a subject over which philosophers, politicians, behavioral scientists, ministers, boy scout leaders, management consultants—you name it—have flown more than a few sorties. There seems to be an omnipresent interest in the subject and an ever-ready supply of commentators prepared to drop whatever wisdom they possess on the unsuspecting victim.

Fortunately, Vic Vroom and Art Jago have written a book that is destined to illuminate the tricky, shifting, leadership terrain. They very wisely eschew any attempt at a grand theory of leadership and instead take aim at those aspects of the issue relating to power sharing by leaders and to participation and influence by those who work with them. Given the deep concerns these days for participation in the workplace, this focus rivets the book squarely on *the* contemporary leadership challenge.

In approaching the subject, there is a refreshing absence of the typical bromides about democracy and worker involvement that frequently accompany books on leadership. There is also no attempt to foist the "one best leadership style" on the unenlightened reader.

Not that the authors strip themselves of all the presuppositions that would gain them entry to the Baconian inductive school. They propose, after all, a prescriptive or normative model of participation that describes how managers should behave in different situations. But the model is *situational* in nature. It specifies when and where different levels of participation are likely to be most effective. Depending on the specific situation, various forms and degrees of participation in decision making are likely to be highly effective—or disastrous.

The five "processes" that Vic Vroom and Phil Yetton discussed in their pioneering work *Leadership and Decision Making* are reinforced by Vic Vroom and Art Jago's latest work. These processes are really increments on the continuum of participation or power sharing. Effective leadership remains an exercise in understanding the requirements of a situation, how much participation is essential for success and what form that participation should take.

The original Vroom-Yetton leadership model has been of enormous significance both in the academic community and in business and government organizational settings. I personally can vouch for its effect on the latter. In Kepner-Tregoe's training and consulting efforts, it has helped managers from Detroit, Michigan, to Hjo, Sweden, cope with the challenges of participation in the workplace. We have seen real and lasting change in decision-making behavior.

The latest empirical research conducted by Vic Vroom and Art Jago and described in their book reaffirms the basic validity of the original model and extends its implications. Their research enhances the original model by adding greater predictive power to it and by making it applicable to a wider range of situations.

*The New Leadership* will be of great interest to both academicians and managers. The rigorous analysis should satisfy the most technically minded. But others should not be intimidated. The bulk of the discussion is easy to understand, there is a rich source of practical insight in the conclusions, and the case material brings the model to life.

Beyond their contribution to understanding the underlying dynamic of the decision-making process, the authors provide a framework—and a language—for managers and workers to talk intelligently and accurately about the tough issue of participation. That alone makes this book a giant step forward in the art and practice of management.

*Benjamin B. Tregoe*, Chairman
*KEPNER-TREGOE, INC.*
*Princeton, New Jersey*

# ACKNOWLEDGMENTS

It is only fitting that a book that discusses the role of collaboration and teamwork in organizations should itself be the result of a collaborative effort. It is almost as hard for each of us to know who wrote the words on the pages that follow as it is to know which one of us first generated the ideas expressed on those pages. Despite our own "geographical dispersion" we have maintained a high level of interaction. Some of our interaction has occurred on those rare occasions when we have been able to spend a few days together in Houston, New Haven, or New York. Due to crowded and conflicting schedules, these meetings have been less frequent than either of us would have preferred, and most of our communication has occurred via telephone or computer network. In all of these modes we have argued, played devil's advocate, and challenged one another's ideas until the product was one in which both of us took pride.

Along the way we have incurred many debts. First and foremost we must thank Ann Vroom and Janet Jago, who provided the "space" and the emotional support required for us to do our work. In addition, both jumped in, when necessary, to comment honestly on crude first drafts of sections presented to them in no particular order and in handwritten form that was often indecipherable.

In addition, we owe a great debt to Sandy McDade, Jim Ragan, and three anonymous reviewers. All read the entire manuscript and cared enough about the importance of the endeavor to confront us with their concerns both major and minor. If the book is readable, it is due to their prodding. If it is not, it is a reflection of the authors' resistance to change.

Pradeep Gupta was the first to suggest the possibility of representing the rules in the Vroom-Yetton model as mathematical functions. Jeffrey Vroom wrote the computer program that produced the individual leadership analyses, the results of which are shown in Chapter 13; Brian Dooling provided valuable technical support in translating this program from its Apple format to an IBM format. We are also grateful to Karen Donegan, who drew endless decision trees and whose wizardry at the word processor made the typing of the manuscript seem much easier than it must have been.

Finally, we would like to express our thanks to our respective institutions, Yale University and the University of Houston, for providing not only technical support but also a climate conducive to scholarship.

*Victor H. Vroom*

*Arthur G. Jago*

# Chapter One

# INTRODUCTION

Several years ago, one of the authors attended an academic symposium and presented a paper that described an early version of the model to be discussed in this book. The model attempted to specify the forms and degrees of employee participation available to a manager and how that person might tailor an approach to a problem based upon an analysis of the circumstance encountered. Autocratic decision making was described as appropriate for some situations; more participative approaches, including group decision making, were described as appropriate for other situations. A central theme was that situational demands determined the effectiveness—and therefore the advisability—of autocratic or more democratic approaches to organizational problems.

As is the custom at scholarly meetings, a member of the symposium had been assigned to critique the paper and highlight its strengths and weaknesses. In that role was an eminent social scientist who, after a very thoughtful and constructive critique, proposed an alternative model of participation for the audience's consideration. In his alternative model, consensus group decision making was recommended for *all* organizational situations.

The author bristled and began preparing a vigorous rebuttal. The rebuttal was to include such examples as the football quarterback who tried to employ group decision making in the huddle and kept running down the 30-second clock. This defense of the model proved to be unnecessary, however, when the critic added that his advocacy of democratic decision making was based not on the fact that it would work best, but rather on his belief that it was morally right!

A few years later the same author was delivering an academic colloquium on the model at the psychology department of a major university. After the presentation, a professor of clinical psychology proposed that instead of urging leaders to behave in a manner that was consistent with a particular situation, we should be encouraging people to be true to their natural inclinations: An autocratic manager should be encouraged to be autocratic and the participative manager to be participative.

Both of the positions taken by the two critics are defensible. Each emphasizes a different set of values relevant to participation. The first views participation as a moral issue, indeed a moral imperative. Participation is a goal to be sought in its own right because it is good and just. It need not be justified in terms of pragmatism.

Each of us should be able to feel some appreciation for this position. We value democracy in government not because of its efficiency but because it legitimizes people's rights to influence decisions that have profound effects on them. For similar reasons we oppose totalitarianism in the Soviet Union and in Latin America and apartheid in South Africa.

Many social scientists have commented on the diffusion of the democratic value from political institutions into the family, into education, and even into the profit-maximizing world of business. We have heard many managers report their belief that "it is good to be participative and bad to be autocratic."

Our second critic stressed a different set of values, which we think of as existential. One should seek not participation but rather authenticity. Participation may be either good or bad depending on the true nature of the leader. "Be true to thyself" applies equally to the involvement of others in decision making as it does to different facets of human relationships.

Although we can understand and appreciate these positions, our own approach differs from both. Participation will be recommended not because it is right or because it is expressive of humanity's essential decency toward others. In all of our models, degrees of participation will be evaluated in terms of their contributions to the goal of effective performance, not as ends in themselves. Our work does reflect values, but these values favor effective organizations and rational decision making. Under some circumstances participation provides a means to these valued ends, but we do not promote it as an end in and of itself or as a device for authentic self-expression.

This is not to say that our two critics are wrong or even misguided. Values can be attacked in terms of their clarity or their consistency but not by reason of cause and effect. We are grateful that both were able to make explicit their value premises, and the clarity with which they have done so makes it easier for us to see and to express the implicit value premises in our own work. We have less sympathy for behavioral scientists who have confused their science with their personal values and have disguised those values in the form of prescriptions for managerial effectiveness.

Our pragmatism has naturally led us to a contingency or situational approach. Wholesale recommendations of participation or across-the-board condemnations of autocratic decision making suggest to us that broadly based values are operating. Viewing degrees of participation in terms of their instrumentality for organizationally valued ends inevitably forces the conclusion that the nature of the situation must be considered in predicting the consequences of leadership acts.

Simple nostrums, such as 9–9 Leadership (Blake & Mouton, 1974) or Theory Y (McGregor, 1960), are inadequate to deal with the nuances and complexities in situational demands. Perhaps the ups and downs in the romance with participative decision making, which we shall outline in Chapter 2, can be attributed to unrealistic expectations created by a noncontingency view of participative management.

Our belief in the necessity of a contingency model has inevitably guided our work in an analytic direction. We have had to identify the situational variables, their role in the process, and then integrate this into sensible models. The models are more complex than anything that has preceded them. Rightly or wrongly, our analytical approach to the management of participation in organizations has produced a model of sufficient sophistication to qualify as a computer-based "expert system."

In so doing, our work has taken on some of the "coloration" of the algorithms found in operations research and in many of the functional areas of management. This makes our models stand in sharp contrast to a more common perception of behavioral science in management as being by nature "touchy-feely." In the latter view, thinking takes second place to emotion, concepts are few and far between, and equations virtually nonexistent.

Our models defy that stereotype by applying methods associated with one domain to another having different long-standing traditions. The territory that we seek to understand clearly lies in the province of the behavioral sciences. However, the maps that will guide our exploration include decision trees, simultaneous equations, and computer simulations historically associated with the province of management science.

This book was written with three distinct audiences in mind. The first is managers—both present and aspiring—who share our impatience with exhortations to embrace the latest management fad and who seek to better tailor their management styles to the requirements of the situation. Many of this group may have been exposed to some of the concepts of the original Vroom-Yetton model in a class, seminar, or workshop; they will find in the pages that follow a way of exploring them in greater depth. To managers, we recommend that you carefully read the next three chapters (2 through 4). These chapters will put the issue of participation in a historical context, discuss the criteria by which it can be evaluated, and introduce a language to be used throughout the book for describing degrees of participation.

The manager then has a choice. Chapter 5 examines more recent "history" by describing what has become known in the literature as the Vroom-Yetton model. First introduced 15 years ago, it has been widely cited and taught. Alternatively, the manager could skip to Chapter 8, which describes a new model that has arisen since that earlier model's introduction. This new model is both more complex and more valid than its predecessor. The description of this model continues through Chapter 12.

The second audience consists of our colleagues and future colleagues in the fields of organizational behavior and organizational psychology. We expect that this group will be more interested in our summaries of research and in some new studies never before published. We also hope that many scholars will be intrigued by new concepts, approaches, and hypotheses, and will find the book a source of fresh research ideas that will ultimately help to establish a firmer foundation for our scholarly discipline.

We think that the academic audience will find greatest interest in Chapters 6 and 7. These chapters summarize what we have learned from studying the management styles of many thousands of managers. Here, we also summarize the empirical evidence concerning the validity of the Vroom-Yetton model. In addition, we encourage our academic colleagues to read the chapters (8 through 12) that describe the new model, and we urge you to join us in finding ways to test these ideas so that ultimately an even better model can be developed. We believe our model and the cause–effect relationships on which it is built to be consistent with our existing knowledge. However, we would be guilty of gross misrepresentation if we did not acknowledge that the relationships are complex and our science is far from mature.

The third audience is the set of professionals who practice the art and science of executive education and organization development. Many of this group will already be familiar with the Vroom-Yetton model, and some will have had firsthand experience in training managers in its use. In addition to the next three introductory chapters, this group should benefit from Chapter 6, which identifies areas in which the Vroom-Yetton model can be improved, and Chapters 8 through 12, which describe the new model we propose to replace it with. Of greatest interest to this group may be Chapter 13, devoted to a training methodology for making these ideas "come alive" for managers.

# CHAPTER TWO

# A HISTORICAL PERSPECTIVE

Ed Philips fidgeted nervously with his pencil. The phone call that he had just received from his division manager meant that he had less time than he had thought to figure out a solution to the production problem in his plant.

As part of a continuing struggle to reduce costs to meet the ever-present challenge presented by foreign competition, he had installed new machines that were highly touted by corporate technical people. He had expected some initial problems as the employees learned to make the most of the new technology. However no one had expected productivity to drop steadily to a level that, now, six months after the machines were put "on line," was only 70 percent of the previous level. In addition to the decrement in quantity of production, quality had fallen off and the number of employee separations had risen.

Philips is quite confident that there is nothing wrong with the new machines. He has had reports from other companies using the machines, and they confirm this opinion. Representatives from the firm that built the machines have inspected them and report that they are operating at peak efficiency.

As manufacturing manager, the decision about what to do next is up to Philips. His four first-line supervisors and his supply manager share his concern that the problem is severe and getting worse, but they appear puzzled about what to do and, in casual discussion, have offered very different ideas about the next steps that should be taken.

Until the phone call from his division manager he had been hoping that time would solve the problem or at least indicate more clearly what course should be followed. Now his boss has told him that he would like to have a report within a week on the steps that Philips plans to take.

The challenge facing Ed Philips can be viewed from two perspectives. Ultimately he has the task of figuring out a plan. This involves difficult judgments about what the cause of the problem really is, what alternative solutions exist for solving problems such as this one, and judgments of the relative merits of the alternative solutions.

This perspective on Ed Philips's challenge causes us to focus on cognitive activities—on defining problems, generating alternatives, and decision making—that must occur prior to the development of the plan. The relevant concepts involve ways of thinking about production systems. Of potential assistance are the algorithms or heuristics of the management scientist for aiding people in such things as problem analysis and decision analysis.

But there is an alternative approach that can be taken to Ed Philips's challenge. He also has the task of selecting a process by which a plan can be devised. Here our focus is on events that occur between people—social events rather than cognitive events—and on their possible contribution to the development of a sound plan. Who should Ed Philips talk to in coming up with a solution? How much should he share about the problem with those who work for him? Should he call a group meeting? If he opts for a group meeting, should he play the role of decisionmaker or of chairman?

This second focus is the one that we will adopt in this book. The underlying processes are participation in decision making or, to put it more broadly, the issue of the most appropriate style of leadership. In selecting this for our focus we are not negating the value of the first perspective. We view the cognitive and social aspects of organizational decision making as complementary.

Ed Philips's challenge is but one of thousands that he will face during his managerial career. Each day managers in organizations of all kinds—public, private, and not-for-profit—are faced with deciding "how to decide." Should they encourage the participation of others in the decisions they are called upon to make and the problems they must solve? If so, who should participate? In what way and to what degree?

Managers may not always be conscious of the choices that they make. Particularly among those who have been managing for some time, choices about who to involve and when to involve them can become automatic or implicit. They result from habits or routines acquired over the years. Nonetheless the opportunity for choice still exists and, we shall argue, will have important consequences for the manager, his or her subordinates, and for the organization of which the manager is a part.

## AN AGELESS ISSUE

The topics that we address in this book—participation in decision making and leadership styles—are indeed contemporary ones. The highly publicized General Motors Saturn project is but one of about two hundred new design plants that are experimenting with wide-scale, comprehensive programs of employee participation in decision making.

While the questions to be explored are contemporary, they also have a timeless quality. For centuries practitioners and observers of leadership have concerned themselves with appropriate forms and degrees of participation. Let us illustrate the enduring nature of the debate concerning participation by taking a brief trip back through time to see how the issues with which we shall deal have been regarded at a few selected points in recorded history.

We begin our journey in the year A.D. 529 with the Benedictine Rule written by St. Benedict for the guidance of abbots in selecting appropriate leadership styles to use in monasteries:

> As often as any important business has to be done in the monastery, let the abbot call together the whole community and himself set forth the matter. And, having heard the counsel of the brethren, let him take counsel with himself and then do what he shall judge to be most expedient. Now the reason why we have said that all should be called to council, is that God often reveals what is better to the younger. Let the brethren give their advice with all deference and humility, nor venture to defend their opinions obstinately; but let the decision depend rather on the abbot's judgment, so that when he has decided what is the better course, all may obey. (1952, p. 25)

The advice provided by St. Benedict was consultation in a group that includes the entire community. But in a latter passage, St. Benedict recognized that the process to be used may depend on the issue to be decided: "But if the business to be done in the interests of the monastery be of lesser importance, let him use the advice of the seniors only."

A thousand years after St. Benedict addressed the leadership styles of abbots, Machiavelli addressed the same kind of issue—the social processes to be invoked in decision making—when he provided the following advice to ambitious rulers:

> For there is no other way to guard oneself from flatterers than by letting men know that you will not be offended by being told the truth; but when everyone is able to tell you the truth, you lose their respect. Therefore a wise prince should adopt a third means, choosing wise men for his state, and only to those should he allow the freedom to speak truthfully to him, and only concerning those about which he asks, nothing else. But he

should ask them about everything, and listen to their opinions, and afterward deliberate by himself, in his own way; and with these councils and with each one of his advisors he should act in such a way that everyone may see that the more freely he speaks, all the more he will be acceptable; aside from these he should not want to hear any others, he should carry through what was decided and be firm in his decisions. (1964, p. 199)

Machiavelli shares with St. Benedict an emphasis on the importance of consultation prior to decision making. He is less explicit, however, on the nature of the forum within which the consultation should occur. While the leader is counseled to consult only with "wise men," it is unclear whether they should be consulted individually or in a group.

In passing, we should note that it is St. Benedict, not Machiavelli, who stresses the necessity of varying the approach with the nature of the issue to be decided. More than fourteen hundred years later this point of view came to be more formally known as "contingency theory"—a subject to which we will return later.

## THE ERA OF THE CRAFTSMAN

Ideas about the appropriateness of participation in modern organizations have evolved and continue to evolve. We have come a long way from the pronouncements of St. Benedict and Machiavelli to current theories on participative management, semiautonomous work groups, self-managing work groups, and quality-control circles. The course has not been an even one. Our conception of the appropriate division of labor between workers and management and the extent to which the former should be encouraged to participate in managerial decision making has changed markedly throughout recorded history. Many managers would be shocked to learn that just about a century ago many workers had far more control and influence than they have today. The prevailing issue in the journals of that time was not the nourishment of participative management but rather the reestablishment of management authority.

The later part of the nineteenth century was the era of the craftsman. Iron molders, glass blowers, mule spinners, typographers, and puddlers were just a few of the craftsmen that "did the work" of American industry. The jobs which they carried out would have scored very high on a contemporary measure of job enrichment. These workers were highly skilled, and their learning had come not from books but from arduous years of apprenticeship. They typically hired and fired their own helpers, whom they paid out of their earnings.

Collectively these craftsmen exerted even more influence. Montgomery (1979) provides us with a description of the iron rollers of the Columbus Iron Works in Ohio in the mid-1870s:

The three twelve-man rolling teams, which constituted the union, negotiated a single tonnage rate with the company for each specific rolling job the company undertook. The workers then decided collectively, among themselves, what portion of that rate should go to each of them (and the shares were far from equal, ranging from 19 ¼ cents, out of the negotiated $1.13 a ton, for the roller, to 5 cents for the runout hooker); how work should be allocated among them; how many rounds on the rolls should be undertaken per day; what special arrangements should be made for the fiercely hot labors of the hookers during the summer; and how members should be hired and progress through the various ranks of the gang. To put it another way, all the boss did was buy the equipment and raw materials and sell the finished product. (pp. 11–12)

In many industries the autonomous craftsman hired whole teams of helpers, and the practice of inside contracting evolved. A craftsman might have forty helpers all of whom he hired and trained. He unilaterally determined their job assignments and had the capacity to fire them without recourse to any rules.

The craftsman-contractor was often more highly paid and possessed a degree of control vastly exceeding that of many higher-level managers in modern corporations. This power was reflected in enhanced status within the community. As Williamson notes:

A contractor would hire those who lived near his own home, and in many cases the names of half a dozen of his own relatives were on the payroll. For this reason, a large contractor was an important figure in his neighborhood. It was not at all unusual for a youngster who wished to become an apprentice to a contractor to mow the latter's lawn and do all sorts of odd jobs for the privilege. (1952, p. 91)

Inside contracting was a dominant organizational form during the latter part of the nineteenth century, particularly in high-technology industries. Waltham Watch, Singer Sewing Machine, Pratt and Whitney, Baldwin Locomotive, and the Winchester Repeating Arms Company are among the companies studied by historians for which inside contracting accounted for a major part of the total payroll.

Contracting, however, came under fire from many sources. From the standpoint of management, the contractors made a lot more money than would the foremen who would ultimately replace them (Clauson, 1980). From the standpoint of workers, the contracting system merely substituted one group of entrepreneurs for another. These entrepreneurs wore blue collars, came from the ranks of labor rather than the elite, and, perhaps of greatest importance, were working on behalf of their own interests rather than the interests of management. However, the costs were continued exploitation of the vast majority of workers and the obscuring of the lines between employers and employees in the workplace.

The trade union movement began to increase in strength in the 1890s and sought to regulate the behavior of members. Montgomery (1979) cites the sixty-six rules for working contained in the bylaws of the window-glass workers. They included the stipulation that full crews had to be present at each pot setting; that blowers and gatherers should not work faster than at the rate of nine rollers per hour; that no work was to be performed on Thanksgiving Day, Christmas, Decoration Day, or Washington's Birthday; and that no work would be performed between June 15 and September 15.

Frequently such rules prohibited piecework and the employment of helpers. The rules, viewed as securing the group welfare of workers, were typically not negotiated with the employer. Rather they were passed unilaterally by local unions or by the delegates at a national convention. Members who were asked to do anything that would violate rules of their union were instructed to refuse and, if pressured, to pack their toolboxes and walk out.

The reader should note the adversarial and defensive posture of the rules adopted. They rest on a perceived cleavage between the interest of management and workers. The rationale underlying the rules was not increasing return on invested capital, or increasing the quality or quantity of the products produced, but was rather protecting the security of the workers. The processes were participative, but the shared goals of those participating were antagonistic to those of management.

## SCIENTIFIC MANAGEMENT

The worker control that characterized much of American industry during the latter part of the nineteenth century presented a critical problem for the owners and managers of that time. The hero—from their standpoint—was Frederick Winslow Taylor, whose first book, *Scientific Management*, was published in 1911.

For Taylor the principal problem did not lie in workers' lack of knowledge and ability but rather in the lack of knowledge possessed by their managers:

> And yet these foremen and superintendents know, better than anyone else, that their own knowledge and personal skill falls short of the combined knowledge and dexterity of all the workmen under them. The most experienced managers therefore frankly place before their workmen the problem of doing the work in the best and most economical way. (1911, pp. 32–33)

The problem that preoccupied Taylor was the workers' abuses of the control that they had been given. In the pursuit of their own self-interest, workers restricted output, concealed from management how fast jobs could really be done, and saw that they and those that followed them did jobs no faster than they had been done in the past. The "dragon" that Taylor sought to slay was loafing and soldiering by workers.

The essence of Taylor's "scientific management" was the replacement of workers' control by a management that gave the orders, directed the work, and monitored the results of that work. Much has been written about the specifics of Taylor's methods, or Taylorism, so we can be brief here. First and foremost was a reaffirmation of Adam Smith's principle of division of labor. To reestablish management control, tasks had to be simplified, with the one best way of doing each job determined by the methodology of motion study. Consequently "brain power" was removed from the shop floor. Planning, problem solving, and thinking became management rather than worker activities. Workers should have the responsibility for doing work, not for deciding how it should be done.

A second component of Taylorism was the introduction of a piecework compensation system to combat the perceived laziness of workers and the additional insidious element of social pressures to restrict output. Workers were to be given economic incentives to perform jobs effectively, which would be sufficient in size to offset what was thought to be their natural proclivities for conforming to "the principle of least effort."

Taylor's ideas were exceedingly influential in reshaping American industry. Through his writings and workshops, along with those of his associates, "scientific management" became the dominant motif for organizing production processes by the mid-1920s. In fact many scholars argue that Taylor's methods and theories still provide the direction for much of today's management practice. Braverman states:

> It is impossible to overestimate the importance of the scientific management movement in the shaping of the modern corporations and indeed all institutions of capitalistic society which carry on labor processes. The popular notions that Taylorism has been superseded by later schools of industrial psychology or human relations . . . represent a woeful misreading of the actual dynamics of the development of management. (1974, pp. 86–87)

Taylor's scientific management undoubtedly reestablished management control in the American corporation. Concepts of worker participation, employee involvement, and workplace democracy had no place in the managerial vocabulary of the first quarter of the twentieth century.

## PARTICIPATIVE MANAGEMENT

However, the concept of power sharing and participation began to resurface in the academic world in the 1930s. It is hard to point to a single key actor in this resurgence. Elton Mayo, a faculty member at the Harvard Business School and the architect of the famous Hawthorne experiments conducted in the Western Electric Company from 1929 to 1945, was clearly an early and major proponent. His books, *The Social Problems of an Industrial Civilization* and *The Human Problems of an Industrial Civilization*, pointed to some of the societal and corporate costs of the scientific management movement.

A second key figure was Kurt Lewin, a prominent social psychologist at the University of Berlin who fled his homeland just prior to World War II. His abhorrence of the dictatorial methods in Nazi Germany provided the motivation for an impressive set of experiments conducted by Lewin and by his disciples, many of which pointed to the efficacy of worker participation in decision making. If Mayo provided the philosophical rationale for the resurgence of worker participation in a post-Taylorian world, Lewin provided much of its empirical foundation.

In the 1950s and 1960s a number of behavioral scientists, disillusioned with the more traditional methods, sought to develop a new vision of management that was true to the earlier works of Mayo and Lewin. Argyris, then at Yale, Likert at Michigan, and McGregor at MIT each outlined a version of participative management. In these proposals the emphasis was on worker participation rather than on the worker control that typified the pre-Taylorian era. The recommendations of the behavioral scientists for increasing worker involvement in decisions were directed primarily at management rather than at trade unions or workers. Accordingly, the emphasis was no longer on worker influence as a device for self-protection against a potentially malevolent set of owners and managers. Instead, participation was acknowledged to play an important role in overcoming resistance to change, in motivating workers, and in instilling a community of purpose throughout the organization.

The new participative management proposed by behavioral scientists in the 1950s and 1960s stood in sharp contrast with the Taylorism of the first quarter-century. Taylorism stood for management control and the necessity of intelligent "programming" of workers in the one best way of carrying out productive labor. The advocates of participative management stressed worker choice and discretion under such rubrics as "management by objectives," "job enrichment," and "semiautonomous work groups."

Scientific management and participative management were fundamentally opposed to one another. To move toward one was inevitably to move away from the other. Scientific management and participative management were protagonists engaged in an unending battle.

One forum for this battle lay in the intricate experiments and field studies designed by behavioral scientists to describe the different effects of autocratic and democratic leadership styles or, more generally, to ascertain the effects of what has come to be known in the research community as PDM—participative decision making.

Fortunately, for our purposes, many recent reviews of the research results on the efficiency of PDM exist, making another summary on our part unnecessary. Locke and Schweiger (1979), Yukl (1981), and Schweiger and Leana (1986) have provided comprehensive reviews of the growing body of evidence concerning the effects of participation in decision making.

Their conclusions provide little to cheer about, either for advocates of a top-down autocratic approach or for those who advocate participation. There is in fact tremendous variability in the results from one study to another, leading Schweiger and Leana to conclude that "essentially, no single approach, whether autocratic, consultative, or totally participative, can be effectively employed with all subordinates for all types of activities" (1986, p. 159).

While researchers were seeking to provide an objective foundation for theories of leadership and supervision, organizational and managerial life continued. Managers in organizations did not wait for the research results to show a definitive pattern before adopting a position on using participative methods. Research and practice are, at best, loosely coupled activities.

Lawler (1986) has argued that most American managers of the 1960s were reluctant to tamper with a management system that had enabled their organizations to dominate world markets. Their managerial methods were held up by many, including Servan-Schreiber in his best-selling book *The American Challenge* (1968), to be a model for the rest of the world. Behavioral scientists wrote and talked about participative management, but few managers found it necessary to listen.

Writing at the time, Leavitt (1958) argued for a more moderate position: that both scientific and participative management were having an important influence but at different places in the organizational hierarchy. Taylorism had become the dominant organizational philosophy at the lowest levels in most organizations. Thus workers on assembly lines, tellers in banks, clerk-typists in insurance companies, and the like had their jobs subjected to time and motion studies and ended up with very limited opportunities for self-expression, initiative, or discretion. Taylorism won the day.

Several levels above the rank and file, one encountered managerial activities that seemed inherently less programmable and for which participative management seemed to prevail. Beginning at middle management one could see the trappings of participative management. It is here, rather than at the rank and file, that one is likely to see programs such as management by objectives and to see emphases on team building and consensus decision making.

Leavitt's conclusion, written three decades ago, may be less timely today. Rocked by foreign competition American management methods, particularly in manufacturing, are no longer viewed as a model for the world. In fact, our slow productivity growth and mounting trade deficits are seen by many American managers as reflections of the inadequacy of our traditional managerial methods. The voices of change are not just those of behavioral scientists but include many top executives desperately trying to retain market share in the face of lower-cost and higher-quality foreign products.

One of the solutions to the challenge is increased worker involvement in decision making. Quality circles, self-managing work groups, quality-of-work-life programs, and high-performance work teams are but a few of the organizational devices that aspire to increase productivity through increased participation. About forty companies have constructed high-involvement plants different in virtually all respects from conventional manufacturing facilities and designed from ground up to engender worker commitment. Several large corporations, including Honeywell, Westinghouse, General Motors, Ford, Xerox, and Motorola, have gone further and publicly committed themselves to using more participative approaches to the management of people.

However, the path to participative management is neither smooth nor clear. Most programs encounter resistance, and many fail to live up to expectations. As Lawler (1986) puts it:

> It would be nice to report that all is going well as we make this transition to participative approaches to management. The good news is that there is a great deal of activity; the bad news is that much of it is poorly conceived, uses the wrong approaches and is destined to fail. (p. 4)

Our brief excursion through the pages of history—from St. Benedict to recent "high-involvement" management practices—should leave us with a healthy respect for the complexity of the issues of leadership and participation. We should be skeptical of simplistic solutions to the problem, whether they be Likert's System 4 (1961), McGregor's Theory Y (1960), or Ouchi's Theory Z (1981). History teaches us that while the problems are timeless, the solutions are difficult if not unattainable.

Almost two decades ago one of the authors, after reviewing the evidence regarding the effects of participation, wrote:

> The critics and proponents of participative management would do well to direct their efforts toward identifying the properties of situations in which different decision-making approaches are effective rather than wholesale condemnation or deification of one approach. (Vroom, 1970, pp. 239–240)

In this book we accept this challenge. If participation is to be more than fad or current fashion fluctuating in importance with the swing of a pendulum, it is critical that we understand the processes by which it works and the situations that affect those processes. Throughout the succeeding pages we recount our efforts to develop a contingency theory of participation—one which purports to specify the situations in which various forms and degrees of participation are likely to be effective or to fail miserably.

# CHAPTER THREE

# EVALUATING
# PARTICIPATION

## *The Criteria*

In common parlance the term *participation* means "taking part." One participates in varsity sports, in a group discussion, or in the company's profit-sharing plan. The nature of the "part" or role played varies somewhat with the activity described. Most frequently the role is an active one. One participates when one "contributes to" something.

When applied to decision making the term acquires a more precise meaning. Following the tradition of French, Israel, and Ås (1960) and of Vroom (1960), we will define participation in this context as *influence* resulting from a person's assuming an active role in a decision-making process. The amount of an individual's participation in a given decision made by a group or organization is represented by the amount of influence that person has had on the plans or decisions agreed upon.

For some purposes it can be useful to distinguish between actual and *perceived* participation—the latter term referring to the extent to which the individual feels that he or she has influenced the decision. Sometimes perceived participation is much larger than actual participation. In such instances, people believe that their impact on the decision is substantially greater than it is in fact. (Some leaders and managers have been known to encourage such false views as a conscious strategy of manipulation!) The reverse is also logically possible, although perhaps less common. Individuals may have influence but be unaware of it (perceived participation is much less than actual participation). The motivational effects of participation discussed later in this chapter are more closely linked to perceived participation while the effects on decision quality are more closely linked to actual participation.

Another distinction that is helpful in some of our finer-grained analyses concerns the difference between the *opportunity* for participation and the *exercise* of actual participation. Laws give people access to the ballot box, the right to attend meetings, and the right to vote on decisions. Thus, they create opportunities for participation. Whether people exercise their franchise and seek to influence the choices made is a matter of their own volition.

Similarly, a manager may convene a group meeting in order to gain ideas or to achieve consensus, thereby creating an opportunity for participation. But that manager cannot force people to participate against their will. Viewed more broadly actual participation requires both facilitating systems—such as laws and democratic leaders (both of which create opportunities for influence)—and a set of individuals willing to take advantage of these opportunities.

Let us now turn to forms of actual participation in formal organizations. We shall distinguish two patterns of participation. As we shall see they are different in many respects, but the most basic and fundamental difference resides in whether the opportunities for participation are codified in the law.

## LEGISLATED PARTICIPATION

Many instances of participation have their origins in legal systems. Worker councils in Yugoslavia, codetermination in West Germany, and union representation on boards of directors in Sweden and Norway are but a few examples of legally mandated opportunities for workers to participate in the governance of organizations. Locke and Schweiger (1979) refer to these as examples of "forced" participation since the necessity of involving workers comes not from management initiative or discretion but from the law. We prefer the term "legislated" because the fact that an activity is mandated by law does not necessarily mean that the principal motive for its performance is external force. Laws often give expression to people's prior conceptions of justice, and their passage and the resulting changes in people's behavior often cause changes in attitudes as individuals come to internalize laws. The Supreme Court's landmark decision in 1954 outlawing segregated schools affected the behavior of many Americans. Furthermore, as the Court noted in its decision, the behavioral changes mandated by the decision were expected to result in further changes in attitudes and values to make them consistent with the behavior.

Legislated participation involves the creation of formal social systems for the purpose of making specified kinds of decisions. Legal statutes cover such issues as the name of the decision-making body, who is eligible for membership, how members are selected and replaced, and how differences of opinion will be resolved (for example, by majority vote). The United States Senate, the board of trustees of a college, and the board of directors of a corporation are examples of such social systems.

Frequently formal decision-making bodies create opportunities for participation that are both direct and indirect. Those who are official members of the decision-making body participate directly in decision making. Those who are not members may have indirect opportunities for influence through their role in the election of representatives to the official body.

To summarize, in legislated participation the opportunities for participation are rights written in law. Furthermore the bodies that make decisions and the rules by which these bodies operate are formal. Finally, for organizational members whose influence is through representation, the nature of the opportunities for participation is indirect.


## INFORMAL PARTICIPATION

In sharp contrast to legislated forms of participation stands participation that occurs between managers and their subordinates. A manager faced with the task of developing an operational plan for achieving an organizational objective may seek the advice and counsel of his or her subordinates prior to making that decision because "it makes sense to do so," not because the law requires it.

Such instances of participation are informal in character and derive their characteristics from relationships between individuals rather than from legal statutes. The opportunities for informal participation are always voluntarily initiated by managers and almost always direct in nature. They may take many forms ranging from casual conversations around the watercooler to group meetings for the purpose of setting goals and solving problems.

It is informal participation that is most frequently proposed by management theorists, including McGregor, Likert, Bennis, Argyris, and Ouchi. Here the issue of participation merges with the issue of leadership style. Differences among leaders characterized as authoritarian-autocratic or democratic-participative are rooted in the manner in which they provide those who work with them with opportunities to share in the development of plans and the making of decisions.

Interest in formal or legislated systems of participation in the workplace is most common in Europe. In contrast, the informal face-to-face variety is more characteristic of North American and Japanese management. A basic premise on which this book rests is that the latter form of participation is far more relevant to the effective management of people and the all-important question of productivity than is the former.

One reason for this is that the types of decisions with which informal face-to-face participation deals are more likely to correspond to most workers' interests and to their beliefs about appropriate sharing of managerial power.

Lawler, Renwick, and Bullock (1981) asked several thousand workers how much influence they felt they should have and how much they did have in each of seven decision-making areas. Workers felt that their influence was much more appropriate in how they did their own work and in the scheduling of their own work. They felt it was much less appropriate to have influence in broad organizational policies and in hiring and promotion decisions.

A second reason for the greater potential of informal participation is the greater ease with which it can be made situational. By this we mean that participation of the second variety can be more effective because it can be tailored to the time, place, and circumstance. There is no need for a manager to consult equally on all problems with all subordinates or under all circumstances. There is room within nonlegislated participation for it to vary intelligently with situational demands, and for the amount and form of participation to evolve with changing relationships and tasks.

Now that we have defined participation and related concepts we are in a position to examine its likely effects and the ways these effects are produced. We will avoid such global criteria as productivity or organizational effectiveness and look instead at more specific outcomes that are relevant to the organization in its efforts to attain its goals. These are: (1) job satisfaction, (2) quality of decisions, (3) commitment to decisions, (4) development, and (5) time.

## JOB SATISFACTION

Evidence that participation enhances employees' satisfaction with their jobs, their morale, and their attitudes toward their managers is quite compelling. Most people enjoy participating and value work environments that afford them the opportunity to do so.

There are two reasons why people prefer opportunities to participate and to exercise their own discretion. Through influence in decision making one can affect the nature of decisions made so that it reflects one's own interests and concerns. Voting behavior in elections can be largely understood as an instrumental act with people "voting their pocketbooks." Similarly, student participation in university governance is usually directed toward the improvement of faculty teaching, in which students have an obvious interest, as opposed to the improvement of faculty research.

But it would be a mistake to conclude that all interest in participation stems from its instrumentality in the servicing of other goals. To those involved, participation can also be an end in itself. It affords people a chance to be involved in decisions that are important to them, to utilize their talents in a meaningful way, and to be a significant part of a group endeavor. These activities, inherent to the participative process, are valued by most people.

It is certainly understandable that something like participation, valued initially for instrumental reasons, could come to be valued for its own sake. Psychologists have long noted the tendency for means to become ends. *Functional autonomy* (Allport, 1937) is but one of a number of concepts that refer to a learning process that would result in people taking satisfaction from participating in decisions independent of the usefulness of that participation in attaining other objectives.

In an earlier book, one of the authors (Vroom, 1960) studied the personality characteristics of workers whose job satisfaction was enhanced by participation. These individuals were egalitarian in terms of their beliefs and values (as measured by a test known as the F-scale) and scored highly on a measure of need for independence. On the other hand, the job satisfaction of those who were authoritarian and of those who were low in need for independence was unaffected by participation.

Many have speculated that more and more people in our society value participation in its own right. Compared to several decades ago, today the practice of autocratic leadership creates more resentment and resistance, and democratic-participative methods elicit more positive responses. While the evidence for this fact is largely anecdotal, the conditions appear right for the learning of a "motive to participate." As our socializing institutions—such as the family and primary and secondary education—have become less rigid and more oriented to self-expression, they provide more opportunities for individuals to be proactive rather than reactive in the pursuit of their goals. These are conditions that would be expected to strengthen individuals' desire to participate in decisions affecting them.

The effect of participation on job satisfaction is clearly relevant to people's decisions about whether to remain in jobs. Turnover rates and, to a lesser degree, absenteeism rates have been shown in many research studies to be related to job satisfaction. There is little evidence, however, that job satisfaction has a direct effect on raising productivity or efficiency (Vroom, 1964; Iaffaldano & Muchinsky, 1985).

The effects of participation on job satisfaction are certainly relevant to those concerned with increasing the quality of working life. However, the relatively weak connection between satisfaction and performance causes us to look to other criteria to constitute the foundation for our pragmatic view of participation.

## QUALITY OF DECISIONS

Here we consider the effects of participation on the kinds of decisions made within organizations, most particularly on the analytical or impersonal aspects of decisions. Maier (1963) has coined the term *decision quality* to refer to the variable that we have in mind. A high-quality decision is one that, if implemented, is likely to attain the goals of the organization. It is a well-reasoned decision, consistent with available information and with organizational objectives and goals.

The term *decision quality* has its origins in laboratory research on problem solving. A high-quality solution was an elegant, often insightful solution that "worked." Translating that concept into business decision making is relatively easy. Much of what occurs in organizations in the private sector can be thought of as problem solving and as its close relative, decision making. The widespread use of optimization techniques in business management testifies to the importance of obtaining analytically sound or *high-quality* decisions.

Decision quality becomes somewhat more slippery as a term when used in conjunction with many public sector decisions. For example such questions as tax reform have, as a core component, conflicts among the interests of various groups of stakeholders. What is considered a high-quality decision from the standpoint of one group of stakeholders may be considered low in quality to another. As one old sage put it, "In the private sector, we optimize; in the public sector, we compromise."

We must be careful not to overlook the increased use of analytic methods in decision making in the public sector or fail to recognize the influence of "politics" in the private sector. The important point is that the term *decision quality* implies an objective function—a criterion or set of criteria by which the results of decisions can be judged unequivocally. In some social systems and in some kinds of decisions these criteria are obtainable; in others they are not.

There is a great deal of conventional wisdom concerning the effects of participation on decision quality. The expression "two heads are better than one" implies a synergistic effect. On the other hand, the expression "A camel is a horse designed by a committee" implies quite the reverse. Undoubtedly both kinds of effects can occur. The problem is to predict what might happen in any given instance.

The effects of participation on decision quality are undoubtedly highly complex. The conditions that influence whether enhanced participation will benefit or detract from the quality of decisions include (1) the goals of participants, (2) the knowledge possessed by participants, (3) the size of the group, (4) disagreement among participants, and (5) the nature of the problem itself.

### Goals

We noted earlier in this chapter that participation tends to be goal directed. People typically seek to influence decisions in a direction that is consonant with their own goals. Sometimes these are personal goals and the effects of participation are self-serving. We saw in the second chapter how craftsmen in the latter part of the nineteenth century frequently used their influence over decision processes to protect their own interests against those of owners and managers, whose interests they viewed as antagonistic.

There is nothing insidious about this phenomenon, nor is it restricted to rank and file workers. Managers are frequently concerned with "building" and "protecting" their own "empires," and U.S. senators have been known to direct lucrative defense contracts to their own states.

The implications of personal interests for who should participate in decision making is formally recognized in the judicial process: In it, both jurors and judges are subject to disqualification if they have a personal stake in the outcome. No such mechanisms exist in organizational decision making, perhaps because having a stake in the outcome is an inevitable part of organizational life.

There are two situations in which the tendency to put personal goals over organization goals presents a problem for participative systems. One involves a cleavage or conflict in goals that splits the organization horizontally. Perhaps the goals of owners or directors may diverge from those of the managers. Alternatively, the senior managers may have different interests than those of lower-level managers, or the goals of lower-level managers may diverge from those of rank and file workers. Representative situations include a possible merger between two similar organizations (realizing economies of scale but jeopardizing managerial positions) or a possible plant closing and related move of manufacturing capacity to an offshore site (taking advantage of cheaper foreign labor). It is easy to see how who participates, and to what degree, would affect both the nature and the quality of the decisions made.

The second situation involves conflicts that exist among departments or functions. The lines of cleavage are drawn vertically rather than horizontally. A prototypical situation involves competition among different businesses or product lines or among research teams for scarce resources. Here the risk is that, in the absence of a common goal, the involvement of the groups with divergent interests in the solution would be nonproductive.

The common ingredient of both situations is a lack of congruence between organizational goals and those held by individual members. There is little doubt that such conflicts—when they occur—do and should limit the amount and degree of participation in decision making.

But not all organizational decisions involve such conflicts in interests among the possible participants. For many decisions there is what Sherif (1958) has described as a *superordinate goal* or what Maier (1963) terms "a mutual interest." The various participants are confronted with a "win-win" (as opposed to "win-lose") situation. When managers and workers (or different departments) share common objectives, the infighting and "company politics" are typically replaced by problem solving. Synergy is a typical concomitant of such situations.

Many readers will be familiar with the kinds of survival situations frequently used in management training to illustrate synergistic decision making. People are stranded on the moon, in the desert, or in the arctic and are asked to rank some number of items (usually fifteen) in terms of usefulness for their survival. They are asked to do this individually and then as a group. Both individual and group decisions are then compared with those of the "experts"—typically revealing that the group score exceeds that of the average individual and frequently exceeds that of the best person in the group.

For our purposes, the interesting thing about these exercises is that they inevitably give people a shared goal. They are all "in the same boat," united by the shared objective of survival. The task confronting the group is not one of deciding whose interests are paramount but rather whose perspectives, ideas, and information should be incorporated into the group decision. It is intriguing to speculate that the resurgence of interest in employee participation stems from the fact that competition—particularly but not exclusively foreign competition—has created its own set of survival situations.

### Knowledge Possessed by Participants

The decisions reached by organizational members reflect not only their goals and objectives but also their knowledge and information. The quality of those decisions is influenced by the extent to which those participating in the decision possess the information they need to generate and evaluate alternatives. Many low-quality decisions are well intentioned but suffer from a lack of critical information on the part of decision makers.

One of the most frequently cited benefits of participation is the greater information and larger variety of perspectives that it brings to bear on the decision-making process. The extent to which these benefits are realized depends on where the needed information is located. Synergy is more likely to occur when each of the possible participants possesses some but not all of the needed information to solve the problem. Therefore, "large" problems requiring the knowledge and expertise of people from a number of functions or specialties are most likely to demonstrate the potential superiority of group decision making.

This is not meant to suggest that autocratic leaders are incapable of making high-quality decisions but rather to suggest that such results are most likely to occur when the decisions in question fall within the expertise of the decisionmaker. Moving from an autocratic to a participative decision-making mode cannot decrease and, more frequently, will increase the total information on which the decision can rest. Such a transition from individual to group decision making generates another requirement. Having the information is one thing; knowing who possesses it is another. A participative decision-making system can fail if it puts its trust in the "wrong" participants. As Yetton and Bottger (1983) have pointed out, the synergistic properties of group decision making require a mechanism for sorting out experts from nonexperts and good ideas from those destined to fail.

These two factors—goals and knowledge—play a key role in the situational leadership theory put forth by Hersey and Blanchard (1982). Goals and knowl-edge are the two ingredients of the "maturity" of followers that is the central benchmark in the Hersey-Blanchard theory of the leader's choice of an appropri-ate style. Those styles that involve power sharing, including delegation and group participation, are seen as applicable when dealing with followers who are high in maturity.

### Size of Group

Increasing the size of the group typically increases the total information available to the group. This is indeed a benefit. But increasing group size also brings with its some costs, namely, problems of coordinating the efforts of members. In larger groups, compared with smaller ones, members are more likely to hold back on information, and such information is more likely to get lost or overlooked even if expressed. In general the problem of weighing individual contributions in accordance with their merit becomes much more difficult.

A social psychologist, Ivan Steiner, has developed a model for expressing both the positive and negative effects of increasing group size and for examining the cost-benefit tradeoff (1972). He argues that the relationship between group size and total information (which he refers to as *potential productivity*) is negatively accelerated and exhibits diminishing returns from successive incre-ments in size. On the other hand, the relationship between group size and difficulties in coordination (which he refers to as *process losses*) is positively accelerated, exhibiting greater difficulties with successive increments in size.

Whether the model is correct in detail is perhaps less important than the fact that it enables us to think about the costs and benefits of increasing group size. Its implication—that smaller groups are more likely to suffer from not having the needed informational resources and larger ones from problems of coordination—carries with it a ring of truth.

### Disagreement Among Participants

Irving Janis (1982) has written at length about a phenomenon that he calls "groupthink." He likens groupthink to a disease that impairs group decision making. The characteristics of groupthink have been identified by examining a number of historical fiascoes in which groups made very poor decisions despite the competence of individual members and the information to which they had access. Among the groups studied, using available historical records, were Neville Chamberlain's inner circle, which supported the appeasement of Hitler during 1937 and 1938; President Kennedy's inner circle that supported the invasion of Cuba at the Bay of Pigs; and President Johnson's close advisors who supported the decision to escalate the war in Vietnam. The common ingredients included a tendency for decisionmakers in each of these groups to avoid raising controversial issues, to refrain from questioning one another, and to refrain from dissenting from an emerging consensus. Janis sees these ingredients as particularly characteristic of highly cohesive groups and of groups in which members share the same values and beliefs. Diversity in group members is consistent with analytical thinking, as is a set of group norms that legitimizes intellectual challenge, disagreement, and dissent in the search for answers to difficult problems.

Peter Drucker sounds a similar warning:

> Decisions of the kind the executive has to make are not made well by acclamation. They are made well only if based on the clash of conflicting views, the dialogue between different points of view, the choice between different judgments. The first rule in decision-making is that one does not make a decision unless there is disagreement. (1973, p. 472)

Alfred P. Sloan, Jr., the architect of many of General Motors' organizational structures and policies, is reported to have said at a meeting of one of that company's top committees: "Gentlemen, I take it we are all in complete agreement on the decision here." Everyone around the table nodded assent. "Then," continued Mr. Sloan, "I propose we postpone further discussion of this matter until our next meeting to give ourselves time to develop disagreement and perhaps gain some understanding of what the decision is all about" (quoted in Drucker, 1973, p. 472).

The reader may well have noted that we are telling only half of the story in our discussion of disagreement. It may be true that differences of opinion, confrontation, the challenge of one another's views (and the like) may aid in the search for truth. On the other hand, they may contribute to disharmony, anger, and polarization. To put it metaphorically, conflict may lead to heat as well as to light.

The problem is to identify which of these two outcomes is liable to take place. How can conflict be effectively managed so as to maximize the "light" and minimize the "heat"? We will return to this question later in Chapter 9 and offer here only a partial answer. If the conflict revolves around means rather than ends, the likelihood that it can result in the kind of hard-headed thinking envisaged by Janis, Drucker, and Sloan is substantially increased. When people agree on an objective to be obtained and disagree only on how it may best be attained, there exist a number of mechanisms— discussion, data collection, experimentation, to name just a few—by which the differences are capable of being resolved.

### Nature of the Problem

A half-century ago an experimental psychologist, Robert Thorndike (1938), conducted a simple experiment showing that groups are vastly superior to individuals in solving crossword puzzles, but that individuals are superior to groups in constructing them. The significance of this finding transcends by far the enterprise of crossword puzzles or even word games in general. How are the tasks of solving and of constructing crossword puzzles different? Both are complex and are capable of taxing one's abilities. Both are also made up of multiple parts. But here the similarity ends.

In solving crossword puzzles, each part of the puzzle has but one correct answer, and the parts are only loosely coupled with one another. Thus we can begin the puzzle in the "across" column or in the "down" column or jump back and forth among them without sacrificing efficiency.

However, in designing a crossword puzzle there is no single correct solution, and the key task is coordinating earlier steps with later steps. Any word will do as long as it fits together with previous selections and does not obstruct those that will come later in sequence. Order and sequence—instead of being irrelevant—are of great import. Instead of being loosely coupled, the parts of the problem are tightly coupled with one another. Questions of fit, coordination, and sequencing of the parts become highly significant.

Composing a symphony, writing a novel, or painting a great "masterpiece" are far more similar to the design of a crossword puzzle than to its solution. Groups are as notoriously bad at such activities as they are at the simpler enterprise of writing reports. They can discern when a report should be written, the issues it should address, and to whom it should be sent. However, the task of stringing together intricate sequences of words and paragraphs and sections is more conducive to individual cognitive processes.

In Chapter 9, we will revisit the analytical outcomes of participation. This later chapter will show how many of the factors we have identified can be incorporated into a model that could be used by managers to assess the likely quality of decisions that would occur as a consequence of various decision processes.

## COMMITMENT TO DECISIONS

Many of the arguments for increasing participation in decision making stem not from its role in producing better decisions but rather from its role of stimulating commitment to the execution of those decisions. "People support what they help to build" is an adage that attests to the positive motivational consequences of involvement in decision making. By creating opportunities for subordinates to influence decisions, a manager frequently reduces resistance and secures a shared feeling of ownership over decisions that results in smoother and more expeditious implementation of decisions.

It is this potential consequence of participation that has received the most attention from management theorists. Douglas McGregor's Theory Y viewed participation and delegation as motivating subordinates toward organizational objectives and integrating their goals with those of the organization.

One of the earliest experiments on participation supported the integration mechanism by showing that workers' resistance to change in work methods could be reduced by involving them in the nature of the changes (Coch & French, 1948). Similarly, Rensis Likert viewed his System 4—the participative group approach—as a motivational technique for the management of organizations. Effective organizations, to Likert, are made up of cohesive work groups, members of which strive hard to achieve the goals they have set for themselves.

Although the evidence for participation's effects on acceptance of and commitment to decisions is quite compelling, the data contain a few discordant elements. French, Israel, and Ås (1960) tried to replicate the Coch and French experiment described above. The original investigation was conducted at the Harwood Manufacturing Company in the United States. The attempted replication took place in a Norwegian factory. The authors attribute the lack of beneficial effect to the fact that a substantial number of workers did not view their participation as "legitimate." They reason, with considerable empirical support, that for participation to produce commitment it must be viewed as "right" and "proper" by the parties involved.

A similar conclusion seems to follow from an experience reported by Alfred Marrow (1964) from his perspective as chairman of the Harwood Manufacturing Company. His firm opened a new plant in Puerto Rico and naturally began implementing many of the highly participative practices that had worked so successfully in the company's mainland operations. To his chagrin, these methods did not work. Through exit interviews the company discovered that many employees felt the opportunities for participation under the company's unique democratic atmosphere reflected unfavorably on the capabilities of its leadership. Further, workers perceived their involvement in setting goals and making decisions as illegitimate. Chapter 10 will incorporate the factors implied by these and other studies into a contingency model of participative leadership.

## DEVELOPMENT

Learning theorists tell us that practice is necessary for the development of a skill. A corollary to this truth is that one can tell what skills a person is developing in any endeavor by the skills that he or she is practicing. Football players practice during the week, and their developed skills are evident on the weekend. Actors practice during rehearsals, and their developed skills are evident when the play opens. However, watching football on a Sunday afternoon does not develop one's talents as a football quarterback, nor do monthly visits to the local theater develop one's dramatic abilities.

The same principle governs what people learn during the decision-making process. Those who make decisions learn the skills necessary to that endeavor;

those who simply carry out the decisions of others develop the skills relevant to decision execution but not to decision making!

First of all, participative leadership practices, such as delegating important decisions to subordinates and involving team members in meetings for planning and decision making, provide practice not afforded by more autocratic styles. The resulting development of decision-making capabilities increases the reservoir of talents on which the organization can subsequently draw. The *human capital* of the organization is enhanced—an outcome that becomes particularly important when these talents can be put to use during expansion or in meeting new challenges.

Second, the developmental benefits of participation are not restricted to enhanced technical and problem-solving skills. Those forms of participation that take place in groups also develop relationships among team members. In addition to practice in relating to the decision, group processes allow participants some practice in relating to one another. Competitive relationships thrive under more autocratic leadership practices and under those styles that stress interaction with subordinates on a one-on-one basis. Conversely, group methods that involve subordinates in a team promote collaborative and collegial relationships. Working through common problems can lead to the mutual sharing of information, experience, and skills. Team members learn to trust and rely on one another as they recognize the unique resources each member brings to the group.

Third, there is some evidence that participation affects not only the relationships of individuals with one another but with the larger enterprise. McGregor refers to the beneficial effects of participation on integrating individual goals with those of the organization. Likert stresses the impact of participative management on loyalty, both to the group and, indirectly, to the larger system of which the group is a part.

Finally, participation provides the opportunity to broaden an individual's skills and competencies for what might be called "self-management." Lawler (1986) reports that participative structures promote such self-reliant skills, which become evident in the form of less need for extensive staff support within the organization.

These four by-products of participation—individual decision-making skills, team building, loyalty to the organization, and self-management—are only loosely subsumed by the term *development*. Each by-product is desirable in its own right, and each can be construed as an increase in the human capital of the organization.

In Chapter 11 we will revisit the developmental consequences of participation. At that time we will propose additional complexities to these relations. Participation in decision making may have developmental benefits, but in some types of decisions these benefits may be inconsequential.

## TIME

So far each of the outcomes of participation that we have examined represents a possible benefit. Participation can increase job satisfaction, the quality of the decision, commitment to the decision, and the development of subordinates. To be sure, such benefits are not always present, and it is not hard to imagine circumstances under which each outcome would not occur. Nonetheless the overall picture is one of potential benefit.

Lawler (1986, pp. 38–39) provides a list of the possible costs of participation. Included in his list are salary and training costs, program support costs, and costs associated with resistance of middle management and other organizational groups. Many of the items on Lawler's list of costs are not inevitable consequences of participation but are instead dependent upon other situations and conditions, including the type of participation introduced. However, there is one item on his list that is *inherent* in the use of participation. To put it succinctly, participation takes time—and time is a valuable and sometimes scarce commodity.

In general, participation increases the response time of decision-making systems. Group meetings take time to arrange. Rapid decisions, often necessary to deal with emergencies, may preempt the participation of others. Consensus decision making has no role in the quarterback's huddle or on the bridge of a naval vessel during a delicate docking maneuver. Many writers, in analyzing the implications of the consensus decision making practiced in Japan, have commented on the length of time required by extensive deliberations. They argue that Japanese companies can be slow to respond to problems (or opportunities) because issues are informally discussed until a consensus emerges (Drucker, 1971).

There is another sense in which time is relevant to an evaluation of participation. Not only does involving others slow down decision practices, it also uses up the time of those organizational members who are participating in the decision. Group meetings take up the time not just of the leader but of all who are present. Participative organizations make extensive use of meetings, and each meeting reduces the amount of time left over for organization members to carry out either the decisions reached or their regular responsibilities. Mintzberg (1973, p. 39) reports that a typical top-level manager may spend 69 percent of working time in scheduled and unscheduled meetings—a figure that may be substantially higher in highly participative organizations.

Both meanings of time—the ability of the organization to respond to the need for rapid decision making and the total amount of time consumed—represent costs of participation. A sensible framework for deciding when and where participative decision processes ought to be employed must weigh these costs against the potential benefits we have cited earlier.

In the next chapter we provide a formal language of participation and in the chapter after that move to models of leadership style and of participation. The language and models will make use of the analyses developed so far, but in a form that integrates the concepts into a specific framework. This structure should be of value to leaders and managers faced with the necessity of solving problems and making decisions in specific organizational situations.

# CHAPTER FOUR

# FORMALIZING A LANGUAGE OF PARTICIPATION

In the second chapter we took a historical view of the role of participation, examining some of the "ups and downs" in management's romance with participative methods. Our third chapter adopted a more analytical view, distinguishing different forms of participation, different outcomes in terms of which its efficacy can be judged, and different situations affecting the likelihood of each outcome. Both preceding chapters point to the complexity of the phenomenon and to the difficulty of doing justice to it with simple concepts. In Chapter 4 we add to the complexity. Here we suggest that a more differentiated language is necessary to describe the form or amount of influence that a manager affords subordinates in the making of a particular decision.

The noun *participation* is like many in the English language—temperature, speed, height, and weight, to name just a few—that do not refer to discrete objects or events. Instead, participation is an attribute of a relationship between persons and decisions and can vary in amount or degree.

The point may seem obvious, but it can have very significant consequences. A company that announces its intention to run its plant in a participative manner may create very different expectations in the minds of managers, workers, and the union. To some it may mean that workers as a group will run the plant; to others it may mean that workers will be consulted; to still others it may mean that management will explain the rationale behind its actions.

Anthropologists have noted that the number of words that exist within a language to refer to an object reflects the importance of that object within the culture using the language. Thus, the Eskimos have over a dozen words for snow, permitting such distinctions as falling snow, granular snow, snow newly drifted, and snow mixed with water.

Less frequently recognized is the fact that increases in importance of objects within a given culture are accompanied by the introduction of new words into the language. Thirty years ago we had one word for computers. Today we find it necessary to distinguish among minicomputers, microcomputers, work stations, and mainframes.

As with computers, the concept of participation has increased in importance over the last 30 years. We need, accordingly, to have a linguistic capability of making finer distinctions among forms of participation. Just as Eskimos need to distinguish among kinds of snow in order to give one another accurate information relevant to travel, so do managers and workers need to be able to distinguish among forms of participation.

Beginning with the next chapter we will be describing our efforts to develop a normative or prescriptive model to guide managers in their use of participative methods. Our models will make use of some of the criteria— quality, commitment, time, and development—discussed in the previous chapter.

Here we describe an essential component of each of these models: a language for describing amounts of participation afforded subordinates in managerial decision making. Consider a manager in an organization. Also consider an organizational problem to be solved or a decision to be made. The problem or decision may be important or trivial, complex or simple, but *it must fall within the manager's area of freedom or discretion.* In other words, it must be a decision problem on which the leader is expected or permitted to act. We are not interested in those decisions that must be referred elsewhere in the organization, including those to senior managers further up in the organizational hierarchy.

To these two entities—a manager and a decision problem—we add a third ingredient. There must be one or more "others" within the same organization who are affected by the problem. Vroom and Yetton (1973) use the term *subordinates* to refer to this group. But there is nothing magic about that term. Although most of our work has concerned this group, we recognize that the concepts can also be applied to a teacher and students, a chief executive officer and the board of directors, or a project manager and other members of a project team. In specifying the amount and form of participation, it is only necessary that one have the relevant "other" or set of others clearly in mind.

The kinds of decision problems in which we are interested include the following:

- A president of the United States must decide how to respond to a diplomatic initiative from another chief of state.

- A college professor is approached by a student who suggests that classes be held off campus during a strike of campus clerical personnel that has produced a picket line ringing campus buildings.
- A director of an emergency ward in a hospital must submit a plan showing adequate coverage of the ward during the Christmas–New Year holiday period when most of the staff are seeking time off.
- A mayor of a major U.S. city learns that he must deal with public protest stemming from the unexpected departure of a major league football team for another city.
- A chief operating executive is concerned about a progressive loss of market share in one of the product divisions for which she is accountable.

## DEFINING DECISION PROCESSES

Vroom and Yetton (1973) distinguish between "individual problems" and "group problems." An individual problem is one that has potential effects on only one person. For example, if only one of a manager's direct reports was involved in a problem, it would be classified as an individual problem (for example, the last of the preceding examples). A group problem, by definition, has effects on more than one of the manager's direct reports.

### Group Problems

We will talk first about the kinds of decision processes that apply to group problems. Table 4–1 contains a set of five alternative decision processes potentially applicable to group problems. Each process is designated by a letter followed by a number. A stands for autocratic; C stands for consultative; and G stands for group. Autocratic and consultative processes each have two variants designated by the roman numerals I and II.

These five processes can be thought of as steps on a scale of participation or power sharing. As one moves from AI through GII, there is a progressive increase in the opportunities provided for subordinates to influence the decision. GII, with its emphasis on consensus among subordinates, is most participative; AI is least participative.

Many people have adopted the taxonomy shown in Table 4–1 for a variety of purposes. Kepner-Tregoe, Inc., a leading organizational development and research firm, has developed Table 4–2 for expressing degrees of participation or involvement.

Some colleagues have proposed the addition of a sixth type of decision process that is even more participative than GII. Perhaps called DII, this would describe instances in which the leader delegated or empowered the group to make the decision without the leader's presence. This practice is frequently found in semiautonomous work groups in which workers meet to exchange jobs and even elect their leader. However, after much thought and

TABLE 4–1    Types of Management Decision Methods—
Group Problems

| SYMBOL | DEFINITION |
| --- | --- |
| AI | You solve the problem or make the decision yourself using the information available to you at the present time. |
| AII | You obtain any necessary information from subordinates, then decide on a solution to the problem yourself. You may or may not tell subordinates the purpose of your questions or give information about the problem or decision on which you are working. The input provided by them is clearly in response to your request for specific information. They do not play a role in the definition of the problem or in generating or evaluating alternative solutions. |
| CI | You share the problem with the relevant subordinates individually, getting their ideas and suggestions without bringing them together as a group. Then *you* make the decision. This decision may or may not reflect your subordinates' influence. |
| CII | You share the problem with your subordinates in a group meeting. In this meeting you obtain their ideas and suggestions. Then *you* make the decision, which may or may not reflect your subordinates' influence. |
| GII | You share the problem with your subordinates as a group. Together you generate and evaluate alternatives and attempt to reach agreement (consensus) on a solution. Your role is much like that of chairperson, coordinating the discussion, keeping it focused on the problem, and making sure that the critical issues are discussed. You can provide the group with information or ideas that you have, but you do not try to "press" them to adopt "your" solution, and you are willing to accept and implement any solution that has the support of the entire group. |

Reprinted from *Leadership and decision-making* by Victor H. Vroom and Philip W. Yetton by permission of the University of Pittsburgh Press. © 1973 by University of Pittsburgh Press.

debate we elected to treat this practice as an admissible variant of GII—or GII without the leader present.

We can illustrate the meaning of the five processes shown in Table 4–1 with a specific example. Let us consider the director of a hospital emergency ward. The problem is to formulate a plan providing for coverage of the ward by physicians during the popular holiday period. In AI, the director formulates a plan based on knowledge already available. While hospital policy places some constraints on the solution, requiring that there be at least one specialist in internal medicine and one surgeon on duty at all times, there is still plenty of opportunity left for the leader's judgment. Jewish physicians are scheduled to work on Christmas; Christian physicians are scheduled for the Jewish High Holy Days; those who worked last New Year's Eve are given this year off; and the like.

All of these considerations are important, but an attempt to implement them may cause the leader to become aware of gaps in knowledge. This possibility leads naturally to AII, in which the leader fills in identified gaps in knowledge

**TABLE 4–2  Kepner-Tregoe Adaptation of Decision Processes**

| | AI | AII | CI | CII | GII |
|---|---|---|---|---|---|
| *Who is involved* | Leader | Leader and others individually | Leader and others individually | Leader and others in group | Leader and others in group |
| *Nature of involve-ment* | Unassisted decision | Individuals respond to specific questions | Individuals provide data, rec-ommendations, one-on-one | Group shares data and analyzes | Group shares data, ana-lyzes, and reaches consensus |
| *Who makes decision* | Leader | Leader | Leader | Leader | Group |

*Source:* Weiss (1976). Reprinted by permission of Kepner-Tregoe Inc.

through asking questions. Are you planning to go away over the holidays? Would you rather work Christmas or New Year's day? In AII, subordinates have a chance to influence the decision, but only through their responses to information requested from them.

Both consultative processes, CI and CII, give subordinates the opportunity to address the entire problem. With CI the consultation occurs on a one-on-one basis. The leader talks to subordinates individually. In CII the leader calls a group meeting. This introduces the added ingredient that each "consultant" can hear the advice provided by each other "consultant."

With both consultative modes the leader makes the final decision, but only after those affected have had their opportunity to influence that decision. Our director of the emergency ward would have the benefit of the advice of each of the physicians but would probably have the unenviable task of judging the relative merits of the conflicting interests.

The last alternative, GII, shares with CII the fact that there is a group meeting between leader and subordinates. However, in GII the decision is made by the entire group, not just the leader. Our director of the emergency ward calls a meeting of the physicians, describes the properties of an acceptable solution, for example, at least one internist and one surgeon must be on duty at all times, and then serves as moderator or chairperson of a meeting aimed at reaching a mutually acceptable plan.

### Individual Problems

Not all the decision problems confronting managers affect the entire team as in the hospital case just cited. Some affect only one subordinate and are termed *individual problems*. The distinction between group and individual

problems is not original in our theorizing. Although an advocate of both participation and group interaction, Likert (1961) recognized the fact that there were
some matters in which the leader and a single subordinate should make decisions
together.

> The leader strengthens the group and group processes by seeing that all
> problems *which involve the group* are dealt with by the group. He never
> handles such problems outside of the group nor with individual members
> of the group. While the leader is careful to see that all matters which
> involve and affect the whole group are handled by the whole group, he
> is equally alert not to undertake in a group meeting agenda items or tasks
> which do not concern the group. Matters concerning one individual member
> and only that member are, of course, handled individually. (p. 196)

Although Likert does not go on to suggest how decision problems should
be handled with individual subordinates, we have taken that additional step.
Table 4–3 contains the set of decision processes potentially applicable to individual problems. Three of them (AI, AII, CI) are common to the previous list
for group problems. A manager can inform an individual subordinate of a

**TABLE 4–3    Types of Management Decision Methods—
Individual Problems**

| SYMBOL | DEFINITION |
|---|---|
| AI | You solve the problem or make the decision yourself using the information available to you at the present time. |
| AII | You obtain any necessary information from the subordinate, then decide on a solution to the problem yourself. You may or may not tell the subordinate the purpose of your questions or give information about the problem or decision on which you are working. The person's input is clearly in response to your request for specific information. He or she does not play a role in the definition of the problem or in generating or evaluating alternative solutions. |
| CI | You share the problem with the relevant subordinate, getting the person's ideas and suggestions. Then *you* make the decision. This decision may or may not reflect your subordinate's influence. |
| GI | You share the problem with one of your subordinates, and together you analyze the problem and arrive at a mutually satisfactory solution in an atmosphere of free and open exchange of information and ideas. You both contribute to the resolution of the problem with the relative contribution of each being dependent on knowledge rather than on formal authority. |
| DI | You delegate the problem to one of your subordinates, providing the person with any relevant information that you possess, but giving the person full responsibility for solving the problem alone. Any solution that the person reaches will receive your support. |

decision that has already been made in much the same way he or she might inform a group of subordinates. A manager can also obtain specific facts or consult with a single subordinate prior to making the decision. Missing from the list are CII and GII, the two processes that involve group meetings. Bringing a group together to discuss an issue that affects only one of the members of that group is generally not a good idea, at least not as a result of a unilateral action by the manager. In their place are two new decision processes—GI and DI.

GI is a group decision made by a manager and a single subordinate. It requires consensus between these two persons before the decision is made. McGregor's Theory Y (which he termed management by integration and self-control) made much use of this method of solving problems and making decisions. In his outline for management by objectives, McGregor proposed that each manager enter into a discussion with each subordinate to reach agreement about such matters as the requirements of the subordinate's job and the targets to be attained within the forthcoming work period. McGregor recognized that setting objectives works best when the goals or objectives don't come from top–down or from the bottom–up but rather are jointly worked out by both parties. Cognizant of the fact that the manager's input in such a dialogue is liable to have substantially more weight than that of the subordinate, McGregor proposed that the latter's views be obtained first, usually by drafting the list of job requirements or goals.

DI is delegation of the decision to the subordinate. The subordinate is charged with solving the problem or making the decision within the area of freedom available to the manager. This process provides for maximum participation or influence by the subordinate and occupies, for individual problems, a status analogous to that of GII for group problems.

To illustrate these options, let us focus on a chief operating executive worried about what to do about a progressive loss of market share in one of the product divisions. The affected subordinate is the division manager. Once again the issue is how to decide. The alternatives describe different amounts of opportunities for participation afforded that person.

AI is clearly a possibility particularly when the CEO believes that she has the solution to the problem and when the competence and trustworthiness of the division manager are in question. In such a case the decision may be to replace the division head—an alternative that lends itself to the AI alternative.

AII involves further data collection. For example, more frequent reports may be requested on orders, shipments, returns, and so forth, to permit a more sensible judgment by the CEO of what to do.

CI and GI are similar to one another in the sense that both involve a face-to-face meeting between the CEO and the division head. However, in CI the decision is made by the CEO after consultation; in GI the decision is not made until both parties have examined all relevant alternatives and have reached agreement on the action to be taken. Finally, in DI the CEO empowers the division manager to deal with the problem and pledges support regardless of what that manager should decide.

## DECISION PROCESSES AND LEADERSHIP SKILLS

So far we have dealt exclusively with the methods or processes available to a leader in solving organizational decision problems. We will show later (in Chapter 6) that the leader's choice of method is indeed very important. Ineffective decisions frequently result from using a decision process that is inappropriate to situational demands. However, the results encountered depend not only on one's method but also on one's skill in using it. A surgeon may choose a correct operating procedure, but its success also depends on the surgeon executing that procedure in an appropriate manner.

Autocratic leadership methods require different skills than more participative methods. To employ AI effectively a leader must be intelligent enough to make a high-quality decision. The person must be able to identify alternatives, seek and assimilate information relevant to these alternatives, and rationally make a choice. It is also helpful if the leader is "charismatic" or, at the very least, skilled in the art of persuasion. Autocratic methods or decision processes require skills both in decision making and in inspiring others.

Group methods such as GII and CII require a very different set of skills, namely the skills of a facilitator or discussion leader. The evidence is clear that the quality of decisions made by groups depends markedly on the extent to which the leader is skilled in facilitating group discussion.

Fortunately, for our purposes, the skills required to lead problem-solving groups have been well researched by the late professor Norman Maier and his colleagues at the University of Michigan (Maier, 1963; Maier, 1970). Maier's recommendations to a leader for effectively implementing consensual group decision making (what we call GII) are unique in that they are based on controlled experiments rather than on speculation.

It should be noted that Maier was not addressing the skills required for leading a group therapy session nor those for chairing a session of Parliament. He was explicitly concerned with small face-to-face groups, like those in organizations, brought together to solve a problem affecting each member. One group member is the formal leader and is assigned the responsibility for solving the problem.

Maier's group leadership skills are not designed to manipulate the group toward a solution that the leader has previously generated. Instead they are skills that the leader should use in involving the group in cooperative problem solving.

The starting point for such a group meeting is a *problem*, defined as a gap between where we are or what we have (that is, the present state) and where we would like to be or what we would like to have (the desired state).

Whether the gap is large or small, the purpose is to eliminate it. The task of the group is to find one or more courses of action that will change the existing state into the desired one. How the leader behaves affects, in no small way, the degree to which this task will be accomplished.

### Stating the Problem

Maier maintains that the way in which the problem is initially stated may well determine the subsequent course of the meeting. Thus, some key skills involve stating the problem in such a way that it is likely to elicit collaborative efforts to solve it. One of the most important principles for stating problems, in order to stimulate effective work by groups, is that a mutual interest is identified. The goal or desired state must be one that the group members must wish to attain. The problem of how to reduce unit costs by 30 percent may not involve a mutual interest unless the group has already worked through the necessity of cost reduction in order to attain some more ultimate objective.

In addition, the statement of the problem should not imply a single solution or one favored by the leader. The existence of more than one potential response to the situation should be explicit, or at least implicit, in the way the problem is posed to the group. Otherwise, the leader is presenting a solution to the group rather than a problem, and the likely result of any deliberation is a foregone conclusion. As Maier points out, "How can we reduce the number of personal phone calls?" is not a statement of a problem but rather an exhortation to reduce the use of telephones for personal purposes.

Leaders should also avoid stating problems in terms of choices among alternatives (for example, "Should we do X or Y?"). Rather, the leader should identify the underlying problem to which these alternatives—and probably others—are potential solutions. Group members should have an opportunity to participate in the generation of alternatives, not just in choosing among them.

Finally, Maier argues that problems should not be located *in* group members but rather *in* the situation. If the leader describes the problem as laziness or irresponsibility of group members, one can expect defensiveness rather than creative problem solving. When the leader considers the problem as a "gap" between present and desired behavior patterns by group members, it would be prudent to refocus the problem in terms of the situations that induce those behaviors. Consider the differences in likely reactions of group members to the accusation of laziness versus their likely response to a problem statement such as "How can we make the work environment and the work itself more challenging?"

### Conducting the Discussion

In AI, AII, CI, and CII, the leader makes the decision. In GII the leader necessarily relinquishes some control over the nature of the decision to be reached. However—and this is very important—the leader maintains control over the group process. Managers should not underestimate the importance of this role nor its likely consequences for the effectiveness of decisions emerging from the group.

In many respects the skills necessary to effectively conduct the discussion vary with the nature of the problem being discussed. If the problem requires creativity, it is frequently a good idea to separate in time the *alternative generating* process from the *alternative evaluation* process. Brainstorming, as defined by Osborne (1953), is one method proposed for encouraging creativity. The listing of ideas, on a flip chart or blackboard, occurs at the initial stage of the meeting. During that time a moratorium is placed on evaluating ideas. The rationale is simple. The criticism of an idea during this stage may squelch not only that idea but also many other ideas in the minds of group members. Only after all ideas have been generated does the group proceed to evaluate and ultimately select among them.

The requisite skills also vary with the degree to which the problem has emotional overtones. Strong feelings or emotions on the part of group members require a method that Maier terms *free discussion*. The leader should be nondirective, establishing a permissive climate by demonstrating acceptance of the members' right to express their feelings. The leader imposes no structure on the discussion and instead permits the structure to emerge from within the group. Free discussion, similar to the one-on-one "nondirective interview," is conducive to uncovering hidden agendas, to airing of grievances, and to identifying and resolving interpersonal conflicts.

In contrast, Maier proposes what he terms the *developmental discussion* when the group's principal tasks are problem solving and information processing. The objective of developmental discussion is to increase decision quality by synchronizing the discussions of issues so that people discuss the same aspect of the problem at the same time. The leader divides the problem into subparts and engages the group in discussing them in a logical sequence.

While specific leadership activities may vary with the nature of the problem, other activities are relatively common across all problems. The leader should avoid dominating the discussion and instead encourage group members to do most of the talking. The goal is to involve all participants by asking exploratory questions, encouraging task-based disagreement, and refraining from directly judging or evaluating members' ideas. Maier cautions against premature closure and argues that the leaders' role should be to keep attention focused on the problem where solution possibilities are likely to be richest. The leader should protect those group members who may express a minority view and ensure that such views receive a fair hearing. More broadly, the leader's behavior should legitimize the taking of a minority viewpoint, and this behavior should be a model for all group members. Norms of healthy conflict should be encouraged.

Above all the leader should avoid personally advocating a "pet" solution to the problem, because that solution is liable to be accorded much more weight than might be justified by its merits. In a similar vein, the leader should emphasize that ownership of any idea or suggestion does not reside in the individual proposing it but rather within the entire group. Pitting "Jim's solution" against "Sandy's solution" is likely to pit Jim against Sandy as well as the two alternatives. Ideas should stand on their merits, not on the personalities of those suggesting them. Similarly, when the group reaches a decision it should also be owned by the group. The winners and losers that emerge from a meeting should be alternatives, not people.

### Reaching the Decision

One of the principle functions of the leader is to provide periodic summaries, thereby enabling the group to keep track of its progress. Differences of opinion that are likely to have characterized the earlier and middle stages of the meeting are likely to give rise to convergence in which differences are gradually reduced.

When polarization occurs and differences threaten to disrupt the group, Maier proposes that the leader use what he terms the "two-column method." In this approach all group members engage in the task of building a list of the advantages and disadvantages of each of the proposed alternatives.

The objective is to achieve consensus or "a meeting of the minds." However, consensus does not mean unanimity among group members' initial preferences. Indeed, unanimity of view is impossible in many circumstances. It does mean a final decision that each and every member of the group can stand behind and support. If it is not unanimity of view, it is a level of full agreement just short of unreserved unanimity. This definition of consensus suggests another important dimension of the leader's role within the group: *consensus testing*. Silence does not indicate consent, and it is the leader's responsibility within GII to poll group members to ensure that any apparent consensus indeed reflects the wishes of all group members. This further reinforces group ownership of the decision.

There are, however, some situations in which a group cannot reach such full agreement. Maier cautions that such a failure should be regarded not as the leader's problem but rather as the group's problem. The leader should make it the group's responsibility to determine what should be done if consensus is not reached. The group's task is shifted from how to solve the problem to how to decide on a process to deal with the lack of consensus in solving the problem. In the hospital emergency ward case discussed earlier in this chapter, the group might agree to some random process (such as drawing straws) to determine who works which holiday shift. In other instances, the group might agree to abide by a majority vote or to abide by the leader's decision.

There is some evidence that although most managers feel comfortable employing AI, AII, CI, or CII, they lack some self-confidence in carrying out the demands of GII (Jago, 1979). Perhaps this stems from the belief that managers have no control in group decision making or that it represents an abdication of authority or responsibility. Neither is the case. The reason is that GII requires certain unique skills. In the next chapter, and later in Chapters 8 through 12, we will be describing models that purport to specify which of the decision processes is appropriate to various types of decision problems. In these models we will be assuming that the leader understands each of the decision processes and has at least a minimal level of skill in executing them. We realize that there may be instances in which this assumption may be incorrect, and in such cases the recommendations of the models may have to be modified accordingly.

Although not all managers may have the necessary skills to conduct a GII meeting, we do believe that all managers have the aptitude to learn them. We could incorporate the level of skill one possesses as one of the factors that should regulate one's choice of management style. To do so, however, would unnecessarily reduce managerial effectiveness and misrepresent people's ultimate capabilities to learn, grow, and adapt to their environments.

## ILLUSTRATIVE CASES

The models to be described in subsequent chapters are general ones and are designed to fit any decision problem that might confront a manager in an organization. Due to their generality these models may seem abstract, or only "theoretical." To encourage readers to practice linking these models with concrete examples, we will conclude this chapter with eight cases chosen from hundreds of real managerial decisions we have collected from managers. Five of these are group problems; here, the potentially applicable processes are those that have been described in Tables 4–1 and 4–2. The last three problems are individual problems; these lend themselves to one or more of the alternatives shown in Table 4–3.

The reader is encouraged to study the lists of processes and then to decide which should be employed in each of the eight situations. The opportunity to compare those choices with the choices of the models will be presented in later chapters.

---

### CASE 1    PARKING LOT DECISION PROBLEM

You have recently been appointed manager of a new plant, which is presently under construction. Your team of five department heads has been selected, and they are now working with you in selecting their own staff, purchasing equipment, and generally anticipating the problems that are likely to arise when you move into the plant in three months.

Yesterday you received from the architect a final set of plans for the building, and for the first time you examined the parking facilities that are available. There is a large lot across the road from the plant intended primarily for hourly workers and lower-level supervisory personnel. In addition, there are seven spaces immediately adjacent to the administrative offices, intended for visitor and reserved parking. Company policy requires that a minimum of three spaces be made available for visitor parking, leaving you only four spaces to allocate among yourself and your five department heads. There is no way of increasing the total number of spaces without changing the structure of the building.

Up to now there have been no obvious status differences among your team, which has worked together very well in the planning phase of the operation. To be sure, there are salary differences, with your administrative, manufacturing, and engineering managers receiving slightly more than the quality-control and industrial-relations managers. Each has recently been promoted to the new position and expects reserved parking privileges as a consequence of the new status. From past experience you know that people feel strongly about things that would be indicative of their status. So far you and your subordinates have been working together as a team, and you are reluctant to do anything that might jeopardize this relationship.

*Review the decision processes in Table 4–1 and decide which comes closest to what you would do were you the manager in the above situation. For future reference circle your choice below:*

AI        AII        CI        CII        GII

## CASE 2    COAST GUARD CUTTER DECISION PROBLEM

You are the captain of a 210 ft. medium-endurance coast guard cutter, with a crew of nine officers and sixty-five enlisted personnel. Your mission is general at-sea law enforcement and search and rescue. At 2:00 A.M. this morning, while en route to your home port after a routine two-week patrol, you received word from the New York Rescue Coordination Center that a small plane had ditched 70 miles offshore. You obtained all the available information concerning the location of the crash, informed your crew of the mission, and set a new course at maximum speed heading for the scene to commence a search for survivors and wreckage.

You have now been searching for 20 hours. Your search operation has been increasingly impaired by rough seas, and there is evidence of a severe storm building to the southwest. The atmospherics associated with the deteriorating weather have made communications with the New York Rescue Center impossible. A decision must be made shortly about whether to abandon the search and place your vessel on a northeasterly course to ride out the storm (thereby protecting the vessel and your crew, but relegating any possible survivors to almost certain death from exposure) or to continue a potentially futile search and incur the risks it would entail.

You have contacted the weather bureau for up-to-date information concerning the severity and duration of the storm. While your crew are extremely conscientious about their responsibility, you believe that they would be divided on the decision of leaving or staying.

*Review the decision processes in Table 4–1 and decide which comes closest to what you would do were you the captain in the above situation. For future reference circle your choice below:*

AI      AII      CI      CII      GII

## CASE 3    NEW MACHINES DECISION PROBLEM

You are the manufacturing manager in a large electronics plant. The company's management has always been searching for ways of increasing efficiency. They have recently installed new machines and put in a new, simplified work system, but to the surprise of everyone, including yourself, the expected increase in productivity was not realized. In fact, production has begun to drop, quality has fallen off, and the number of employee separations has risen.

You do not believe that there is anything wrong with the machines. You have had reports from other companies that are using them, and the reports confirm this opinion. You have also had representatives from the firm that built the machines go over them, and they report that the machines are operating at peak efficiency.

You suspect that some parts of the new work system may be responsible for the change, but this view is not widely shared among your immediate subordinates, who are four first-level supervisors, each in charge of a section, and your supply manager. The drop in production has been variously attributed to poor training of the operators, lack of an adequate system of financial incentives, and poor morale. Clearly this is an issue about which there is considerable depth of feeling within individuals and potential disagreement among your subordinates.

This morning you received a phone call from your division manager. He had just received your production figures for the last six months and was calling to express his concern. He indicated that the problem was yours to solve in any way that you thought best, but that he would like to know within a week what steps you planned to take.

You share your division manager's concern with the falling productivity and know that your people are also concerned. The problem is to decide what steps to take to rectify the situation.

*Review the decision processes in Table 4–1 and decide which comes closest to what you would do were you the manager in the above situation. For future reference circle your choice below:*

AI      AII      CI      CII      GII

## CASE 4    R & D PROJECTS DECISION PROBLEM

You are the head of a research and development laboratory in the nuclear reactor division of a large corporation. Often it is not clear whether a particular piece of research is potentially of commercial interest or merely of "academic" interest to the researchers. In your judgment, one major area of research has advanced well beyond the level at which operating divisions pertinent to the area could possibly assimilate or make use of the data being generated.

Recently, two new areas with potentially high returns for commercial development have been proposed by one of the operating divisions. The team working in the area referred to in the previous paragraph is ideally qualified to research these new areas. Unfortunately, both the new areas are relatively devoid of scientific interest, while the project on which the team is currently engaged is of great scientific interest to all members.

At the moment, this is, or is close to being, your best research team. The team is very cohesive, has a high level of morale, and has been very productive. You are concerned not only that they would not want to switch their effort to these new areas, but also that forcing them to concentrate on these two new projects could adversely affect their morale, their good intragroup working relations, and their future productivity both as individuals and as a team.

You have to respond to the operating division within the next two weeks indicating what resources, if any, can be devoted to working on these projects. It would be possible for the team to work on more than one project, but each project would need the combined skills of all the members of the team, so no fragmentation of the team is technically feasible. This fact, coupled with the fact that the team is very cohesive, means that a solution that satisfies any team member would very probably go a long way to satisfying everyone on the team.

*Review the decision processes in Table 4–1 and decide which comes closest to what you would do were you the manager in the above situation. For future reference circle your choice below:*

**AI    AII    CI    CII    GII**

## CASE 5    PURCHASING DECISION PROBLEM

You have recently been appointed vice president in charge of purchasing for a large manufacturing company. The company has twenty plants, all located in the Midwest. Historically, the company has operated in a highly decentralized fashion with each of the plant managers encouraged to operate with only minimal control and direction from the corporate office.

In the area of purchasing, each of the purchasing executives who report to the plant manager does the purchasing for his or her plant. There seems to be little or no coordination among them, and the relationships that do exist are largely ones of competition.

Your position was created when it began to appear to the president that the company was likely to face increasing difficulty in securing certain essential raw materials. In order to protect the company against this possibility, the present haphazard, decentralized arrangement must be abandoned or at least modified to meet the current problems.

You were chosen for the position because of your extensive background in corporate purchasing with another firm that operated in a much more centralized fashion. Your appointment was announced in the last issue of the company house organ. You are anxious to get started, particularly since the peak buying season is now only three weeks away. A procedure must be established that will minimize the likelihood of serious shortages and secondarily achieve the economies associated with the added power of centralized purchasing.

*Review the decision processes in Table 4–1 and decide which comes closest to what you would do were you the manager in the above situation. For future reference circle your choice below:*

**AI      AII      CI      CII      GII**

---

## CASE 6    CLIENT COMPLAINT DECISION PROBLEM

You are regional manager of an international management consulting company. You have a staff of six consultants reporting to you, each of whom enjoys a considerable amount of autonomy with clients in the field.

Yesterday you received a complaint from one of your major clients regarding the effectiveness of the job being done by one of your people. The nature of the problem was not made very explicit, but it was clear that the client was dissatisfied and that something would have to be done if you were to restore the client's faith in the company.

The consultant assigned to work on that contract has been with the company for six years. Trained in systems analysis and one of the best in that profession, this person is capable of superb performance and for the first four or five years was a model for the more junior consultants. More recently, however, there has been a marked change in attitude. What used to be identification with the company now seems to be replaced with an arrogant indifference. This change in interest has been noticed by the other consultants.

This is not the first complaint that you have had from a client. Several months ago another client told you that the consultant had seemed to him at times to be under the influence of drugs.

It is important to get to the root of the problem quickly if your major client is to be retained. Your consultant has invaluable skills and experience and would be almost impossible to replace. Your instincts tell you that this person must be "salvageable," but how?

*Review the decision processes in Table 4–3 and decide which comes closest to what you would do were you the manager in the above situation. For future reference circle your choice below:*

**AI    AII    CI    GI    DI**

---

## CASE 7    LIBRARY SPACE DECISION PROBLEM

You are the head librarian in corporate headquarters of a large multibillion dollar company. Your library maintains most business periodicals, reference works, and textbooks dealing with various facets of business management. Recently you have acquired a small collection of works of fiction and "best sellers," which can be borrowed by employees for their personal reading. To take on this additional function it was necessary to acquire additional space and to hire an assistant librarian, with whom you have developed a close working relationship.

The new space was previously used for storage and is in substantial need of redecoration before it can be of much use. As a first step it must be painted, and you have made arrangements with the maintenance department to do that next week. You have just received a color chart showing available colors, any one of which would be acceptable. You must notify maintenance of your choice by late afternoon.

*Review the decision processes in Table 4–3 and decide which comes closest to what you would do were you the manager in the above situation. For future reference circle your choice below:*

**AI    AII    CI    GI    DI**

---

## CASE 8    HIRING DECISION PROBLEM

Six months ago you were brought in as manager of research and development of a large pulp and paper firm. Your appointment was brought about by a policy decision to phase out the long-range basic research program on which the company had embarked ten years ago and to develop a research program more immediately applicable to the company's needs. You realized that your assignment would be a difficult one—the total budget was to be cut 25 percent over that under which your predecessor operated—but it was a challenge and a significant increase in responsibility over your previous job.

Your previous reputation as a hard-nosed cost-conscious manager was not helped when you had to let several of your subordinates know that they had six months in which to find new employment. One of the others, a specialist in data analysis whom you did not want to lose, found a better job and resigned, giving only two-weeks notice. You tried to persuade this person to rethink the matter, but it was clear to you that this individual was very unhappy over the changed mission of the R & D function and with the "arbitrary dismissal" of several close friends. This departure will be a loss. The individual's superb technical skills more than compensated for deficiencies in other areas.

You began a search for a successor immediately, hoping to find someone who could start work before the month is up. The requirements for the position are quite clear-cut. You need a person who is competent in multivariate analysis and experimental design, who is experienced in working with computers, and who is knowledgeable, concerned, and interested in solving applied problems in an industry such as yours.

A phone call to your previous employer produced a couple of candidates, and you have interviewed both of them, checked out their recommendations, and made an assessment of their qualifications. You have also learned of a potential candidate in your present organization. This candidate appears to have the kind of educational background that you require, but you don't know anything about the person's familiarity with computer programming. The individual most knowledgeable about this should be your present data analysis specialist. You hope to reach a decision among the three candidates by next week.

*Review the decision processes in Table 4–3 and decide which comes closest to what you would do were you the manager in the above situation. For future reference circle your choice below:*

AI    AII    CI    GI    DI

## SUMMARY

In this chapter we have described the range of alternatives available to managers for deciding both group and individual decision problems. The alternatives can be placed on a continuum of participation by subordinates or power sharing by the manager. AI is least participative for group and individual decision problems while GII and DI are the most participative.

These alternatives require different skills. The success to be expected is dependent not only on the leader's choice of method but also on his or her skill in the implementation of the method chosen. Leadership skills applicable to the GII processes were described.

Finally, eight decision problems were described and the reader encouraged to think of the most appropriate process for each. Undoubtedly, certain options seemed more likely to be successful than others, and the most effective process for one case may have been different than the most effective process for another case. This issue of the relative effectiveness of these decision processes will guide our inquiry in many of the subsequent chapters.

Our basic assumption—that of a situational or contingency theory—is that the most effective decision process will vary with the situation. Delegation or consensus decision making by groups may be exceptionally effective in some situations but disastrous in others.

Our goal is the development of a roadmap to enable managers to select the most effective decision process for each situation that they encounter. The criteria of effectiveness will include many that were discussed in the previous chapter including decision quality, commitment, time, and development.

The next chapter will present a simple model—widely known as the Vroom-Yetton model. Chapters 8 through 12 present a more complex model that lends itself to a personal computer. The reader who is familiar with the Vroom-Yetton model or who feels comfortable with complex expert systems may choose to skip to Chapter 8.

# CHAPTER FIVE

# SITUATIONAL THEORIES OF PARTICIPATION

## *The Vroom-Yetton Model*

Most of the widely known theories of leadership style do not consider differences in situational requirements. McGregor's Theory Y, Likert's System 4, Ouchi's Theory Z, and Blake and Mouton's 9–9 Leadership Style are noncontingency theories. They share a view that there is one best approach to managing— usually involving decision making by consensus and delegation—that is universal in its application. To be sure, most of these theorists acknowledge some role for the situation in implementing their universal prescription. Likert, for example, states:

> Supervision is . . . always a relative process. To be effective and to communicate as intended, a leader must always adapt his behavior to take into account the expectation, values and interpersonal skills of those with whom he is interacting. . . . There can be no specific rules of supervision which will work well in all situations. Broad principles can be applied in the process of supervision and furnish valuable guides to behavior. These principles, however, must be applied in a manner that takes fully into account the characteristics of the specific situation and of the people involved. (1961, p. 95)

To Likert and others, this situational relativity is a matter of individual fine tuning and is incapable of further specification. There are some theorists, however, who have put forth contingency theories that have attempted to be specific about the way in which styles of leadership should be related to situational requirements. While this book is not about leadership in general, or even contingency theories of leadership in general, we will digress briefly to consider four theories of this type. All four are precursors of our work, and the differences among them should prove instructive.

## FIEDLER'S CONTINGENCY MODEL

The most thoroughly researched of situational theories is Fiedler's Contingency Model of Leadership (1967). Fiedler has developed a short personality test that can be used to distinguish leaders. The test, deceptively simple, requires leaders to think of the person with whom they "could work least well." That person is then rated on a set of eight-point scales anchored at either end by a set of adjectives such as pleasant–unpleasant, and friendly–unfriendly. Fiedler calls this measure the Least Preferred Co-worker Scale (LPC) and refers to those with low scores, that is, who describe their least preferred co-worker in relatively unfavorable terms, as *task motivated.* Similarly, those with high scores, who view their least preferred co-worker in relatively favorable terms, are called *relationship motivated.*

Defining leadership styles in terms of motivations rather than behavior makes it difficult to see the direct relevance of this personality characteristic for participation. At times Fiedler describes task-motivated leaders as autocratic and describes relationship-motivated leaders as participative, but, in later elaborations of the theory, he acknowledges that it is not quite as simple as this.

Fiedler and his colleagues have examined the relationship between leaders' LPC scores and objective criteria of group or organizational performance. Many different types of groups have been studied, including basketball teams, army tank crews, and crews working in open-hearth steel shops. The correlations varied over an extremely wide range. In some situations high-LPC leaders were highest in performance; in others they were low performers.

This variation in results was most perplexing. However, Fiedler found that much of this apparent inconsistency could be explained by classifying the situations on three dimensions: (1) the degree of structure involved in the group task, (2) the amount of power given to the leader by virtue of his or her position, and (3) the quality of interpersonal relationships between the leader and other members. To Fiedler, these dimensions have one thing in common. Each pertains to a different aspect of the "favorableness of the situation." Thus, a highly favorable situation is characterized by high-task structure, high-position power, and positive leader–member relationship.

Relationship-motivated leaders (with high LPC scores) are found to be more successful in moderately favorable situations. On the other hand, those who are task motivated (with low LPC scores) tend to be more successful in both highly unfavorable and highly favorable situations. Equating task-motivated leadership with autocratic leadership and relationship-motivated leadership with participative leadership leads us to the conclusion that autocrats do best in extreme situations (either very favorable or very unfavorable). Participative leaders do best when the situation is at neither extreme of favorability.

We will not recite here the rationale given by Fiedler for these assertions. Nor will we take sides in the deep controversy over the extent to which the theory is consistent with available evidence (for example, McMahon, 1972; Ashour, 1973; Schriesheim & Kerr, 1977; Vecchio, 1983). Our present concern is with the extent to which it helps provide present and aspiring leaders with a basis for thinking and acting intelligently about issues of power sharing and participation.

On this criterion we find the Fiedler model wanting. It does not provide any guidance to leaders in carrying out their roles effectively. It could provide some help in leader selection and placement, or in what Fiedler calls "organizational engineering"—altering the situation to fit the personality characteristics of the leader. In fact, LEADER MATCH (Fiedler & Chemers, 1984) is a programmed learning instruction manual that enables leaders to learn what their leadership style is (by taking the LPC test) and then how to score situations based on the components of situation favorableness. These two factors—the leader's personality and the favorableness of the situation—enable the user to determine in which types of situations the theory predicts success. The text suggests ways to change situations (by increasing or decreasing their favorableness) when they do not match one's LPC score.

While the Fiedler model is a good example of a situational leadership theory, its validity has been called into question, and it does not address many of the issues of interest to us in this book. Since leadership style is assumed to be a relatively stable and enduring personality characteristic, it is neither modifiable by training nor does it provide for flexible adaptation of one's style to the situation. To quote from Fiedler:

> The alternative method would call for training the leader to develop a flexible style and to adapt his leadership style to the particular situation. The author is highly pessimistic that this training approach would be successful. There may be some favored few who can be effective in any leadership situation and some unfortunate few who would find it difficult to lead a troop of hungry Girl Scouts to a hot dog stand. However our experience has not enabled us to identify these individuals. Nor have we found it possible to identify those who can switch their leadership style as the occasion demands. It would seem more promising at this time, therefore, to teach the individual to recognize the conditions under which he can perform best and to modify the situation to suit his leadership style. (1967, pp. 254–258)

Our focus on leader behavior rather than on leader traits leads us to a different conclusion. With regard to autocratic versus participative behavior, it is far easier to adapt one's choice of a decision-making method to the demands of the specific situation than it is to change the features of the decision that may conflict with one's behavioral preferences. Managers may feel more "comfortable" in some situations than in others. Unfortunately, some uncomfortable situations can neither be changed nor ignored.

## HERSEY AND BLANCHARD'S SITUATIONAL LEADERSHIP

While basically a situational leadership theory dealing, at least tangentially, with the subject of participation, Fiedler's contingency theory says little about how leaders can effectively manage the individuals, groups, and external challenges that they face. Our second example of a contingency theory, proposed by Paul Hersey and Ken Blanchard, does address the behavior of leaders that is required to deal with various situations. If Fiedler's contingency theory can be thought of as derivative of the focus on leadership as a trait and on the measurement of individual differences, the Hersey-Blanchard theory is a contingency theory built on the Michigan and Ohio State investigations into leader behavior carried out in the late 1940s and 1950s. Hersey and Blanchard (1982) distinguish four leadership styles—*telling, selling, participating,* and *delegating*—each of which they view as appropriate in some kinds of leadership situations. The situational variable in the Hersey and Blanchard theory is the *maturity* of subordinates, defined in terms of their "readiness to tackle the task facing the group."

A low level of maturity among subordinates requires a telling mode. As the level of maturity of followers increases, the transition should be made to selling followed by participating. Finally, the mature group is most effectively lead by delegation.

Hersey and Blanchard refer to the model as a life-cycle theory and draw an analogy between leader–follower and parent–child relations. Just as parents should relinquish control as a function of the increasing maturity of their children, so too should leaders share more decision-making power as their subordinates acquire greater experience with and commitment to their tasks.

The Hersey-Blanchard model is different from Fiedler's in several ways. Representing leadership in terms of what a leader does, rather than what he or she is, permits the model to be used in leader training rather than in selection and job engineering as is the case with Fiedler's approach. As a consequence, the Hersey-Blanchard life-cycle model has been widely used in training managers and executives, rivaling in this respect the Blake-Mouton *managerial grid* (Blake and Mouton, 1964), an earlier two-dimensional noncontingency theory. Its usefulness for such purposes stems from the possibility of leaders varying their styles with their assessment of the maturity level of subordinates. There is also no reason why a given leader could not adopt a delegating mode with one subordinate and a selling mode with another if they were at different ends of the maturity spectrum.

While the behavioral focus of the Hersey-Blanchard theory lends itself to a wider range of applications than was true for the Fiedler model, these applications are limited by an oversimplified concept of situational demands. It substitutes only one dimension—the maturity level of subordinates—for Fiedler's three components of situation favorableness encompassing characteristics of the task, the leader, and the followers. Intuitively it seems reasonable to expect the effectiveness of power-sharing methods, like participation and delegation, to be governed by such additional factors as the nature of the problem to be solved and perhaps even the traditions of the organization in which the decision is embedded. The analogy of parent–child relationships is, at best, a partial and misleading one. While Hersey and Blanchard define maturity of subordinates in relation to the group task, their analysis does not explicitly recognize that groups may have "multiple maturities" depending on such things as external demands, role requirements, tasks, and information.

Another limitation of the Hersey-Blanchard model is the absence of research of the kind that would be needed to validate either the model in its entirety or its components. In order to carry out this research it would undoubtedly be necessary to clarify, both conceptually and operationally, the precise meaning of the terms contained in the model, especially the maturity of subordinates. These terms evoke strong images, but the nature of the image can potentially vary among persons.

## HOUSE'S PATH–GOAL THEORY OF LEADERSHIP

House's (1971) "path–goal" theory of leadership has generated far greater research than the Hersey-Blanchard model and has produced at least as much supportive evidence for its position as has Fiedler's model. Building on the work of Evans (1970), House and his associates argue that a leader's most important role is that of motivating subordinates. This is accomplished by clarifying *paths* to desired *goals* and by providing subordinates with rewards to supplement those that may be found in the environment (House & Dessler, 1974; House & Mitchell, 1974).

The theory deals with four types of leader behaviors: directive, supportive, participative, and achievement oriented. For our purposes we are concerned with the theory's treatment of participation. Here the theory makes two predictions (House & Mitchell, 1974):

- Participation is appropriate when subordinates are assigned a challenging task that is also ambiguous.
- In other tasks, participation is most appropriate if subordinates have a high need for independence and are "antiauthoritarian" in their personalities.

When compared to Fiedler's model, path–goal theory clearly deals more specifically with the concept of participation and its expected effects. When

compared to the Hersey-Blanchard model, the contingencies governing participation are a bit more complex and do not rest on poorly conceptualized variables.

Nonetheless, we find the treatment of participation in path–goal theory
to be incomplete. The efficacy of participation depends on additional factors
beyond those two elements of the task and two personality characteristics
included in the theory. Specifically, we find that the absence of any treatment
of the decision situation, within which participation would occur, to be a
serious omission in the approach. Although the tasks assigned to subordinates
may be relevant, they seem less important in determining the optimal degree
of participation than the nature of the problems or decisions requiring action
by the leader.

Although research has confirmed several elements of path–goal theory,
we are also concerned about the lack of research specifically testing its propositions regarding participation. In a recent and exhaustive review of available
studies, Indvik (1986) found insufficient evidence to confirm path–goal's participation hypotheses.

## THE ORIGINAL VROOM-YETTON MODEL

In 1973, the senior author and a colleague, then a graduate student and now
a professor at the Australian Graduate School of Management, published what
has come to be called the Vroom-Yetton model (Vroom & Yetton, 1973). The
model was in the spirit of Fiedler, Hersey-Blanchard, and House in the sense
that it dealt explicitly with situational differences. In some ways it was similar
to each. It shared with Hersey-Blanchard and House the emphasis on leader
actions rather than personality. It shared with Fiedler and House a broader
conception of situational characteristics, embracing not only subordinates' qualities but also the task to be performed and certain ingredients of the context
within which the task had to be carried out.

But it was different in major respects from each of the other three approaches. First, its focus on the amount and form of participation of decision
making was explicit. It did not profess to deal with all of leadership or of
what leaders do. Instead it concentrated only on those aspects bearing on
power sharing by leaders and on participation and influence by those who
work with them.

A second difference lies in what is meant by the term *situation*. For
Fiedler the situation is a role that must match the qualities of the leader; for
Hersey-Blanchard, it is the maturity level of the subordinate(s) being lead;
for House, it is the subordinates' assigned task. For Vroom and Yetton, the
situation is a problem or decision faced by the leader.

Each problem or decision is thought to represent a distinctive combination
of characteristics that ought to influence the leader's choice of leadership style.
For example, different leadership styles or amounts of participation may be

prescribed for complex decisions than for simple ones even though both might be faced within the course of a given day.

We will discuss first the part of this model that applies to group problems, defined in the previous chapter as decision problems affecting more than one of the manager's subordinates. At the core of the model is a method for choosing among five decision processes ranging from AI (most autocratic) to GII (most participative). (See Table 4–1 for a description of these decision processes.) This is accomplished through a situational analysis using seven "problem attributes." To determine the most effective decision-making process the leader evaluates the status of the immediate decision on the following seven factors:

### Attribute A: The Importance of the Decision Quality

In Chapter 3 we used the term *decision quality* to refer to the technical aspects of the decision. A decision is of high quality to the extent to which it is consistent with the organizational goals to be attained and with potentially available information. A high-quality solution "solves the problem" or has a high likelihood of doing so.

Here we introduce a related concept—the *importance* of decision quality. Certain decisions do not require a high-quality decision. In fact, in such situations the leader should be indifferent to the alternatives, provided they meet other requirements such as acceptance by subordinates. For example, the director of the emergency ward in the previous chapter should be indifferent concerning who works at what times as long as the ward is adequately staffed and the physicians are willing to implement whatever is decided.

On the other hand, a manager cannot be indifferent to alternative strategies for regaining market share, nor can a surgeon be indifferent about what surgical procedures to use. Both decisions have a substantial analytical component, and the effectiveness of the decision will be dependent, in large measure, on the consistency of the chosen alternative with organizational goals and available information.

Problem attribute A performs two functions in the model. First of all, it affects the importance of other attributes. If decision quality is important, then other qualities become critical to an effective decision—most notably, where information exists pertinent to achieving a high-quality decision and how that information is to be processed.

A second function of this problem attribute is a more direct one. All other things being equal, major decisions in which the quality of the decision is of considerable importance warrant more participative processes.

### Attribute B: Leader's Information Relevant to the Problem

If a problem or decision possesses a quality requirement, information is needed to permit the intelligent creation and evaluation of alternatives. This attribute refers to the extent to which the leader possesses sufficient information to solve the problem or make the decision without the aid of subordinates. Vroom and Yetton intend the term *information* to refer to technical data relevant to the external consequences of alternatives, and not to information concerning what solution would most "please" subordinates. In general, the model prescribes a more participative choice by the leader when he or she does not possess the information.

### Attribute C: Extent to Which the Problem Is Structured

Decision scientists frequently refer to decision problems as "well structured," "well programmed," or "programmable." A structured problem is one in which the decisionmaker is familiar with all three of the following problem components: (1) the current state, (2) the desired state, and (3) the mechanisms for transforming the former into the latter. The alternative courses of action and the criteria against which they are to be evaluated are all known. These are the problems for which optimization techniques of the type developed in the decision sciences are potentially applicable.

On the other hand, decisionmakers are frequently much less experienced in dealing with the problems they face. The present state may not be clearly understood and may require diagnosis. Creativity is required in inventing new solutions, or analysis is required to clarify the goals or desired state. Such problems are ill formulated by the standards of the management scientist.

What role does this attribute play in selecting a decision-making process? Leavitt (1958) argues that the methods of management science are uniquely suited to well-structured and programmable decisions. It is the unstructured problems that require participative management, group processes, and brainstorming. The role of this problem attribute in the Vroom-Yetton model is similar—recommending more group-oriented processes, such as CII and GII, for problems that are less well formulated or understood.

### Attribute D: Importance of Acceptance of Decision by Subordinates to Effective Implementation

Maier (1963) has proposed that the effectiveness of decisions is dependent not only on their quality but also on their acceptance by subordinates. Furthermore he has proposed that decisions vary in the degree to which they require acceptance by subordinates. This attribute has much in common with problem attribute A (importance of quality) in the sense that it regulates the effects of other factors. But it differs in that it addresses the need for acceptance and support in getting the decision implemented.

Two factors enter into our judgments concerning the importance of acceptance. First is the role that subordinates must play in the execution of the decision. If they are not to be involved at all in decision execution, the need for their acceptance is minimal. (One may wish to obtain the benefit of their ideas and thinking, but the purpose of this involvement would be to enhance decision quality, not acceptance.) Maier refers to such situations as "outsider problems."

Second, if subordinates will be executing the decision, the role that they will be playing may require only a set of routine and preplanned steps requiring little thinking or judgment on their part. These situations require compliance by subordinates but not their acceptance or commitment. Both of these latter terms imply voluntary and enthusiastic support of the kind that would be needed to execute decisions in the absence of control systems and well-defined directives. Because participation tends to produce feelings of acceptance and joint ownership over the decision, the model treats the existence of an acceptance requirement as a sign that more participative decision processes are required.

### Attribute E: Probability that the Leader's Decision Will Be Accepted by Subordinates

While participation in decision making tends to produce acceptance, we should not lose sight of the fact that there are circumstances under which autocratic decisions will be readily accepted by subordinates. French and Raven's theory (1959) about the bases of power in social relationships provides at least part of the answer concerning when autocratic decisions will be accepted. Three of their bases of power are likely to produce acceptance of the leader's decisions. They are (1) legitimate power, (2) expert power, and (3) attraction or referent power.

Legitimate power comes from mutual endorsement of the "rules of the game." It is the power base of the umpire in a baseball game or the linesman in a tennis match. While closely akin to the concept of formal authority, French and Raven are careful to point out that legitimate power works only when those whom one is trying to influence accept the influence attempt as legitimate. If one's subordinates believe that the leader should make the decision or that it is the leader's right to do so, then the leader possesses legitimate power.

Expert power is the power base of most professionals. People act on the recommendations of their doctors, lawyers, and accountants—and even of some teachers and professors! In each case the influence is conditional on their belief that such professionals have superior knowledge or expertise about the issue in question. Similarly, in organizations one is more likely to accept and endorse the decisions of those leaders and managers whom one believes to be knowledgeable and informed and to oppose (or ignore) decisions of leaders whom one believes to be ignorant and uninformed.

As is true with legitimate power, to be effective the expertise must be "in the eyes of the beholder." It is not the mere possession of knowledge that counts in decision acceptance but rather the belief on the part of others that you have that knowledge.

One should note that both expert and legitimate power are highly "decision specific." The baseball umpire can call balls and strikes but can't tell batters to bat on the left or the right side of the plate; the doctor can tell us what to do to treat our sprained ankle but not how to vote. In organizations, when leaders and managers attempt to exert influence over others in areas in which they have neither legitimacy nor expertise, their capacity to gain commitment to decisions which they make autocratically is governed by what French and Raven term *attraction* or *referent* power.

Attraction power is based on positive feelings toward the leader. The feelings may involve trust, respect, or admiration. The term *charisma* embodies an extreme form of attraction power.

The reader may have noted the absence of mention in our discussion of power of control over rewards and punishments. Managers in organizations typically have some control over work assignments, salaries, and promotional opportunities of their subordinates. Doesn't this give them power over them? The answer is a clear "yes . . . but!" The influence that comes from possession of rewards and punishments, unaccompanied by one of the other power bases, is likely to cause compliance rather than acceptance. People carry out the decision because they "have to" not because they "want to."

This statement is not meant to denigrate the usefulness of rewards and punishments to influence subordinates but rather to define their role more precisely. In getting people to do things that can be monitored, measured, and observed, they are very useful. However, to gain such intangibles as commitment and acceptance of decisions, they take a poor second place to legitimacy, expertise, and attraction.

The likelihood of acceptance of an autocratic decision made by a leader depends not only on that leader's power but also on the particular decisions he or she makes. Some decisions are inherently easier to sell than others. Subordinates are likely to be far more supportive of a pay raise of 25 percent than a 25 percent increase in workload even though both came from the top without their input. The amount of the three types of power needed must be assessed in relation to the requirements of a particular decision. In the Vroom-Yetton model, greater participation is prescribed when the leader lacks the power required to "sell his or her own decision."

### Attribute F: Congruence of Organizational and Subordinate Goals

Almost a half-century ago, Mary Parker Follett described the skills of the effective organizational leader in these words: "Above all, he should make his co-workers see that it is not his purpose which is to be achieved, but a common purpose, born of the desires and the activities of the group" (1941, pp. 142–144). Common purposes pave the way for joint decision making. Involving others in decision making is more likely to result in synergy when differences exist—differences not in the ends to be achieved—but rather in the means of achieving them. Thus, the Hersey-Blanchard model discussed earlier in this chapter prescribed greater use of power-sharing methods in dealing with more mature subordinates who could be trusted to pursue organizational objectives. In the Vroom-Yetton model, goal congruence plays a similar function: In the context of a particular decision, shared goals and objectives are a signal of greater potential benefit from the use of more participative methods.

### Attribute G: Conflict or Disagreement Among Subordinates

The seventh and final problem attribute in the Vroom-Yetton model deals with conflict or disagreement among subordinates. At first glance, conflict might be thought of as the opposite end of the dimension that we have termed goal congruence. It is certainly true that one of the sources of goal incongruence is a set of group members deadlocked in a struggle over whose goals are to be paramount. But on reflection, one can see that there can be congruent goals but considerable conflict or disagreement over how to achieve them. Conflict can exist over means as well as ends.

Conflict plays no role in the Hersey-Blanchard model, but is one of the elements that enters into the measurement of an unfavorable situation in Fiedler's contingency model. From our perspective there are four seemingly reasonable propositions that one might make about the consequences of conflict, each of which has implications for participative decision making:

1. Conflict among people increases the time that they will require to make joint decisions.
2. Conflict among people may polarize and be a source of divisiveness in subsequent relationships.
3. Conflict among people can lead to clearer thinking and better decisions.
4. Conflict among people is a sign that they should interact more (rather than less) frequently in an attempt to resolve their differences.

The first two of the above statements imply that one should avoid conflict. The presence of conflict or disagreement should result in more autocratic practices. In contrast, the third and fourth imply that one should confront conflict. Its presence should be a sign to utilize more participative practices, encouraging those with different opinions to interact with one another in the context of solving problems.

In the Vroom-Yetton model conflict plays a much smaller role than any of the other six attributes. The role is primarily *conflict-confronting* rather than *conflict-avoiding* and flows naturally from the fourth statement above. Where acceptance or commitment on the part of subordinates is of importance, the presence of conflict or differences should signal a need for a more participative solution in which differences can be resolved in advance of making the decision. This can be accomplished without impairing decision quality, and the time spent in doing so should be more than repaid in smoother execution of the decision.

### Climbing a Decision "Tree"

Each of the seven problem attributes is represented by a yes–no question. These questions are shown in Table 5–1. A manager faced with a particular problem to solve or decision to make can diagnose situational demands by answering each of the seven questions. Answers provide the basis for selecting among the decision processes (AI through GII).

Much of the work of the model is performed by a set of seven rules. These are rules of thumb or guidelines, each of which utilizes two or more problem attributes as signs indicating the need to eliminate alternatives from consideration because of the risk they pose to either decision quality or decision acceptance.

Shown in Table 5–2, the rules are of two types. The first three are quality rules—so named because they are intended to protect the quality of the decision. The next four are acceptance rules, which perform a similar function for the acceptance of the decision.

Figure 5–1 shows a *decision tree*—the simplest tree to show the effects of the seven rules. The questions relating to each problem attribute are arranged at the top of the figure. To use the tree, one selects a problem that is within one's area of freedom or area of discretion and is also a problem that has potential effects on more than one subordinate. One then enters the decision tree at the extreme left at *state the problem* and asks the first question: Does the problem possess a quality requirement? The answer, *yes* or *no*, denotes

**TABLE 5–1    Problem Attributes**

| | |
|---|---|
| *Question A* | Does the problem possess a quality requirement? |
| *Question B* | Do you have sufficient information to make a high-quality decision? |
| *Question C* | Is the problem structured? |
| *Question D* | Is acceptance of decision by subordinates important for effective implementation? |
| *Question E* | If you were to make the decision by yourself, is it reasonably certain that it would be accepted by your subordinates? |
| *Question F* | Do subordinates share the organizational goals to be attained in solving this problem? |
| *Question G* | Is conflict among subordinates over preferred solutions likely? |

*Source*: Vroom, Yetton, & Jago (1976).

**TABLE 5–2    Rules Underlying the Model—Group Problems**

### 1. The Leader Information Rule

If the quality of the decision is important and the leader does not possess enough information or expertise to solve the problem alone, then AI is eliminated from the feasible set.

### 2. The Goal Congruence Rule

If the quality of the decision is important and subordinates are not likely to pursue the organizational goals in their efforts to solve this problem, then GII is eliminated from the feasible set.

### 3. The Unstructured Problem Rule

In situations in which the quality of the decision is important, if the leader lacks the necessary information or expertise to solve the problem alone, and if the problem is unstructured, the method of solving the problem should provide for interaction among subordinates likely to possess relevant information. Accordingly, AI, AII, and CI, which provide no interaction among subordinates, are eliminated from the feasible set.

### 4. The Acceptance Rule

If the acceptance of the decision by subordinates is important for effective implementation, and if it is not reasonably certain that an autocratic decision will be accepted, AI and AII are eliminated from the feasible set.

### 5. The Conflict Rule

If acceptance of the decision is important, is not reasonably certain if the decision is made autocratically, and disagreement among subordinates over possible solutions is likely, the methods used in solving the problem should enable those in disagreement to resolve their differences with full knowledge of the problem. Accordingly, under these conditions AI, AII, and CI, which permit no interaction among subordinates and therefore provide no opportunity for those in conflict to resolve their differences, are eliminated from the feasible set. Their use runs the risk of leaving some of the subordinates with less than the needed commitment to the final decision.

### 6. The Fairness Rule

If the quality of the decision is unimportant but acceptance of the decision is important—and not reasonably certain to result from an autocratic decision—the decision process used must generate the needed acceptance. The decision process should permit the subordinates to interact with one another and negotiate among themselves the method of resolving any differences with full responsibility for determining what is fair and equitable. Accordingly, under these circumstances AI, AII, CI, and CII are eliminated from the feasible set.

### 7. The Acceptance Priority Rule

If acceptance is important, not reasonably certain to result from an autocratic decision, and if subordinates are motivated to pursue the organizational goals represented in the problem, then methods which provide equal partnership in the decision-making process can generate far greater acceptance without risking decision quality. Accordingly, AI, AII, CI, and CII are eliminated from the feasible set.

A. DOES THE PROBLEM POSSESS A QUALITY REQUIREMENT?

B. DO YOU HAVE SUFFICIENT INFORMATION TO MAKE A HIGH-QUALITY DECISION?

C. IS THE PROBLEM STRUCTURED?

D. IS ACCEPTANCE OF DECISION BY SUBORDINATES IMPORTANT FOR EFFECTIVE IMPLEMENTATION?

E. IF YOU WERE TO MAKE THE DECISION BY YOURSELF, IS IT REASONABLY CERTAIN
   THAT IT WOULD BE ACCEPTED BY YOUR SUBORDINATES?

F. DO SUBORDINATES SHARE THE ORGANIZATIONAL GOALS TO BE ATTAINED IN SOLVING THIS PROBLEM?

G. IS CONFLICT AMONG SUBORDINATES OVER PREFERRED SOLUTIONS LIKELY?

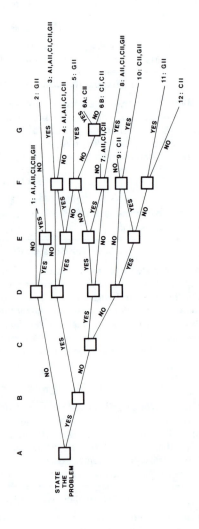

**FIGURE 5–1**  Decision Tree Governing Group Problems—Feasible Set (Vroom, Yetton, & Jago, 1976)

a path that leads to another box signifying another question by the letter immediately above the box. The process continues until one encounters a "terminal node" (that is, an endpoint on the tree) designated by a number (called the "problem type") and one or more of the alternative decision processes. At this point, all seven rules have been applied, and decision processes that threaten either decision quality or acceptance have been eliminated. What is left over is called the *feasible set*.

For some problem types there is only one alternative remaining in the feasible set. For the majority of problem types there are two or more feasible alternatives.

Assume that one has coded a problem as problem type 7. (The problem has a quality requirement; you do not have enough information; the problem is structured; you do not need acceptance by your subordinates [or your decision will be accepted by them]; and your subordinates do not share the organizational goals.) The feasible set includes AII, CI, and CII. (AI is eliminated by Rule 1; GII by Rule 2.) Each of these three alternatives is deemed equally likely to generate any needed decision quality or decision acceptance.

How should one choose among these remaining alternatives? Several bases for choice seem sensible. One could, for example, choose the decision process that one is "best at carrying out"; or the one that is most consistent with one's personality; or the one that has most frequently been used in the past. However, the model looks not at the leaders' skills, propensities, or past behavior but rather at the external consequences of the alternatives.

Vroom and Yetton propose two alternative ways of choosing within the feasible set, each based on a different consequence of participation. The most widely cited model is called *Model A*, and is shown in Figure 5–2. Also called the "Time-Efficient model," Model A is based on the premise that more participative methods are slower than those that are less participative and use up more time on the part of each of those who are involved in the decision. Consequently Model A's prescription for each problem type is the most autocratic alternative within the feasible set. (The reader who compares Figure 5–1 with Figure 5–2 will realize that, operationally, Model A selects the leftmost of the feasible responses identified in Figure 5–1.) For problem type 7, AII is the Model A choice.

Model A is a short-term model. It is focused on the effectiveness of the immediate decision and expends the least amount of time required to achieve that objective.

*Model B* is another basis for choosing within the feasible set. It is based on the observation made in the previous chapter that participation has developmental consequences. Termed the "Time-Investment model," Model B selects the most participative alternative within the feasible set (that is, the rightmost of the feasible responses in Figure 5–1). For problem type 7, CII is the prescribed choice. In fact by glancing down the righthand side of Figure 5–1,

A. DOES THE PROBLEM POSSESS A QUALITY REQUIREMENT?

B. DO YOU HAVE SUFFICIENT INFORMATION TO MAKE A HIGH-QUALITY DECISION?

C. IS THE PROBLEM STRUCTURED?

D. IS ACCEPTANCE OF DECISION BY SUBORDINATES IMPORTANT FOR EFFECTIVE IMPLEMENTATION?

E. IF YOU WERE TO MAKE THE DECISION BY YOURSELF, IS IT REASONABLY CERTAIN
   THAT IT WOULD BE ACCEPTED BY YOUR SUBORDINATES?

F. DO SUBORDINATES SHARE THE ORGANIZATIONAL GOALS TO BE ATTAINED IN SOLVING THIS PROBLEM?

G. IS CONFLICT AMONG SUBORDINATES OVER PREFERRED SOLUTIONS LIKELY?

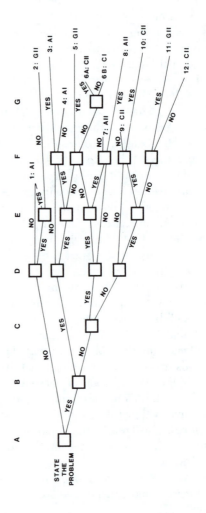

**FIGURE 5-2** Decision Tree Governing Group Problems—Model A: Time Efficient (Vroom, Yetton, & Jago, 1976)

the reader can verify that Model B prescribes a group meeting, either CII or GII, for each of the problem types.

In the Vroom-Yetton model, Models A and B—the Time-Efficient and Time-Investment models respectively—are regarded as antithetical models representing extremes. Both seek to make choices that are consistent with the analytical and behavioral consequences of participation represented by the decision rules, but they differ in the values they place on time and development. Within the constraints imposed by the rules, Model A places exclusive weight on time and no weight on development; Model B places no weight on time and exclusive weight on development.

## APPLYING THE VROOM-YETTON MODEL

The best way of understanding the model is to see how it can be applied to concrete problems. For this purpose we return to the first five illustrative group problems discussed in Chapter 4. The reader is encouraged to compare his or her preferred method of dealing with each situation with the methods prescribed by the model.

### CASE 1    PARKING LOT DECISION PROBLEM

*Synopsis*

> You have four preferential parking spaces that can be allocated among yourself and five department heads, all of whom are expecting the privilege.

*Analysis*

A.   Does the problem possess a quality requirement?   *No*
D.   Is acceptance of the decision by subordinates important for effective implementation?   *Yes*
E.   If you were to make the decision by yourself, is it reasonably certain that it would be accepted by your subordinates?   *No*

*Synthesis*

| | |
|---|---|
| Problem Type | 2 |
| Feasible Set | GII |
| Model A | GII |
| Model B | GII |

This problem is similar to the situation, discussed in the previous chapter, faced by the director of the emergency ward trying to schedule his physicians during the Christmas holidays. One of its central characteristics is the absence of any analytical ingredient. The manager should be indifferent about who parks where. While of little importance to the organization, such problems can be important to people, at least in part because of their symbolic value. Maier (1963) sees such problems as involving the element of fairness and points to the low likelihood of acceptance of both autocratic and consultative methods.

---

## CASE 2    COAST GUARD CUTTER DECISION PROBLEM

### Synopsis

As captain of a coast guard cutter you must decide whether to abandon a search (thereby protecting your ship from a storm) or continue the search with risks to your vessel and crew.

### Analysis

A.  Does the problem possess a quality requirement?  *Yes*
B.  Do you have sufficient information?  *Yes*
D.  Do you need acceptance of your subordinates for effective implementation?  *Yes*
E.  If you were to make an autocratic decision, is it reasonably certain that it would be accepted by your subordinates?  *Yes*
F.  Do your subordinates share the organizational goals to be attained in the solution of the problem?  *Yes*

### Synthesis

| | |
|---|---|
| Problem Type | 3 |
| Feasible Set | AI, AII, CI, CII, GII |
| Model A | AI |
| Model B | GII |

---

In this situation, the rules do not eliminate any of the alternative decision processes. The entire burden of selecting among them rests on the relative weights applied to time and development. Model A—the Time-Efficient model—prescribes AI; Model B—the Time-Investment model—prescribes GII. Given the emergency nature of this particular problem most managers would undoubtedly place substantially more weight on time rather than development.

## CASE 3   New Machines Decision Problem

*Synopsis*

> Although you do not know why, the expected productivity of newly installed machines has not been realized despite their operation at peak efficiency. The first-line supervisors reporting to you have different views about the likely source of the problem.

*Analysis*

> A.   Does the problem possess a quality requirement?   *Yes*
> B.   Do you have sufficient information to make a high-quality decision?   *No*
> C.   Is the problem structured?   *No*
> D.   Is acceptance of the decision important for effective implementation?   *Yes*
> E.   If you were to make the decision by yourself, is it reasonably certain that it would be accepted by your subordinates?   *No*
> F.   Do subordinates share the organizational goals to be attained in solving this problem?   *Yes*

*Synthesis*

| Problem Type | 11 |
|---|---|
| Feasible Set | **GII** |
| Model A | **GII** |
| Model B | **GII** |

The attentive reader may remember this as the problem with which we began Chapter 2. Here the rules eliminate four of the five decision processes leaving only GII. Each of the problem attributes (including "subordinate conflict," which is not needed for generating the feasible set) signals potential benefits from maximum participation of subordinates.

## CASE 4   R & D Projects Decision Problem

*Synopsis*

> You must choose which projects an R & D team will be assigned. Current projects are appealing to the team; proposed projects will be profitable but are devoid of scientific interest.

*Analysis*

A. Does the problem possess a quality requirement? *Yes*
B. Do you have sufficient information to make a high-quality decision? *Yes*
D. Is acceptance of the decision by subordinates important for effective implementation? *Yes*
E. If you were to make an autocratic decision, is it reasonably certain that it would be accepted by your subordinates? *No*
F. Do subordinates share the organizational goals to be attained in solving this problem? *No*
G. Is conflict among subordinates over preferred solutions likely? *No*

*Synthesis*

| | |
|---|---|
| Problem Type | 6B |
| Feasible Set | CI, CII |
| Model A | CI |
| Model B | CII |

For this problem type, the feasible set is restricted to the two consultative modes. Model A prescribes CI, and Model B prescribes CII. AI and AII are eliminated by Rule 4 and GII by Rule 2.

## CASE 5   PURCHASING DECISION PROBLEM

*Synopsis*

As new vice president of purchasing, you inherited a purchasing system decentralized among twenty midwestern plants. New procedures must be established, to be implemented by local purchasing managers, that minimize shortages of raw materials and achieve the economies of scale associated with a more centralized system.

*Analysis*

A. Does the problem possess a quality requirement? *Yes*
B. Do you have sufficient information to make a high-quality decision? *No*
C. Is the problem structured? *Yes or No*
D. Is acceptance of the decision by subordinates important for effective implementation? *Yes*
E. If you were to make the decision by yourself, is it reasonably certain that it would be accepted by your subordinates? *No*
F. Do subordinates share the organizational goals to be attained in solving this problem? *No*
G. Is conflict among subordinates over preferred solutions likely? *Yes*

*Synthesis*

| | |
|---|---|
| Problem Type | **6A** or **12**[*] |
| Feasible Set | **CII** |
| Model A | **CII** |
| Model B | **CII** |

---

[*] Depending upon problem structure.

---

Case 5 is our paraphrase of the beginning of a popular case entitled *The Dashman Company*, published by the Harvard Business School. The complete case also includes a description of the autocratic directive sent out by the actual vice president, requiring each purchasing executive to give the head office advance notice concerning all contracts in excess of $10,000. The case ends with a terse description of the outcome of this directive:

> During the next six weeks the head office received no notices from any plant that contracts were being negotiated. Executives in other departments, who made frequent trips to the plants, reported that the plants were busy, and the usual routines for that time of year were being followed.

## EXTENSION TO INDIVIDUAL PROBLEMS

The concept of participation is equally applicable to understanding a manager's interactions with individuals. In the model, there are common principles in deciding to share one's decision-making power in managerial decisions affecting a single subordinate and in those affecting an entire group. For example, delegating a decision to a single subordinate tends to produce in that person a feeling of ownership or commitment to that decision that is seldom achieved with more autocratic methods. Similarly, it tends to be a source of growth and development, giving people opportunities to use skills untapped by leaders who restrict them to carrying out decisions made at higher levels. Furthermore, whether delegation results in higher-quality decisions depends on such things as the knowledge and talents of both leader and subordinate as well as on their commitment to use these talents in the pursuit of organizational objectives.

The model developed by Vroom and Yetton for individual problems uses a set of decision processes (shown in Table 4–3) ranging from AI (most autocratic) to DI (most participative). It preserves as closely as possible the format, structure, and logic used in the model for group problems. Consequently it also makes use of problem attributes and rules. Table 5–3 shows a minor

**TABLE 5–3   Rules Underlying the Model—Individual Problems**

#### 1a. THE LEADER INFORMATION RULE

If the quality of the decision is important and the leader does not possess enough information or expertise to solve the problem alone, then AI is eliminated from the feasible set.

#### 1b. THE SUBORDINATE INFORMATION RULE

If the quality of the decision is important and the subordinate does not possess enough information or expertise to solve the problem alone, then DI is eliminated from the feasible set.

#### 2a. THE GOAL CONGRUENCE RULE

If the quality of the decision is important and the subordinate is not likely to pursue the organizational goals in an effort to solve this problem, then DI is eliminated from the feasible set.

#### 2b. THE AUGMENTED GOAL CONGRUENCE RULE

Under the conditions specified in the previous rule (that is, quality of decision is important, and the subordinate does not share the organizational goals to be attained in solving the problem), GI may also constitute a risk to the quality of the decision taken in response to an individual problem. Such a risk is a reasonable one to take only if the nature of the problem is such that the acceptance by the subordinate is critical to the effective implementation of the decision and the probability that an autocratic decision will be accepted is low.

#### 3. THE UNSTRUCTURED PROBLEM RULE

In situations in which the quality of the decision is important, if the leader lacks the necessary information or expertise to solve the problem alone, and if the problem is unstructured, the method of solving the problem should provide for interaction with the subordinate and the opportunity for that person to contribute to the generation of alternatives. Accordingly, AI and AII, which do not provide these opportunities, are eliminated from the feasible set.

#### 4. THE ACCEPTANCE RULE

If the acceptance of the decision by the subordinate is important for effective implementation, and if it is not reasonably certain that an autocratic decision will be accepted, AI and AII are eliminated from the feasible set.

#### 6. THE FAIRNESS RULE

If the quality of the decision is unimportant but acceptance of the decision is important—and not reasonably certain to result from an autocratic decision—the decision process used must generate the needed acceptance. The decision process should permit the subordinate to determine what is fair and equitable. Accordingly, under these circumstances AI, AII, and CI are eliminated from the feasible set.

#### 7. THE ACCEPTANCE PRIORITY RULE

If acceptance is important, not reasonably certain to result from an autocratic decision, and if the subordinate is motivated to pursue the organizational goals represented in the problem, then methods that provide equal partnership in the decision-making process can generate far greater acceptance without risking decision quality. Accordingly, AI, AII, and CI are eliminated from the feasible set.

revision of the Vroom-Yetton rules for individual problems proposed by Vroom and Jago (1974).

One of the attributes used in the group model—conflict among subordinates—is omitted from the list and is replaced by subordinate's information. The latter situational characteristic is a key part of a new rule, the *subordinate information rule*, which eliminates delegation from the feasible set when the problem possesses a quality requirement and the subordinate lacks the necessary information and expertise to solve the problem.

The decision tree for individual problems is shown in Figure 5–3. The tree shown reflects the feasible set and, therefore, contains all of the alternatives remaining after the rules have been applied.

As was the case for the group problem model, several alternatives remain for many problem types. One can make more specific prescriptions by taking advantage of the relative importance to the manager of time and of development. The Model B or developmental choices are, as before, the most participative of feasible responses. By assigning to time a zero value, one encourages the leader to utilize only CI, GI, and DI, the three most participative processes in our original list in Table 4–3.

A complication arises, however, in deriving the prescriptions of Model A—the Time-Efficient model. The complication stems from the fact that, in individual problems, maximizing the subordinate's involvement in the decision is not necessarily inefficient from the standpoint of time.

In talking about group problems we made the case that the time required by a decision-making process was directly related to its participativeness. GII requires more time than CII and so on down the scale until one reaches AI. However this argument loses force when the decisions affect only a single subordinate. DI is more participative than GI but is not less time efficient.

Clearly delegation can be a very time-efficient method of solving many problems. To order the five methods in terms of the total amount of time they require would not yield an ordering in terms of participativeness. Vroom and Yetton (1973, p. 193) propose that differences in the time requirements of the various processes for individual problems are not nearly as large as they are for group problems. They propose that AI requires the least time, followed by DI, AII, CI, and GI, in that order. Accordingly, the Model A prescriptions are shown in Figure 5–4.

In working with managers over many years we have frequently heard people say that they were firm believers in delegation but didn't place much faith in participation. McGregor made a similar observation more than a quarter of a century ago (1960, p. 125). The preceding discussion has suggested one possible rationale for such assertions. Consensus decision making and delegation are similar in many of their properties but differ markedly in the amount of time they consume. Those who use delegation but avoid group meetings are acting as if they placed a very high priority on time and attached little or no weight to the consequences of power sharing.

A. DOES THE PROBLEM POSSESS A QUALITY REQUIREMENT?

B. DO YOU HAVE SUFFICIENT INFORMATION TO MAKE A HIGH-QUALITY DECISION?

C. IS THE PROBLEM STRUCTURED?

D. IS ACCEPTANCE OF DECISION BY THE SUBORDINATE IMPORTANT FOR EFFECTIVE IMPLEMENTATION?

E. IF YOU WERE TO MAKE THE DECISION BY YOURSELF, IS IT REASONABLY CERTAIN THAT IT WOULD BE ACCEPTED BY YOUR SUBORDINATE?

F. DOES THE SUBORDINATE SHARE THE ORGANIZATIONAL GOALS TO BE ATTAINED IN SOLVING THIS PROBLEM?

H. DOES THE SUBORDINATE HAVE SUFFICIENT INFORMATION TO MAKE A HIGH-QUALITY DECISION?

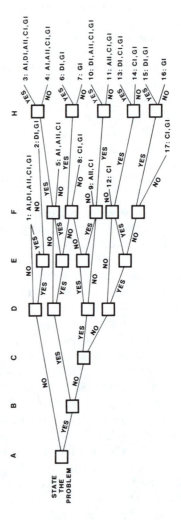

**FIGURE 5-3** Decision Tree Governing Individual Problems—Feasible Set (Vroom, Yetton, & Jago, 1976)

72

A. DOES THE PROBLEM POSSESS A QUALITY REQUIREMENT?

B. DO YOU HAVE SUFFICIENT INFORMATION TO MAKE A HIGH-QUALITY DECISION?

C. IS THE PROBLEM STRUCTURED?

D. IS ACCEPTANCE OF DECISION BY THE SUBORDINATE IMPORTANT FOR EFFECTIVE IMPLEMENTATION?

E. IF YOU WERE TO MAKE THE DECISION BY YOURSELF, IS IT REASONABLY CERTAIN
   THAT IT WOULD BE ACCEPTED BY YOUR SUBORDINATE?

F. DOES THE SUBORDINATE SHARE THE ORGANIZATIONAL GOALS TO BE ATTAINED IN
   SOLVING THIS PROBLEM?

H. DOES THE SUBORDINATE HAVE SUFFICIENT INFORMATION TO MAKE A HIGH-QUALITY DECISION?

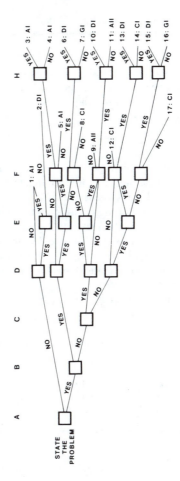

**FIGURE 5-4** Decision Tree Governing Individual Problems—Model A: Time Efficient (Vroom, Yetton, & Jago, 1976)

73

## Applying the Individual Model

We can see how the individual model operates by applying it to the three individual problems that concluded Chapter 4.

---

### CASE 6   CLIENT COMPLAINT DECISION PROBLEM

*Synopsis*

A major client has complained about one of your most competent subordi-nates, who recently has seemed indifferent about his work. The client was not very clear about the problem, but it is clear your goodwill with the client is at stake.

*Analysis*

A.   Does the problem possess a quality requirement?   *Yes*
B.   Do you have sufficient information to make a high-quality decision?   *No*
C.   Is the problem structured?   *No*
D.   Is acceptance of the decision by the subordinate important for effective implementation?   *Yes*
E.   If you were to make the decision by yourself, is it reasonably certain that it would be accepted by the subordinate?   *No*
F.   Does the subordinate share the organizational goals to be attained in this problem?   *No*
H.   Does the subordinate have sufficient information to make a high-quality decision?   *Yes*

*Synthesis*

| | |
|---|---|
| Problem Type | 17 |
| Feasible Set | CI, GI |
| Model A | CI |
| Model B | GI |

---

This is an important problem threatening the loss of a major client. It was brought about by the substandard performance of a single subordinate, which seems not to be a matter of ability but rather of motivation. At this point you have decided not to fire the subordinate, meaning that any actions to be taken must be taken by that person and, hence, require his or her acceptance. The only feasible methods are CI and GI, the former being the Model A method while the latter is that prescribed by Model B. AI is eliminated by both Rule 1 and Rule 4. You don't have the information needed to know what action to take, and the subordinate's commitment is necessary. AII is also eliminated on two separate grounds expressed by Rule 3 and Rule 4. AII is inconsistent with the fact that you don't understand what the problem is and with the fact that the subordinate's acceptance is required. Finally, DI is eliminated as a viable method by Rule 2a. The importance of the problem combined with apparent indifference toward organizational goals by the subordinate makes delegation a risky option.

---

## CASE 7    LIBRARY SPACE DECISION PROBLEM

### Synopsis

You (and/or your assistant) must decide what color to paint the walls of a new room being added to the library. The assistant will have responsibility for the room.

### Analysis

A.   Does the problem possess a quality requirement?   *No*
D.   Is acceptance of the decision by the subordinate important for effective implementation?   *No*

### Synthesis

| | |
|---|---|
| Problem Type | 1 |
| Feasible Set | **AI, AII, CI, GI, DI** |
| Model A | **AI** |
| Model B | **DI** |

---

In many respects, this is a trivial problem that will not have a significant impact on the organization regardless of which method is employed. The fact that the feasible set is full reflects this state of affairs. The time-efficient Model A prescribes AI. A manager pressed for time could make the decision autocratically and inform the subordinate of the chosen alternative. On the other hand, the time-investment Model B prescribes DI. Delegating the decision to the person in charge of the new collection could have developmental value.

---

## CASE 8    HIRING DECISION PROBLEM

*Synopsis*

> You must replace a talented subordinate who has decided to leave due to your dismissal of several of his close friends and colleagues. You have several candidates in mind, including one from another department within the organization. However, you do not know if this candidate has a particular required skill. The current subordinate is likely to have this information.

*Analysis*

> A. Does the problem possess a quality requirement? *Yes*
> B. Do you have enough information to make a high-quality decision? *No*
> C. Is the problem structured? *Yes*
> D. Is acceptance of the decision by the subordinate important for effective implementation? *No*
> E. Does the subordinate share the organizational goals to be attained in this problem? *No*

*Synthesis*

> | | |
> |---|---|
> | Problem Type | 9 |
> | Feasible Set | AII, CI |
> | Model A | AII |
> | Model B | CI |

---

This individual problem is different from the previous ones in the manner in which the subordinate is identified. Since your specialist in data analysis is leaving, his acceptance of the new appointment is of no import. It is important, however, to gain the information possessed by that specialist. Two methods are potentially of value—AII and CI. AII is the Model A solution while CI is the Model B solution. They differ in the degree to which the specialist is involved in the decision.

In AII, questions about the technical competence of the candidate(s) would be asked of the outgoing specialist. CI would entail consultation on the broader problem of who would be a suitable replacement.

## WHO SHOULD MAKE UP THE GROUP?

Most of the situations we have considered have been ones in which existing role relationships specified the person or set of persons composing the group. The subordinates who report to the leader were "the group" for group problems, and the single subordinate responsible for a particular function or division became the affected person to be involved (or not be involved) in the process of solving individual problems.

There are some situations in which a natural group does not exist and has to be created. For example, the organization has just merged with a former competitor, and a transition team or task force must be created to plan the timetable and details of the actual consolidation of activitives of the two firms.

Vroom and Yetton (1973, p. 40) maintain that there are two potentially separate sets of considerations involved in forming a decision-making group. The group should include those persons whose support and cooperation is necessary to implement the decision. We can call this the *acceptance set*. It should also include those persons with the knowledge and expertise necessary to develop a plan of high quality. We can call this the *information set*.

Sometimes these two sets of persons are the same; sometimes they overlap; and occasionally they are distinct. The criteria of acceptance and knowledge are useful guidelines for composing committees and task forces of many kinds to deal with broad nonrecurring kinds of problems.

The same kinds of issues may be applicable within an existing work team set up for other purposes. Sometimes a team discovers that the ultimate implementation of the solution requires the commitment of persons who are not team members. One alternative is to broaden the composition of the team to include such individuals. For example, members of a client system are often included in deliberations of a team of external consultants when their support is going to prove necessary in implementing the decision.

Similarly, a team may discover that collectively it does not possess the needed knowledge to solve the problem it has been assigned. A broadening of the team composition to include others, perhaps an organization member or an external consultant who possesses that knowledge, is one realistic possibility for dealing with the "information shortfall" that has been recognized.

# CHAPTER SIX

# EVALUATING
# THE VROOM-YETTON MODEL

The Vroom-Yetton model was designed to be consistent with the empirical evidence concerning the consequences of participation available at the time of its development. By scientific standards, however, acceptance of the model requires more than its apparent consistency with prior evidence. The model itself must be put to the test to determine precisely what its predictive power is. To argue that the model is "reasonable" is not enough. It must be demonstrated that its specific contingencies can account for the relative success of different decisions and, by extension, the relative success of different leaders. Although it is unlikely that such evidence ever completely confirms or disconfirms a model or theory, it can provide an indicator of the *degree* of validity the model possesses. Research on the validity of the model might also point to areas of possible improvement.

Seven validation studies have been conducted to assess the true usefulness of the Vroom-Yetton model. In this chapter these studies are summarized, as are directions suggested for the model's improvement.

## VALIDATION STUDIES

Six of the seven comprehensive tests of the Vroom-Yetton model lend themselves to direct comparison. These studies focused on specific behaviors in specific decisions that proved to be either successful or unsuccessful. The seventh study is of a broader design and examines the consequences of following the model for the overall profitability of organizations and for the job satisfaction of subordinates. It is noteworthy that each of the seven studies was restricted to a test of the Vroom-Yetton "group" model. No evidence has been collected to test the validity of that portion of the model that pertains to "individual" problems.

## Managerial Behavior and Decision Success

Of the six studies that focused specifically on the consequences of the model for decision success, three were conducted in the United States (Vroom & Jago, 1978; Zimmer, 1978; Liddell, Elsea, Parkinson, & Hackett, 1986); two in Canada (Field, 1982; Tjosvold, Wedley, & Field, 1986); and one in Austria (Böhnisch, Jago, & Reber, 1987). These studies isolated successful and unsuccessful decisions and examined the leader's behavior in each. All together, a total of 1,545 decisions have been studied, 769 successful decisions and 776 unsuccessful decisions.

The leader's behavior in each situation was determined to be either within the feasible set of decision processes for that problem or outside this set. When the feasible set status of the behavior is compared with the success of the decision, Table 6–1 is produced. *Across all six studies, if a manager's behavior conformed to the normative model the rate of success was 62 percent. On the other hand, if the manager's behavior failed to conform to the model, the rate of success was only 37 percent.*

If the model were perfectly valid, the choice of a feasible behavior would guarantee success and the choice of a nonfeasible behavior would guarantee failure (that is, one diagonal within Table 6–1 would contain all 100 percents and the other would contain all zero percents). Clearly this is not the case, nor would one expect it. No model in the social sciences can predict the consequences of a behavior with perfect accuracy. Predicting the outcomes of organizational decisions is particularly problematic because those decisions are often affected by external factors that could not be known or predicted at the time the decision was made. (Consider the impact on decisions made prior to 1973 of the unexpected OPEC oil embargo.) Sometimes the "right" decision-making process will fail because events could not be anticipated; sometimes the "wrong" decision-making process will succeed in spite of its inappropriateness.

What the data in Table 6–1 do suggest is that some managers might increase their "batting averages" for effective decisions by following the rules contained in the Vroom-Yetton model.

To be sure, there are differences in the estimates that each study makes. The Vroom and Jago study produced evidence most favorable to the model and the Field study produced evidence least favorable to the model. Because the six studies were conducted in three different countries, the differences

**TABLE 6–1    Summary of Six Validation Studies**

| | DECISION EFFECTIVENESS (in percents) | |
| --- | --- | --- |
| | SUCCESSFUL | UNSUCCESSFUL |
| Choice within feasible set | (1)  68 | (1)  32 |
| | (2)  67 | (2)  33 |
| | (3)  61 | (3)  39 |
| | (4)  49 | (4)  51 |
| | (5)  54 | (5)  46 |
| | (6)  67 | (6)  33 |
| Weighted average | **62** | **38** |
| Choice outside feasible set | (1)  22 | (1)  78 |
| | (2)  41 | (2)  59 |
| | (3)  38 | (3)  62 |
| | (4)  36 | (4)  64 |
| | (5)  29 | (5)  71 |
| | (6)  44 | (6)  56 |
| Weighted average | **37** | **63** |

*Note*: (1) Vroom & Jago (1978); (2) Zimmer (1978); (3) Tjosvold, Wedley, & Field (1986); (4) Field (1982); (5) Liddell, Elsea, Parkinson, & Hackett (1986); (6) Böhnisch, Jago, & Reber (1987). Averages are weighted by the number of decisions examined in each study.

may be due to cultural factors. More likely, the differences are due to unique methodological features that distinguish the designs of the six studies.

*Studies 1, 2, and 3*    Each manager within the Vroom and Jago study, the Zimmer study, and the Tjosvold et al. study supplied for two recent decisions the following data: (1) the behavior employed, (2) the success of the decision, and (3) the problem attributes that were present in the situation. Although all the managers were naive to the Vroom-Yetton model at the time the data were collected, the fact that all of the information regarding a decision came from a single source may have inflated estimates of the model's validity. People cannot be totally objective about their own behavior. Knowing how one has handled a problem and knowing its success or failure may have influenced the managers' retrospective judgments about the problem attributes present in the situation. If these managers were at all motivated to rationalize or justify the courses of action that were chosen this motivation may have affected the results. Vroom and Jago (1978) argue that biases, if they exist, would do more to disconfirm the model than to confirm it. However, the actual effect of relying exclusively on self-reported data cannot be estimated.

*Studies 4 and 5*    The Field (1982) and Liddell et al. (1986) investigations eliminated the potential problems of the first methodology but introduced others. Their studies were laboratory investigations employing student subjects in hypothetical situations (for example, an Air Force lieutenant faced with a logistics problem). A randomly selected "leader" was instructed to use one of the five decision processes in handling each case. An outside "expert" was employed to judge the quality of each decision. Members of the group other than the leader (that is, the "subordinates") provided a measure of acceptance. The virtue of these studies is that they do not rely on the retrospective accounts of a manager to provide all the information required to classify a situation. Estimates of the problem attributes, the displayed behavior, and the outcome of the decision were all determined independently of each other.

A serious tradeoff, however, exists in the use of contrived situations. The situations were of no real consequence to the participants in these laboratory experiments. Although they were asked to role-play different characters in certain circumstances, the decisions that were reached were known by all to have no real impact on any of the participants. Under these conditions it is impossible to meaningfully introduce a high need for subordinate acceptance (Attribute D) or, alternatively, a low goal congruence (Attribute F). Under contrived laboratory conditions these attributes have little meaning.

The use of college students as subjects may represent a second tradeoff. Field (1982) reports that 44 percent of his data had to be discarded because his subjects failed to follow instructions. Together these two tradeoffs suggest that these studies may underestimate model validity.

*Study 6*    The methodology of the sixth investigation (Böhnisch et al., 1987), conducted in Austria, is more similar to the first methodology than to the second. Real decisions encountered by actual leaders were the subject of study. However, in an effort to improve on the method, the managers involved in the decisions provided only a portion of the information required to classify a decision. Small discussion groups of managers examined each situation and provided (1) the decision process employed by the manager, and (2) an analysis of the problem attributes present in the situation. Supporting the validity of the method, the study was able to show that the small group judgments were more accurate than a single person's judgments in analyzing written descriptions of standardized cases. Additionally such judgments were thought to be less subject to any self-serving biases that might have existed.

When the methodological differences among the six studies are considered, they suggest that no single study should be relied upon to the exclusion of the other five. The best estimate of model validity is, therefore, the average taken across the six studies.

### Managerial Behavior and Organizational Effectiveness

The seventh study cannot be directly compared to the other six but does provide the most compelling evidence of all. Margerison and Glube (1979) studied 47 owner-operated cleaning franchises in the United States and Canada. The organizational structure, size, and environment of these firms were reasonably constant, providing a natural control of extraneous variables. The leadership behavior of owner-managers was assessed through use of a "problem set," which is described in detail in Chapter 7. Franchise profitability was measured by the ratio of sales revenue to material costs plus payroll. The job satisfaction of employees was measured with a standard questionnaire administered to 241 subordinates of the owner-operators.

Responses to hypothetical problems were used to divide the sample into those owner-operators above and below the median level of overall "agreement with the feasible set." The results indicated that those with above-average conformity to the model had significantly more profitable operations and more satisfied employees.

The results are particularly impressive because three distinct relationships were required to exist: (1) the problem set must be a reasonably valid measure of leadership behavior in decision-making situations, (2) the decisions that a manager makes must impact the profitability of the organization and the satisfaction of subordinates, and (3) the Vroom-Yetton model must be valid. Each link in this chain must exist for the results to emerge as they did. Therefore, the evidence not only supports the validity of the model but also the usefulness of the problem set as a measure of leader behavior and a predictor of managerial success.

### Validity of Component Rules

Although all the evidence suggests that behavior prescribed by the feasible set will be more effective than behavior eliminated from that set, it must be remembered that these prescriptions are determined by the application of seven underlying decision rules (see Table 5–2). While the validation studies provide evidence for the validity of these seven underlying rules in the aggregate, it is conceivable that some rules are contributing nothing to model validity, or are even acting to decrease that validity.

Four of the seven validity studies specifically tested each of the component rules within the Vroom-Yetton model (Vroom & Jago, 1978; Field, 1982; Liddell, et al., 1986; Böhnisch et al., 1987). Each rule receives support in at least two of the four studies, with the exception of Rule 5 (the conflict rule), which received support in only one of the four studies. However, support for Rule

5 is provided by an additional experiment similar to that conducted by Field or Liddell et al. but specifically designed to test only this single rule (Ettling & Jago, in press).

Of course, the failure to support each rule in every study should not be interpreted as evidence that rule validity is suspect. Tests of the individual rules must be conducted on subsets of cases within the validation studies (that is, those situations in which a particular rule applies). In the Vroom and Jago study, for example, there were only eight instances (out of 181 decisions) in which the conflict rule was violated (by the use of AI, AII, or CI in a situation in which subordinate acceptance is required, not certain to result from an autocratic decision, and subordinate conflict is likely). This number is far too small to provide an adequate test of rule validity. The rule might be completely valid, but some of our tests, to date, might be too insensitive to detect it.

## SHORTCOMINGS OF THE MODEL

After reviewing some of the same evidence that we have just summarized, Miner (1984) concludes that no leadership theory surpasses the Vroom-Yetton model in its scientific validity and practical usefulness. In every test attempted, the model is shown to improve the effectiveness of organizational decision making.

At the same time, we have recognized that the model is far from perfect. After approximately sixty scientific books and articles published about the model (including the seven studies directly assessing its validity), and after our work with thousands of leaders in various management development programs around the world, we now recognize several shortcomings of the model. These limitations place a ceiling on its validity and, ultimately, a ceiling on its usefulness as a practical guide for managerial behavior. In the remainder of this chapter these major shortcomings are outlined.

### Model Fails to Differentiate Among Feasible Responses

The structure of the decision rules is such that the rules tell you what *not* to do, not *what* to do. After the rules are applied, a feasible set remains that sometimes contains a single decision strategy but more often contains a variety of strategies from which to choose. These choices can be based on the time requirements of the different strategies (that is, Model A), on the developmental consequences of different strategies (that is, Model B), or on other inclinations or predispositions. The model simply is not very specific in its prescriptions for handling different situations.

The decision tree contained in Figure 5–1 presents thirteen "problem types." If these problem types are found with equal frequency in situations faced by the typical manager, the average feasible set contains 2.38 of the five decision processes. Of course, the thirteen problem types are not equally frequent. If we use the 181 real decisions from Vroom and Jago (1978) to represent the typical mix of problems a manager might face, the average size of the feasible set is 2.66. On the average, the application of the prescriptive model eliminates less than half the behavioral alternatives at the disposal of the manager. In the final analysis, the prescriptive model is not very prescriptive at all!

If a publication like *Consumer Reports* tested products but failed to produce ratings that differentiated these products, the publication would be providing little guidance to its subscribers. Similarly, the Vroom-Yetton model frequently fails to give much guidance when the feasible set for a particular situation contains three, four, or even five decision processes. The underlying rules do too little of the "work" of the model, leaving much to the unique inclinations and proclivities of the individual manager.

### Model Fails to Differentiate Among Nonfeasible Decision Processes

Just as the model fails to differentiate among leader behaviors within the feasible set, it fails to differentiate among behaviors outside that set. The model treats a decision process that violates one underlying rule the same as another decision process that may violate another rule. Additionally, a decision process that violates one rule is treated the same as a decision process that may violate two, three, or four rules.

The model operates according to what mathematicians call a "step-function." Behaviors inside the feasible set are distinguished from behaviors outside the set by a single "step," graphically illustrated by one of the lines in Figure 6–1. This illustrated "step" describes the operation of the model when applied to the sample decision, discussed in depth in Chapter 5, of the R & D director who must choose the projects on which a particular research team must focus. The two consultative strategies (CI and CII) are within the feasible set and predicted to be successful. All other processes (AI, AII, and GII) are outside the feasible set and predicted to be equally unsuccessful.

It is perhaps more reasonable to assume that the behaviors within the feasible set are not all equally effective, and that behaviors outside that set are not all equally ineffective. In the case of the research projects decision, it could be argued that CII would be most effective (because of its expected ability to generate the necessary acceptance and commitment) followed by CI, GII, AII, and AI. AI might be the least preferred alternative in this case because it provides no opportunity for subordinate involvement in the decision and therefore no opportunity to build commitment to a financially viable course of action. These alternative predictions are represented by the second line in Figure 6–1, a "continuous" function not having the dramatic discontinuities (or "steps") of the first line.

DECISION EFFECTIVENESS

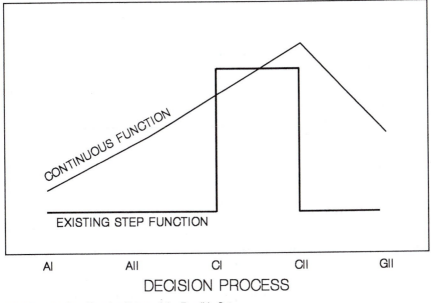

**FIGURE 6-1** Step-Function Nature of the Feasible Set

Actually, some evidence challenging the step-function nature of the feasible set is found in the studies reviewed in this chapter that addressed the validity of the Vroom-Yetton rules. In three of those studies, a relationship was found between the number of rules violated and the degree to which decisions were unsuccessful. Leader behaviors outside the feasible set were not equally ineffective. A behavior that violates two rules is less successful than a behavior that violates one rule; a behavior that violates three rules is less successful than a behavior that violates two rules; and so forth.

### Model Fails to Capture All Meaningful Differences Among Existing Problem Attributes

Perhaps the most frequent reaction that managers have to the Vroom-Yetton model is that it does not permit an answer of "probably yes," "maybe," or "probably no" to any of the seven questions representing the problem attributes. The model makes the assumption that all situations are either black or white, while managers tell us that the most difficult situations they encounter are those that are found in the varying shades of gray. Yes and no answers simply do not capture all the meaningful differences that exist among situations.

For most of the problem attributes the issue is one of failing to recognize that some analyses of situations will be more uncertain than others. In some situations, for example, the leader may not know if subordinates are likely to agree or disagree in their preferred alternatives until well after a decision process has been selected and implemented.

The issue is a bit different, however, for the attributes dealing with quality and acceptance requirements (Attributes A and D). Here the yes–no format of the model fails to capture differences in the *degree* of quality that a decision must possess and, similarly, the *degree* of acceptance that it must generate to prove successful. Uncertainty is not so much the issue as is the relative weight to be given these criteria of success.

At the time of its development, a very practical consideration dictated that each attribute in the model be expressed in its yes–no format. To add a single additional response category would create three branches at each node in the decision tree. The size of the tree grows exponentially until there are over 200 endpoints instead of the existing 13. The model becomes unmanageable, its use virtually precluded by its complexity.

Of course, the problem is only compounded if all three additional response categories ("probably no," "maybe," "probably yes") are included. Finer and finer discriminations among situations cause geometrically larger and larger problems for representing the model in a decision-tree format.

The model therefore applies only to those clear and unambiguous situations that can be represented by firm yes–no answers to the problem attributes. Yet the available evidence suggests that such firm answers may exist for less than one-half the situations a manager may face (Vroom & Yetton, 1973, Table 4–3). Attempting to use the model in other situations is like using the wrong size wrench to loosen a bolt. The tool is being used for a job for which it was not designed, and its expected effectiveness may not be realized as a consequence.

### Important Attributes of the Situation Are Ignored

The model operates on seven features of the situation in determining its prescriptions. While it can be argued that these are the most important variables, they are not an exhaustive list of those characteristics that govern the success or failure of different leader behaviors.

Again, it was a pragmatic consideration that required the list be kept to seven. To add an eighth variable (and a decision rule that the additional problem attribute would invoke) would cause some feasible sets in the decision tree to become empty. The manager attempting to use the model would be left with no prescriptions for certain types of problems.

What variables are candidates for inclusion in the model but precluded by the need to keep the list to seven? Our research evidence and experiences in teaching the model to managers suggest three:

*Subordinate information*    The decision tree asks the manager if he or she has sufficient information to make a high-quality decision but does not ask a similar question regarding the level of subordinate information (except in the individual model). Vroom and Yetton (1973) justify the exclusion of such a question on the grounds that most managers assume their subordinates have any information that they may lack. While this may be a reasonable assumption in most cases, there are times when neither the manager nor the subordinates have the complete information to make a proper decision. Moreover, even when leader information is high, the manager may need to behave differently depending on the level of information and expertise represented within the subordinate group.

Consider the goal congruence rule (Rule 2). It eliminates GII from the feasible set when subordinates are not motivated to use their information and expertise toward the attainment of organizational objectives. A similar case can be made that GII is not entirely appropriate when subordinates have little information and expertise to bring to bear on the problem (regardless of their motivation). In this case, GII does not necessarily represent a severe threat to decision quality, but neither would it be expected to enhance such quality. Setting aside any acceptance considerations that may exist, having a group struggle with an issue with which it is ill prepared to deal seems a poor way of handling the situation.

*Time constraints*    Inevitably there are situations that require an immediate decision and for which there is little time to offer meaningful participation to subordinates. These are most typically emergency or crisis circumstances that cannot be anticipated. Because the prescriptive model does not consider the implications of such severe time constraints, it can prescribe a participative manner of handling a situation when there simply is not sufficient time. Doing almost anything may be better than doing nothing, yet the model would have you do nothing until your subordinates could be consulted.

Some managers with whom we have worked say such emergencies are quite common and represent the major reason why they cannot follow the model's prescriptions. Upon our probing, however, we find that most of these managers are citing a severe time constraint simply to justify or rationalize their preferred autocratic style. When so-called crises are examined, we find that there was almost always ample time to undo a bad decision although the pressure of time was cited as the reason for the poor decision in the first place. President Kennedy and his staff of advisors took the necessary time to deliberate (13 days) before responding to the threat of missiles in Cuba, certainly more of a real crisis than most of those encountered by managers.

On the other hand, some managers do face an unusually high number of actual crises. More often than not, this is a signal that the organization is not properly designed to deal with a turbulent and uncertain environment within which it operates. Major surgery on the organization is required, not more autocratic decision making.

Nonetheless, every manager on some occasion will encounter a situation in which decision-making time is extremely short. Currently, the Vroom-Yetton model is incapable of recognizing or dealing with such situations, as infrequent as they may be—a shortcoming not overlooked by other reviewers of the theory (for example, Van Fleet & Yukl, 1986).

*Geographical constraints*    The model makes the assumption that if a meeting is prescribed, all relevant subordinates can attend. Either a special meeting can be held, or the item can be attached to the agenda of a scheduled meeting. In some circumstances, however, subordinates are geographically isolated, making such meetings impractical if not impossible. These subordinates may be stationed in different states, different regions, or even different countries. Like time constraints, the Vroom-Yetton model is incapable of recognizing or dealing with such circumstances.

### Primitive Contingencies in a Complex Model

Others have suggested that the model may be too complex to be of much practical value to the manager (for example, Filley, House, & Kerr, 1976; Field, 1979). It certainly is the most complex leadership theory available, in a literature that far too often provides overly simplistic solutions to complex problems. We naturally prefer Miner's (1984) conclusion that the model's complexity and specificity provide a practical usefulness surpassed by none.

The shortcoming we do recognize is that the model is too primitive, not that it is too complex. It also oversimplifies complex human phenomena, although perhaps not to the degree displayed by other theories and models. Some of this oversimplification has already been described (that is, the step-function nature of the feasible set). It extends beyond these issues, however, to the core of the existing underlying contingencies.

Models A and B provide examples. Model B suggests that the most participative of feasible decision processes will always be the most developmental. Consider, however, a situation with no quality requirement and no acceptance requirement (that is, a Type 1 situation in Figure 5–1). Model B would have you select GII. But in a situation that is relatively trivial and one that subordinates are concerned little about, will a group-consensus meeting really increase subordinates' managerial and technical skills? On the other hand, Model A suggests that the most autocratic of feasible decision processes will always be the most time efficient. But will a GII meeting always take more time than CI? Perhaps so if the situation is unstructured and conflict exists among subordinates. But what if the situation is relatively structured and conflict-free? One could envision the item being handled more quickly and efficiently at a weekly staff meeting than if the leader consulted each subordinate individually.

These are but two examples of how the model fails to capture the complexities of organizational reality. The model is not too complex; rather, its decision rules are too simple.

The identification of these five shortcomings provides a starting point for the model's revision in the hope of increasing its validity and usefulness. It is clear, however, that an attempt to address these limitations requires major changes in the model's form and substance. In Chapter 8, we introduce the basic features of a new model designed explicitly to remedy the shortcomings discussed in this chapter. The details of this new model are then unfolded in Chapters 9 through 12.

The next chapter, however, continues the research emphasis contained in this one. We turn briefly from normative or prescriptive issues to descriptive ones. Instead of when managers *should* use participative methods, we take up the question of when managers *do* employ participation in dealing with organizational decision problems.

# Chapter Seven

# Use of PARTICIPATION by MANAGERS

The model described in the previous two chapters is a "normative" or "prescriptive" model. It attempts to specify when and where different levels of participation are likely to be most effective. To the extent to which that model is valid, it describes how managers should behave in different circumstances.

Other questions addressed by Vroom and Yetton in 1973 (and in subsequent research by us and others) deal with what managers actually do as opposed to what they "should" do. What kinds of problems and decisions tend to induce managers to involve their subordinates? How do managers differ from each other in their responses to situations? What organizational factors encourage or inhibit the use of participative and autocratic practices? How does the behavior of the typical manager compare to that suggested by the normative model? These are descriptive as opposed to prescriptive questions.

These two perspectives on participation—normative and descriptive—are illustrated in Figure 7–1. The normative perspective is shown at the top of the figure. Here we start with the degree of participation employed by a manager and end with criteria of effectiveness such as decision quality, decision acceptance, time, and development. As we have shown in previous chapters, there is ample evidence that this relationship is not invariant but rather is affected by situational factors illustrated by the vertical arrow in the top portion of Figure 7–1. For example, "lack of information by the leader"—a situational

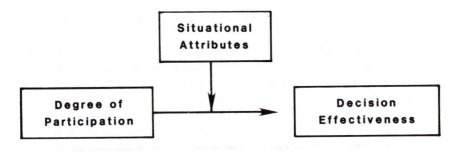

**A NORMATIVE (PRESCRIPTIVE) PERSPECTIVE**

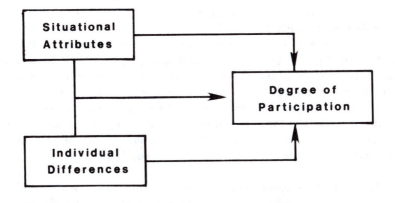

**A DESCRIPTIVE PERSPECTIVE**

**FIGURE 7–1**   Two Perspectives on Participation

variable—can impair the effectiveness of a particular decision-making process such as AI.

The descriptive perspective is illustrated in the lower portion of Figure 7–1. The degree of participation used by a manager now becomes the phenomenon to be explained. The relationships indicated by the arrows suggest the kinds of factors that might be expected to cause managers to be participative or autocratic. Following Lewin (1938), who asserted that behavior is dependent on both person and environment, our diagram distinguishes those causes that are attributable to the immediate environment or situation and those that are attributable to the qualities of the person, including traits or generalized dispositions to be autocratic or participative. The arrows that flow from each of these two factors toward participation denote their status as possible independent causes of participation. The arrow from the midpoint of the line joining these two factors to participation denotes the possible joint, or interactive, effects.

Prior to the publication of the normative model in 1973, most research on participation in organizations employed rather simple scales to attempt to assess a manager's "style." Typically the manager would be asked to indicate a level of agreement with the statement "I involve my subordinates in the decisions that I face" or "I consult my subordinates when a decision comes up." Alternatively, the subordinates of a manager would be asked to agree or disagree with "My boss cares about what I think regarding an issue" or "My supervisor asks my opinion before making a decision."

Such questions assume a leader's participativeness to be the same across situations and that it is an expression of a relatively stable personality trait, or managerial "style." Such questions are incapable of revealing situational influences on participation or differences in the way managers tailor the degree of participation to the demands of situations.

In their earliest efforts to understand the situational causes of a leader's behavior, Vroom and Yetton (1973) employed a research method that they termed *recalled problems*. In this method, a manager is asked to think of a recent decision problem and to provide a written description of it along with the behavior (AI through GII) that best described how he or she tried to solve it. Once the case is written, the manager answers a set of questions about the decision and the situation in which it was made. When many such situations are collected from many different managers, analyses can be conducted to determine how the typical manager responds to circumstances having different attributes.

The method, however, had some serious drawbacks. Because only one or two decisions were collected from each manager, it was impossible to determine how any one manager varied his or her behavior over a wide variety of circumstances. Second, the method relied exclusively on the manager's self-reported behavior and a self-reported analysis of the situation. Although a manager may be able to accurately describe how he or she handled a particular situation, we have found differences among managers in their ability (and motivation) to objectively report the circumstances that preceded their action. It is to be expected that any recollection of events might sometimes be colored by an attempt to rationalize one's actions.

## PROBLEM SETS

These problems were overcome, however, with the development of a standardized *problem set*. From hundreds of the collected "recalled problems," thirty were selected. The basis for their selection was not random but highly systematic. Each of the problem attributes used in the Vroom-Yetton normative model was varied over the situations; and the variation of each attribute was statistically independent of each other attribute (the statistician refers to this as a multifactorial experimental design). For example, the design of the set required fifteen cases in which subordinate conflict over preferred solutions (Attribute G) was likely and fifteen cases in which such conflict was unlikely. For each written case, care was taken to ensure that each problem attribute was represented in an unambiguous manner. What emerged were one- to two-page scenarios, samples of which the reader encountered in Chapter 4. (A complete description of the design and construction of the problem set can be found in Chapter 5 of Vroom and Yetton, 1973.)

Managers are given the set and asked to assume that each situation is real and that they are the depicted leader. The respondents are not asked to solve the problem or make the decision, but rather to describe the process (from the list AI, AII, CI, CII, GII) that they would employ in that circumstance. Completion of the entire set of thirty cases takes between 1½ and 3 hours.

Use of the problem set to address questions of how managers tailor their behavior to situations has two key benefits. First, the cases are standardized and, unlike the use of "recalled problems," do not require the leader or manager to specify which problem attributes are present in or absent from the situation. The facts in each case are fixed and unambiguously portrayed. Second, the design of the set permits an analysis of how a particular manager varies his or her behavior as elements of the situation change. For example, it is possible to compare the behavior displayed in conflict situations with the behavior displayed in situations without conflict. Within each group of cases other situational attributes are controlled.

Of course these benefits are not achieved without a cost. To be precise, the problem set does not measure behavior at all but rather "behavioral intent." What managers say they would do in each of the thirty hypothetical circumstances may be somewhat different than what they would do if actually confronted with the problem or decision. Although the problem set is administered in a manner that provides the respondent with the opportunity for complete anonymity, managers may nonetheless respond with answers perceived to be "appropriate" or "desirable" rather than answers representing an accurate prediction of their own behavior.

There is, however, some evidence that managers' reports of what they would do in standardized problems will predict what they will later do in real situations encountered by them on their jobs. Managers who had completed the problem set some weeks before were asked to provide a written account of a "recalled problem," including how they dealt with it. When behavior in the real situation was compared to intended behavior in the similar (but hypothetical) scenario, significant agreement was found (Jago & Vroom, 1978). Similar behaviors were reported in about two-thirds of the cases. Virtually identical results occurred when the study was replicated in Austria with a German translation of the problem set (Böhnisch, Ragan, Reber, & Jago, 1986).

However, managers' statements of their intended behavior on standardized cases often do not agree with their subordinates' predictions of that behavior (Jago & Vroom, 1975). Specifically, subordinates reported their superiors to be significantly more autocratic than those superiors saw themselves. Although subordinate predictions may themselves be suspect, we cannot be sure that the managers' self-reports are completely accurate and free from bias.

Several different problem sets have been created. Some of these were designed for particular populations. For example, problem sets consisting of military and public sector cases have been created for collecting valid data from these groups. Other problem sets have been designed to answer research questions of interest—including the effects of institutional context and of organizational level on choices of decision processes.

The number of managers worldwide that has completed one of these different versions of the problem set is conservatively estimated to be in six figures. Most of these data were collected within the context of management development programs, and managers were completely unfamiliar with the Vroom-Yetton normative model at the time they completed the instrument. In the remainder of this chapter we will discuss findings that we have learned from the use of this method.

No claim can be made that the data are representative of any population. Nonetheless, the numbers of managers studied and the range of organizations represented provide us with a good deal of confidence in drawing inferences based on this data.

It is noteworthy that most of the research has been based on what were described in Chapter 4 as group problems (for example, problems or decisions affecting more than one subordinate). Comparatively little research has been conducted to determine how managers deal with individual problems. The reader is referred to Vroom and Jago (1974) for a discussion of what has been learned on this issue.

## OVERALL RESULTS

Managers' responses to a problem set provide a basis for understanding the most and least frequently chosen decision processes and for identifying differences between managers' choices and those of the model. In one large sample of 2,631 U.S. managers, each of whom responded to the same set of thirty cases, CII and AI were the most frequent choices with, respectively, 29 percent and 24 percent of total choices; the least frequent choices were AII and GII, accounting respectively for 13 percent and 16 percent of the total number of choices (Table 7–1).

To provide a basis for comparison, Table 7–1 also contains the behavior that the Vroom-Yetton prescriptive model would display across the same set of thirty cases. These percentages reflect how a leader would behave if that leader followed either Model A (the Time-Efficient model) or Model B (the

TABLE 7–1    Distribution of Choices

|  | MANAGERIAL SAMPLE | NORMATIVE MODEL | |
|---|---|---|---|
|  |  | MODEL A | MODEL B |
| AI | 24% | 40% | 0% |
| AII | 13 | 13 | 0 |
| CI | 18 | 3 | 0 |
| CII | 29 | 23 | 40 |
| GII | 16 | 20 | 60 |
| Mean Level of Participation | 4.97 | 4.17 | 9.20 |

Note: AI = autocratic decision making. AII = AI with information collection. CI = one-on-one consultation. CII = consultation in a group. GII = group consensus.

Time-Investment model) consistently. When compared to Model A, the typical manager makes less use of both AI and GII and substantially more use of CI. When compared to the highly participative Model B, the typical manager makes substantially less use of both CII and GII.

## DIFFERENCES AMONG MANAGERS

Although these percentages provide a picture of the average manager, there is a great deal of variation among managers. These differences can be summarized in a single statistic that we call the "mean level of participation." Each choice can be assigned a number from the following scale (the numbers being derived from several statistical techniques discussed by Vroom and Yetton, 1973):

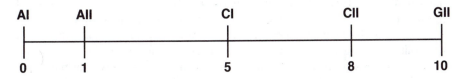

Higher numbers represent greater involvement of subordinates and greater opportunities for them to influence the ultimate decision. AI represents "zero" subordinate participation, GII represents ten units of participation (ten being an arbitrary endpoint representing maximum involvement). AII is assigned one unit of participation, a value very close to that of AI and reflecting the fact that the two processes are very similar. From the standpoint of the subordinate, AII offers little more involvement or more meaningful participation than does AI. CI offers a midrange level of participation. Although CI and CII are both consultative decision processes, CII is given a value a bit closer to GII than it is to CI because it shares with GII the group setting at which the decision is discussed.

The average mean level of participation (MLP) for the sample of 2,631 managers is 4.97. As is the case for other personal traits, the distribution around this mean score is bell-shaped with 90 percent of all managers achieving mean scores varying from 2.92 (the fifth percentile) to 7.02 (the ninety-fifth percentile).

## CORRELATES OF DIFFERENCES AMONG MANAGERS

These differences in level of participativeness (MLP) correlate meaningfully with other measures of leadership style. Vroom and Yetton found that highly participative managers were more likely to believe that "goals of subordinates need not conflict with organizational objectives," that "subordinates are not inherently lazy," and that "they will meet the challenge of increased responsibility"—all elements of McGregor's Theory Y. Bassan (1979) also found participativeness to be negatively correlated with a personality measure of authoritarianism and to be negatively correlated with "initiating structure," a dimension of leader behavior identified in the classic Ohio State studies; it emphasized the regulation of the work environment, the determination of work standards, and the establishment of patterns of work flow. On the other hand, participation was found to be positively correlated with "consideration," the second dimension of leader behavior identified in the Ohio State studies; this latter dimension emphasized the development of two-way communication with subordinates, mutual trust, and concern for subordinate welfare.

MLP has also been found to be related to the gender of the manager. By comparing the responses of female managers with a matched group of males, we have found women to be substantially more participative than men (Jago & Vroom, 1982). These differences are also evident in comparisons of the problem set responses of male and female management students.

These differences between men and women managers are consistent with differences in the pressures that each group encounters in carrying out its roles. Our research suggests that when a manager is perceived as participative, the reactions of close associates are generally positive and unaffected by whether the person is a man or woman. However, women who are perceived to be autocratic tend to elicit much more negative reactions from others than do men who are perceived as autocratic (Jago & Vroom, 1982). Authoritarian behavior on the part of men may be viewed as a sign of decisiveness, but the same behavior on the part of women may be seen as inappropriate and inconsistent with the cultural stereotype of feminine behavior.

Another finding involves the relationship between participation and age. The most autocratic managers we have studied are in their twenties. Participativeness tends to increase throughout the thirties and reaches a maximum during the forties, where it appears to stabilize (Table 7–2). While our findings are cross-sectional rather than longitudinal, the most likely interpretation is that people continue to revise their assumptions about leadership through adulthood.

The ability to update one's theories of leadership through experience should also be reflected in differences in leadership styles among managers with different responsibilities. We have identified a number of relationships between the jobs managers perform and the level of participation they display.

Robert and Vroom (reported in Vroom, 1984) studied differences in degree of participativeness among military officers, private sector managers, managers in government, and academic administrators. The most autocratic predispositions were found in the military, and the most participative tendencies were found in both academic and governmental settings. Private sector managers were midway between these extremes. A second study by Jago (1980), using different research methods, also documents the greater participativeness of managers in government compared with those in other settings. Whether these differences reflect the kinds of people recruited by these different institutions, or are the result of different norms and socialization pressures, cannot be ascertained.

Similar questions are raised by comparisons of participativeness found among managers in different positions within the same organization. We have repeatedly found higher-level managers to be more participative than those at lower levels (Jago 1977; Jago & Vroom, 1977; Jago, 1980; Jago, 1981). The difference appears to be sharpest between first-level and second-level managers.

Is the greater participativeness found at higher levels a reflection of the kinds of people who get promoted, or a reflection of a change in managers' views about the usefulness of participation made after they encounter the demands of higher-level positions? Both factors may be involved, but our educated guess, following research by Lieberman (1956), would attach more

**TABLE 7–2   Participativeness by Age**

| AGE | NUMBER IN SAMPLE | MEAN LEVEL OF PARTICIPATION |
|---|---|---|
| 20–30 | 185 | 4.58 |
| 31–40 | 1099 | 4.89 |
| 41–50 | 845 | 5.08 |
| > 50 | 240 | 5.05 |

Note: Participativeness measured on 0 to 10 scale.

weight to changes in attitudes toward participation induced by the different challenges and responsibilities of managerial positions at higher organizational levels.

Jago (1977) showed that higher-level managers are more likely to encounter decisions for which they have insufficient information and which are unstructured. Both of these situational differences lead managers (and lead the model) toward more participative practices. It is also likely that higher-level managers enjoy the benefits of higher subordinate goal congruence and longer time horizons, both of which would also contribute to more frequent use of participation.

The evidence on the correlates of MLP that we have presented in the preceding pages is supportive of the view that managers' leadership styles frequently change to be consistent with the nature of the responsibilities, opportunities, and pressures with which they must deal. Supporting the same conclusion is evidence that differences exist in the leadership styles of managers representing different functional specialties (Jago, 1980).

The possibility that managers can adapt their leadership style to situational requirements does not mean that all managers adapt or that the degree of adaptation is always optimal. We have all known of managers who failed to recognize the fundamental differences between their new and their old leadership positions and whose performance was seriously compromised as a consequence. In Chapter 13, we will examine an approach to leadership training that is intended to facilitate the unlearning of old, less effective leadership styles and the relearning of new ones.

## PARTICIPATION TRENDS

The MLP score of 4.97 observed on our set of 2,631 managers is significantly higher than the mean of 4.69 reported by Vroom and Yetton for 571 managers in 1973. Although there are many possible explanations for this difference, other observations lead us to the view that managers have become more participative over the last ten to fifteen years. Since 1972 we have been collecting problem set data from about 300 managers per year in one large diversified corporation specializing in the manufacture of electrical equipment. Even though the managers have been selected from the same level in the organization (corresponding roughly to the second level of management), we have seen a continued increase in mean level of participation from 4.40 to 5.25. Each year the mean shows a further increase, reflecting greater frequency of use of the more participative processes of CII and GII and less use of the autocratic methods AI and AII.

Although the evidence from other organizations is less clear-cut, we have reason to believe that increased participativeness is not unique to this particular firm but is generalizable to much of American industry. As Lawler

(1986) points out, the society, the work force, the products produced, and the business environment that exist in the United States today are all very different from those conditions that existed during the era of Taylorism and through World War II. While acknowledging the difficulty of estimating the relative influence of different factors promoting greater use of participation, the fact that managers adapt their styles to situational pressures' leads us to believe that the most likely causes are: (1) greater complexity in the challenges faced by managers, and (2) changes in the labor force.

### Greater Complexity

One of the most formidable of these changes is the greater complexity of decisions required of managers in today's environment. Drucker (1980) describes today's leader as "managing in turbulent times" due to growing technological innovations and structural shifts in previously stable institutions. Contemporary managers, particularly in rapidly changing industries, can seldom possess all of the knowledge necessary to make intelligent decisions by themselves. Increasingly the managerial role is that of integrating the knowledge and talents of specialists in different functions or aspects of technology. Integration of information necessarily requires participation.

The greater complexity is reflected, in part, in changes in the kinds of organizations in which managers work. Within manufacturing, "smokestack industries" have fallen victim to foreign competition, and investment has been in high-tech industries where complexity abounds but continued growth may be found. In addition, the last fifteen years have witnessed a marked increase in the proportion of managers engaged in the delivery of services and a proportionate decrease in manufacturing.

The electrical-products organization that we have studied over the years is no exception to these trends. Its growth has been explosive in the financial services industry where deregulation has created new opportunities and challenges. In addition, this company has pursued an explicit policy of selling off manufacturing businesses, where little or no prospects of growth exist, in favor of ventures dealing with advanced technology.

### Changes in the Labor Force

A related but conceptually different explanation for increased participation puts the cause not in the complexity of problems or decisions but in the changing composition of the labor force. One's subordinates in today's organizations are more likely to expect to become involved in decisions than did their predecessors decades earlier. A manager who uses autocratic methods will encounter greater resistance to such practices today.

The people who populate organizations in the modern world may possess not only a greater desire but also a greater capacity to participate. They tend to be more highly educated and have more to contribute in solving today's organizational problems. Ninety percent or more of those with advanced education become employees—and therefore "subordinates"—in modern organizations, a shift away from the tendency for these individuals to become self-employed professionals (Drucker, 1980, p. 187). Participation and delegation may work better today because more people in organizations are able to accept the responsibilities attendant on participation.

Both of these explanations for the movement toward more participative management seem plausible and are consistent with an adaptability thesis. They are also sufficiently interconnected to make it difficult and probably unnecessary to try to select between them. Greater complexity of decisions, brought about at least in part by moving into new and more sophisticated technologies, tends to attract and require a more highly educated work force, whose talents can be best used through participative decision-making systems and who, increasingly, expect that this will be the case.

## DIFFERENCES AMONG SITUATIONS

Mean level of participation is an average score for a manager and is calculated across all problems. The same scale values for AI, AII, CI, CII, and GII can also be used in calculating means for problems across all managers. In a frequently replicated analysis, we find that mean scores calculated across problems vary about three times as much as do mean scores calculated across persons (Vroom & Yetton, 1973; Vroom & Jago, 1974; Jago, 1977; Steers, 1977). Simply stated, the problem or decision that a manager confronts is potentially a much better predictor of how that manager will behave than is the manager's personality or overall "style."

To illustrate, consider two situations discussed in Chapter 4. The first, presented on page 42, described the captain of a coast guard cutter faced with a decision about terminating a search and rescue mission in the North Atlantic due to a severe storm. The second, presented on page 43, described a manufacturing manager confronted with an unexpected drop in productivity following the installation of new machines.

AI and AII are by far the most frequent processes used in the coast guard problem, with CII and GII almost never selected. On the other hand, the predominant choices on the manufacturing problem are CII and GII, with AI and AII being rarities.

What are the situational factors—dominating the individual factors—that influence managers' choices of decision-making processes? One of the most useful features of the problem set is the counterbalancing of problem attributes within its design. The manner in which problem attributes are distributed within the set allows us to isolate a manager's (or a group's) behavioral response as each attribute changes. With other features of the situation held reasonably constant, we can determine the effect of changes in any one variable. This is accomplished by comparing the level of participation elicited in cases having the attribute with the level of participation elicited in cases not having the attribute. Essentially, a manager's choices on one subset of cases is compared with his or her choices on another subset of cases.

Table 7–3 reveals the percentage of managers who become more (or less) participative when an attribute of the situation is present versus absent. For managers in our sample to be classified in either of these categories, their average behavior must have changed at least .50 points (on our ten-point scale) when problems with the attribute are compared with problems without the attribute. Smaller changes are likely to be unreliable, and these people are classified as showing no behavioral response to the problem attribute (that is, neither an increase or decrease in participation when the condition exists).

### Quality Requirement

Sixty-two percent of our sample is more participative in situations that have a technical component (that is a high-quality requirement) than in situations lacking such a component. These managers appear to be using what Miles (1965) has called a "human resources" approach to participation. According to this view, the manager expects participation to increase the quality of decisions by tapping the full range of experience, insight, and creative ability represented in subordinates. Participation is viewed as less important in situations that are relatively trivial because it would represent an inappropriate and cost-ineffective allocation of the talents and resources of subordinates.

TABLE 7–3  Managers' Responses to Situational Attributes

|  | DEGREE OF PARTICIPATION (in percents) | | |
| --- | --- | --- | --- |
| CONDITION | MORE | LESS | NEITHER |
| When a quality requirement exists | 62 | 21 | 18 |
| When leader information is missing | 68 | 12 | 20 |
| When the problem is unstructured | 76 | 11 | 13 |
| When subordinate acceptance is required | 49 | 24 | 28 |
| When an autocratic decision is unlikely to be accepted | 92 | 2 | 5 |
| When subordinates' goals and organizational goals are congruent | 71 | 8 | 20 |
| When conflict is likely | 19 | 50 | 31 |

On the other hand, 21 percent of our sample show the opposite pattern. These managers are more participative in situations lacking a quality requirement than in situations possessing one. Employees are more likely to be involved in planning departmental picnics, deciding on office decorations, and so forth— situations in which little damage can be done. The assumption may be that such participation can make subordinates "feel" important, as if their opinions were valued.

The remaining 18 percent of all managers reveal neither pattern. They employ about the same level of participation in situations possessing a quality requirement as they do in those that lack such a requirement, but this does not imply that all these managers are the same. Some may be highly participative in both high- and low-quality situations; others may be very autocratic in both types of situations. (These are differences *between* managers as opposed to differences *within* managers.)

### Leader Information

Within the situations requiring a high-quality solution, half depict the manager as missing critical pieces of information and half depict him or her as having complete information. Sixty-eight percent of our sample is more participative in situations where they lack information than in situations where they have full information. This large majority uses participation to gather the necessary facts required to make the best decisions. Another 20 percent displays near equal levels of participation in the two types of situations. Again, for some managers this may be a high level of participation (reflecting a perceived benefit from its use even when the leader already knows all the facts), and for other managers this may be a low level of participation (reflecting no perceived benefit from its use in either condition).

The remaining managers employ greater participation when they have complete information than when they lack information. Although only 12 percent, this percentage is higher than we expected. Some of these managers may equate any display of having less than complete information with a confession of ignorance and incompetence. Involving subordinates in order to increase one's own information may be threatening. When participation is used, it is only in circumstances that provide an opportunity to reveal one's expertise and to show a complete command of the situation.

### Problem Structure

Of those situations in which leader information is low, half are structured (that is, having well-defined goals and alternatives) and half are unstructured (that is, unknown goals or, more typically, an incomplete set of alternatives to evaluate). Over three-fourths of all managers are more participative on unstructured problems than they are on those that are structured. These managers employ participation to help identify goals and generate alternatives in ill-defined situations.

### Subordinate Acceptance

Two-thirds of all problem set cases describe a need to generate subordinate acceptance, and one-third have no such requirement. Forty-nine percent of all managers are more participative when such acceptance is critical to the effective implementation of the decision than when it is not. These managers are exhibiting a behavior pattern consistent with what Miles (1965) has labeled a "human relations" view toward participation (though not to the necessary exclusion of a human resources view). Nearly half of all managers seemingly expect participation to generate commitment to a course of action and to produce cooperation from subordinates. However, a more important indicator of such expectations is found in responses to the next problem attribute.

### Probability that an Autocratic Decision Will Be Accepted

Of those situations requiring subordinate acceptance, half contain evidence that the manager's autocratic decision would be accepted and half suggest such acceptance is unlikely. All but 7 percent of the managerial sample employ greater participation in those situations where the acceptance of an autocratic decision is unlikely. Reflecting the view that participation breeds acceptance, managers are more participative *when acceptance cannot be generated by other means.* If an autocratic decision can be "sold" to subordinates, almost all managers become more autocratic. To a large extent, participation is reserved for those circumstances where autocracy is expected to fail. At least in regard to generating acceptance, if autocratic or participative processes are equally likely to be effective, the manager chooses the autocratic process, thereby saving time. When the effectiveness of the two are not expected to be equal, the vast majority of managers become willing to invest the time necessary to ensure greater acceptance.

### Goal Congruence

Seventy-one percent of all managers are more participative in situations in which subordinates share organizational goals ("win–win" situations) than in situations in which goals are incongruent ("win–lose" situations). A small number of managers show the reverse pattern. When asked, some justify their actions by suggesting that the existence of low-goal-congruence situations are a symptom of poor organizational health. Steps to be taken to rebuild goal congruence include *increased* participation to regain commitment to the organization and its goals. Involving subordinates provides a greater opportunity for them to see—and influence—the larger picture and their role within it.

### Subordinate Conflict

Nineteen percent of all managers respond to the likelihood of subordinate conflict or disagreement by becoming more participative. We call such managers "conflict-confronters," that is, using participation to help resolve decision-based conflict by encouraging all viewpoints to be heard and bringing all issues out onto the table. However, a much larger number of managers (50 percent) are less participative in the presence of conflict. We call such managers "conflict-avoiders." These managers may fear that participation, especially in a group meeting, will become an arena for the conflict to intensify, thus causing "things to get worse." Thirty-one percent of all managers are "conflict-neutral." No other situational attribute has a higher percentage of people who are neutral to its presence or absence.

Earlier in this chapter we noted that managers tended to exhibit more participative patterns in situations that, from a prescriptive perspective, require greater involvement of others. A similar conclusion is suggested by the results shown in Table 7–3. With one important exception, the Model A variant of the Vroom-Yetton prescriptive model displays the same direction of effect in response to each condition in Table 7–3 as does the majority of managers in our sample. For six of the seven attributes, managerial behavior and model behavior respond similarly to changing circumstances. The single exception involves responses to conflict. Due to the "conflict rule," Model A displays what we have defined as a conflict-confronting pattern; as we have seen, most managers display a conflict-avoiding behavioral pattern. Because of the reversal in the direction of change, this may be managers' single most dramatic departure from prescribed behavior.

## DIFFERENCES IN MANAGERS' REACTIONS TO SITUATIONS

Table 7–3 reveals another kind of difference among managers. Differences among managers are reflected not only in frequencies of use of autocratic and participative processes (MLP), they are also evident in the way in which the manager tailors a choice of autocratic versus participative processes for use in different situations. Two managers may have exactly the same MLP score, suggesting a certain similarity in their leadership styles, but may use substantially different *patterns* of when and where participative and autocratic methods are employed. For example, one may be among the 21 percent who are more participative when the problem lacks a quality requirement while the other is among the 62 percent majority who are more participative on problems possessing a substantial quality requirement.

These differences among managers are more complex, but probably more important, than the differences in overall participativeness that have previously been discussed (cf. Jago, 1978). Because these differences involve characteristics of people that reflect how they respond to situations, we represented this in Figure 7–1 as a line connecting participation with the midpoint of the line connecting person and situation.

## AGREEMENT WITH THE NORMATIVE MODEL

When problem set responses are compared to the "feasible sets" that exist for each case, the typical manager in our sample of over 2,500 conforms to the prescriptions of the Vroom-Yetton normative model in twenty-one of thirty cases, or 70 percent of the time. The rate of agreement with the feasible set varies from a low of fourteen cases to a high of thirty cases (perfect agreement).

We can also calculate the rate at which the typical manager chooses the Model A and Model B selections from the feasible set. Agreement with Model A occurs 39 percent of the time, agreement with Model B occurs 24 percent of the time. Other choices are either outside the feasible set or inside the feasible set but between the most autocratic and the most participative of feasible responses. These figures reveal that the typical manager's behavior is apparently governed more by the time-saving considerations reflected in Model A than by the developmental considerations reflected in Model B. However, they also suggest that the behavior of most managers departs substantially from conformity to either Model A or Model B.

Departure from the model inevitably means violation of a rule designed either to protect decision quality or decision acceptance. (These rules were presented in Chapter 5, Table 5–2.) The results from our large sample support a conclusion, made earlier by Vroom and Yetton (1973), that departures from the model are more likely to be attributable to violations of acceptance rules than of quality rules. If these two sets of rules are regarded as equally valid, the typical manager is more likely to have his or her effectiveness impaired due to lack of appropriate attention to issues of commitment than to inattention to issues relative to the technical quality of decisions.

## SUMMARY

In this chapter we examined how managers *do* behave as opposed to how they *should* behave. We began by looking at differences among managers in their mean level of participativeness—or MLP. These scores roughly correspond to what we mean when we characterize managers as either autocratic or participative. Our measure, based on "problem set" responses, correlates meaningfully with other measures of leadership style and reveals differences associated with gender and with the demands of the position occupied by the manager.

We also examined differences among situations and the likelihood that they will produce autocratic and participative behaviors. Situational differences are larger than differences among people but illustrate the general tendency on the part of most managers to adapt their use of leadership practices to the requirements of the situations they encounter.

Finally, we looked at managers' degrees of agreement with the normative model and identified some respects in which the typical manager's choices of decision-making processes are less than optimal.

# CHAPTER EIGHT

# NEW DIRECTIONS FOR A NORMATIVE MODEL

Fifteen years ago, when the book describing the Vroom-Yetton model was first published, the potential for further development was noted. The existing model was compared to a DC-3; envisioned was a supersonic Concorde. Surprisingly, very few changes have been made to the model since its original introduction. Vroom and Yetton (1973) proposed minor changes in the wording of certain questions and proposed the elimination of two attributes that contributed little. They also added a model for individual problems that was later amended by Vroom and Jago (1974). However, with few exceptions these amendments and elaborations were cosmetic rather than substantive.

In this and the next four chapters we will describe a major revision in the model, which the two authors have been working on for the last four years. We have learned much through a decade and a half of joint research (and from the independent research efforts of others), and this new model employs this knowledge to guide leaders in the effective use of both autocratic and more participative methods.

## NATURE OF THE NEW MODEL

The new model shares with its predecessor two key features. First, it employs the same decision processes as those described in Chapter 4. The terms for describing decision processes—AI, AII, CI, CII, and GII, with the addition of GI and DI for individual problems—are common to both new and old models.

Keeping the same decision processes has consequences that we deem valuable. It frees those who have learned the previous terminology from the necessity of having to learn a new language. Furthermore, preserving the same concepts enables us to compare directly the prescriptions of the two models and to discern their relative validity.

We also retain in the new model the criteria against which the effects of participation are to be evaluated. Like its predecessor, the new model is concerned with evaluating the effects of participation on decision quality, decision commitment, time, and subordinate development.

The new model evaluates decision processes in terms of their relative effectiveness. As shown in Equation 8–1 below, decision effectiveness ($D_{Eff}$) is posited to be dependent on decision quality ($D_{Qual}$) and on decision commitment ($D_{Comm}$).

$$D_{Eff} = D_{Qual} + D_{Comm} - D_{TP} \qquad \textbf{(Equation 8–1)}$$

There is a third term in the equation. $D_{TP}$ stands for "decision time penalty." With this term we acknowledge that having sound thinking and a committed group to implement the decision is often not all that is needed to produce effective decisions. Decisions must also be made in a timely manner. Some decisions are made under severe time constraints. The quarterback on a football team has exactly 30 seconds within which to choose and begin the execution of a play before incurring a penalty for delay of the game. Similarly, a landing-signal officer on an aircraft carrier, observing a plane approaching at an imperfect angle or speed for landing, has only a few seconds to decide whether to wave the pilot off or to permit the landing. Tactical decisions are more likely to have time constraints than are strategic decisions. Those decisions involving a close proximity with complex, volatile, and unpredictable systems, equipment, or materials—whether they be the commodities market, an F-18 fighter plane, or a set of gauges monitoring a nuclear reactor—are more likely to generate emergencies with severe time constraints than are policy-making and procedure-setting roles (Van Fleet & Yukl, 1986).

As we shall see later in this chapter, the *time penalty* term will take on a value of zero whenever there are no stringent time constraints limiting the process chosen. When such time constraints exist, decision effectiveness can be reduced by the choice of processes that are likely to exceed these time limits. In the extreme, decision effectiveness is reduced to zero, independent of decision quality and commitment, when there is insufficient time to execute the process chosen.

Decision effectiveness would be the criterion to use if neither time nor development were important. Throughout this book we will be supplementing decision effectiveness with a new and more comprehensive criterion, which we call *overall effectiveness* ($O_{Eff}$). $O_{Eff}$ is greatly influenced by decision effectiveness, but, as shown in Equation 8–2, its values reflect the remaining two criteria affected by degree of participation. Both consequences pertain to effects of the decision process on available "human capital." Independent of the effectiveness of the decisions produced, a decision process can have effects, either positive or negative or both, on the energy and talent available for subsequent work.

$$O_{Eff} = D_{Eff} - \text{Cost} + \text{Development} \qquad \textbf{(Equation 8–2)}$$

Negative effects on human capital occur because decision processes use up time and energy, even in the absence of a time constraint. A four-hour group meeting between a senior executive and seven associates consumes 32 person-hours of time. The value of that time is certainly not zero, although its precise cost varies with the opportunity costs of the meeting. What other activities had to be forsaken by each of the managers in order to participate in that meeting? If critically important activities are not carried out because of time spent in meetings, costs are incurred that must, at the very least, be "traded-off" against the benefits of the meeting. The cost term in Equation 8–2 is intended to represent the value of time lost through use of a given decision process. In a later chapter we will address the methods by which we propose to estimate these costs.

If decision processes can be thought of as depleting available human capital, are there not ways in which they can enhance it? Early in this book we argued that participation in decision making could be developmental. Group meetings consume time, but they also can provide insight, build teamwork, and stimulate identification with organizational goals. The development term in Equation 8–2 is a surrogate for "value added"—the increment in human capital that can accrue through appropriate involvement of others in decision making.

Accounting for development and cost constitute a kind of "fine tuning" of the decision-effectiveness criterion. Much of the time, use of the two criteria $D_{Eff}$ and $O_{Eff}$ will yield identical prescriptions. Where they do yield differences we recommend the use of overall effectiveness ($O_{Eff}$), because it encompasses a wider range of organizationally relevant outcomes.

Of course, it is also possible for managers to weigh these organizationally relevant outcomes according to their own needs and preferences. This is particularly true for the time and development components of the $O_{Eff}$ equation. The pressure of work may dictate that considerations of time be given priority over development. Alternatively, the need to develop the skills and talents of subordinates may dictate that development be given priority over time. At the extremes, one could attach maximum weight to time and zero weight to development or vice versa. Throughout the remaining chapters we will refer to the operation of the model under the first set of conditions as *Time*

*Driven.* Under the second set of conditions the model's operation is labeled *Development Driven.* "Driving" the model in these different directions sometimes leads to different destinations (that is, prescribed decision processes). At other times, it amounts to taking different routes to the same destination.

## PROBLEM ATTRIBUTES

The prescriptions of the new model are based on a manager's analysis of the status of twelve problem attributes. The questions corresponding to these attributes, and the alternatives from which choices are made, are shown in Table 8–1. The reader interested in a more detailed exposition of these attributes, including alternative forms of the questions, is referred to Appendix A.

Four of the questions require estimates of the importance of various criteria using a scale ranging from "no importance" through "critical importance." Six other questions require probability estimates ranging from "no" through "maybe" to "yes." The remaining two attributes—"time constraints" and "geographical dispersion"—permit only dichotomous responses of "no" or "yes." (The reader familiar with the Vroom-Yetton model described in Chapter 5 will recognize an increase in the number of attributes from seven to twelve and an increase in the number of response alternatives from two to five for most attributes. The reasons for these additions should be apparent from the discussion of the shortcomings of the former model in Chapter 6. The reader may also have noticed that the term *commitment* has been substituted for the previous term *acceptance*.)

## MATHEMATICAL FUNCTIONS

The status of a problem on the twelve attributes provides the basis for estimating the relative (overall) effectiveness of the five degrees of participation. Separate estimates are made for each of the four basic criteria—quality, commitment, time, and development—and summed, with any decision-time penalty if constraints exist, in accordance with Equation 8–2 to yield a prediction of overall effectiveness.

It is through Equation 8–2 that tradeoffs are recognized and addressed. Frequently, the decision process that would be optimal for decision quality is not optimal for maximizing commitment. Similarly, the alternative that maximizes development does not necessarily maximize commitment, infrequently maximizes quality, and almost never is optimal from the standpoint of time. Equation 8–2 weighs, evaluates, and combines these alternative considerations.

The task of predicting criteria is accomplished by mathematical formulae that express these criteria as functions of the decision process and the scaled problem attributes. The next three chapters will discuss in some detail how

**TABLE 8–1    Problem Attributes in the Revised Model**

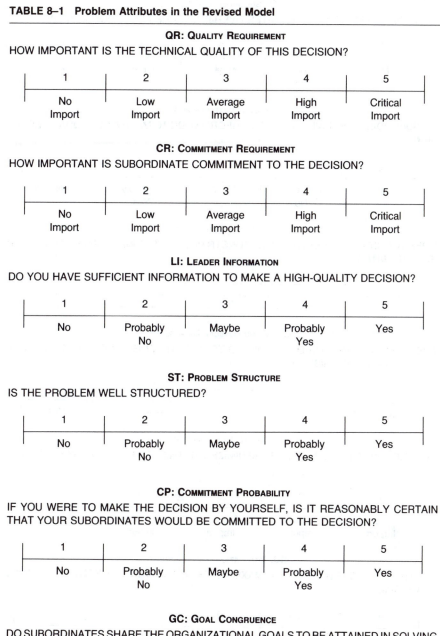

## QR: QUALITY REQUIREMENT
HOW IMPORTANT IS THE TECHNICAL QUALITY OF THIS DECISION?

| 1 | 2 | 3 | 4 | 5 |
|---|---|---|---|---|
| No Import | Low Import | Average Import | High Import | Critical Import |

## CR: COMMITMENT REQUIREMENT
HOW IMPORTANT IS SUBORDINATE COMMITMENT TO THE DECISION?

| 1 | 2 | 3 | 4 | 5 |
|---|---|---|---|---|
| No Import | Low Import | Average Import | High Import | Critical Import |

## LI: LEADER INFORMATION
DO YOU HAVE SUFFICIENT INFORMATION TO MAKE A HIGH-QUALITY DECISION?

| 1 | 2 | 3 | 4 | 5 |
|---|---|---|---|---|
| No | Probably No | Maybe | Probably Yes | Yes |

## ST: PROBLEM STRUCTURE
IS THE PROBLEM WELL STRUCTURED?

| 1 | 2 | 3 | 4 | 5 |
|---|---|---|---|---|
| No | Probably No | Maybe | Probably Yes | Yes |

## CP: COMMITMENT PROBABILITY
IF YOU WERE TO MAKE THE DECISION BY YOURSELF, IS IT REASONABLY CERTAIN THAT YOUR SUBORDINATES WOULD BE COMMITTED TO THE DECISION?

| 1 | 2 | 3 | 4 | 5 |
|---|---|---|---|---|
| No | Probably No | Maybe | Probably Yes | Yes |

## GC: GOAL CONGRUENCE
DO SUBORDINATES SHARE THE ORGANIZATIONAL GOALS TO BE ATTAINED IN SOLVING THIS PROBLEM?

| 1 | 2 | 3 | 4 | 5 |
|---|---|---|---|---|
| No | Probably No | Maybe | Probably Yes | Yes |

**TABLE 8–1** (*continued*)

### CO: Subordinate Conflict

IS CONFLICT AMONG SUBORDINATES OVER PREFERRED SOLUTIONS LIKELY?

| 1 | 2 | 3 | 4 | 5 |
|---|---|---|---|---|
| No | Probably No | Maybe | Probably Yes | Yes |

### SI: Subordinate Information

DO SUBORDINATES HAVE SUFFICIENT INFORMATION TO MAKE A HIGH-QUALITY DECISION?

| 1 | 2 | 3 | 4 | 5 |
|---|---|---|---|---|
| No | Probably No | Maybe | Probably Yes | Yes |

### TC: Time Constraint

DOES A CRITICALLY SEVERE TIME CONSTRAINT LIMIT YOUR ABILITY TO INVOLVE SUBORDINATES?

| 1 | | 5 |
|---|---|---|
| No | | Yes |

### GD: Geographical Dispersion

ARE THE COSTS INVOLVED IN BRINGING TOGETHER GEOGRAPHICALLY DISPERSED SUBORDINATES PROHIBITIVE?

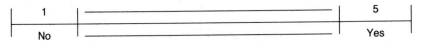

| 1 | | 5 |
|---|---|---|
| No | | Yes |

### MT: Motivation–Time

HOW IMPORTANT IS IT TO YOU TO MINIMIZE THE TIME IT TAKES TO MAKE THE DECISION?

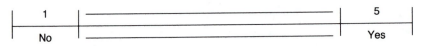

| 1 | 2 | 3 | 4 | 5 |
|---|---|---|---|---|
| No Import | Low Import | Average Import | High Import | Critical Import |

### MD: Motivation–Development

HOW IMPORTANT IS IT TO YOU TO MAXIMIZE THE OPPORTUNITIES FOR SUBORDINATE DEVELOPMENT?

| 1 | 2 | 3 | 4 | 5 |
|---|---|---|---|---|
| No Import | Low Import | Average Import | High Import | Critical Import |

*Note*: See Appendix A for explanations of these problem attributes and their extensions to individual problems.

these formulae operate and the rationale for the role played by problem attributes. For the technically minded, Appendix B contains the formulae themselves. Here we will merely summarize some of the general considerations in developing their mathematical representation.

First and foremost, we wished the functions to be consistent with the accumulated research evidence concerning the effects of participation, or to be derivable from theories of individual, group, and organizational behavior that themselves have been thoroughly evaluated in research. Second, we were mindful of the validity of the Vroom-Yetton model and were committed to retaining those relations that were contributing to that validity. Finally, we sought to capitalize on the things that we had learned through research on the former model and to incorporate attributes that had been repeatedly demonstrated to be missing.

The fulfillment of these aspirations was much more easily attainable with mathematical functions, instead of the use of the analogous, but much cruder, concept of "decision rules" found in the Vroom-Yetton model. When we began formulating mathematical functions to express the rules, we felt at times as if we were replacing a candle with a laser beam. Questions remained as to how strong the beam should be and where precisely it should be focused. However, the medium enabled us, as model builders, to do far greater justice to the accumulating wisdom from research than did the more cumbersome concept of rules.

Let us try to illustrate what we are talking about with an example rather than a metaphor. One of the rules that contributes most to the validity of the Vroom-Yetton model is the rule that eliminates the use of AI and AII when two conditions are present—acceptance is important, and the leader does not have the power to sell his or her solution.

In Figure 8–1 we diagram this rule. The need for acceptance is assumed to exist. The leader's power to sell an autocratic solution either exists or is absent. When absent, AI and AII are predicted not to achieve the acceptance that CI, CII, or GII would produce. When present, all five decision processes are predicted to be successful.

Now, by way of contrast, let us depict this rule as it might be expressed as a mathematical function. The analogous equation itself is of little interest, unless perhaps you are a mathematician. What is of interest is how it would operate. Decision rules and mathematical functions do not lend themselves to direct comparison because the form of their expression is completely different. However, the consequences of their operation can be compared when represented in graphical form.

Figure 8–2 describes how an equation, directly analogous to the acceptance rule, might operate. The reader will recognize that the principal difference is that, in this figure, both axes are now continuous scales rather than dichotomies. This permits finer discrimination to be made in the assessment of the probability that an autocratic decision would generate commitment (the

DECISION ACCEPTANCE

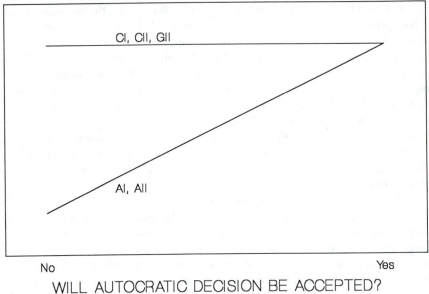

No                                                              Yes

WILL AUTOCRATIC DECISION BE ACCEPTED?

**FIGURE 8–1**   A Graphic Representation of the Acceptance Rule

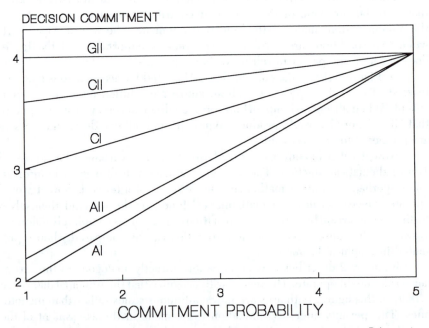

COMMITMENT PROBABILITY

**FIGURE 8–2**   A Graphic Representation of an Equation Analogous to the Acceptance Rule

X–axis). Equally important, it permits finer discriminations to be made among decision processes in assessing their likelihood of achieving the criterion (the Y–axis).

It is clear that decision processes employing higher levels of participation, such as GII and CII, are deemed to produce higher levels of commitment than those that are more autocratic. Their advantage, however, is progressively reduced as the leader's capabilities of selling his or her own decision increase. These differences are totally nullified when the leader's decision is certain to receive commitment from subordinates.

The equation used to produce this example shares a format common to the actual equations employed by the model (Appendix B). Each begins with a value representing the amount of the criterion desired in the situation. In our example, this is *commitment requirement* (CR). Subtracted from this optimal value are quantities representing the degree of risk to the criterion posed by each of the decision processes. In some cases nothing is subtracted, as is the case for GII in Figure 8–2. Under all conditions depicted, GII poses no risk to subordinate commitment. In other cases, however, the amount subtracted can be substantial (for example, AI when the probability that subordinates will be committed to an autocratic decision is remote).

The equation for determining the *time penalty* term ($D_{TP}$) discussed earlier in this chapter provides us with another illustration of the structure of the model. When no time constraint exists, the equation yields a value of zero for $D_{TP}$, thus imposing no penalty on any decision process in Equation 8–1. When the situation becomes an emergency and time is extremely short, more participative processes pose an increasing threat to decision effectiveness. As shown in Figure 8–3, the use of GII under conditions of a severe time constraint would totally nullify the benefits of quality and commitment it might produce. A decision that comes too late to solve the problem is equated with no decision at all.

In this chapter we have introduced the basic structural differences between the previous model and the new one. They share the same language for describing decision processes and many of the same problem attributes employed in diagnosing situations. They also share the same basic set of criteria for evaluating the relative effectiveness of the decision processes. They differ in the way in which judgments of problem attributes are transformed into prescriptions. The new model's use of continuous rather than dichotomous judgments has made it possible to abandon the crude device of rules and to substitute mathematical functions that estimate criteria from judgments of the level of relevant problem attributes. Finally, these structural changes have made it possible to expand the number of problem attributes incorporating factors that we have been forced to overlook until now.

It may seem that the greater promise of validity that the new model brings has been achieved at the expense of substantially greater complexity. Certainly if one had to personally solve the equations referred to in this and

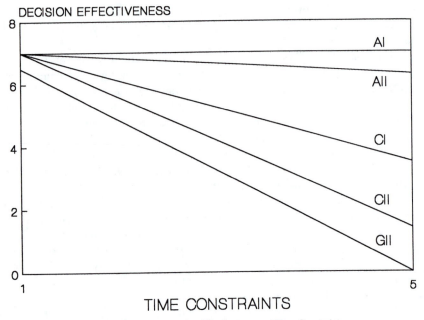

**FIGURE 8–3**  Relationship Between Decision Effectiveness and Time Constraints

subsequent chapters, the costs of this complexity would be very great indeed. Fifteen years ago such considerations loomed large in Vroom and Yetton's reluctance to treat problem attributes as continuous rather than dichotomous. Now, in the era of the personal computer, we are much less fearful of analytical complexities and cumbersome calculations. In Chapter 12, after all the intricacies of the new model have been described, we will show how the personal computer may be used in no more time than it takes to "climb a decision tree." However, for those without a computer we will also show how the model can be represented by decision trees if certain limiting assumptions are made.

In the next three chapters we will examine the subsystems of the new model in depth. We will look, successively, at the way in which we have decided to treat decision quality, decision commitment, and the two components of what we have chosen to call human capital—time and development.

# CHAPTER NINE

# ANALYTICAL OUTCOMES
# IN DECISION MAKING

## *Decision Quality*

As we mentioned in Chapter 3, a popular exercise in management development programs in every corner of the world is known by several different names: the NASA Moon Problem, the Desert Survival Problem, Lost at Sea, and the Subarctic Survival Problem. Although the context changes, the exercise compares the quality of individual versus group decision making—in our language, a comparison of AI and GII. Working individually, participants rank fifteen items according to their importance for survival in some dreaded life-threatening situation. Groups are then formed to consider the same task and to reach a consensus agreement on a set of importance rankings. Both individual and group decisions are then compared to those of a bonafide "survival expert," who provides an objective criterion of success. Groups outperform their average individual members in about four out of five cases; groups outperform even the best individual contained in the group in about two out of five cases (Lafferty & Eady, 1974).

The exercise is typically used in an attempt to demonstrate the superiority of group decisions over individual decisions. However, a more appropriate conclusion is that groups can, *under some circumstances*, outperform individuals. While it would be wrong to think that an autocratic decision will always be of higher quality than a decision in which the input of others is taken into consideration, it would also be wrong to think that an autocratic decision will always be inferior. As in the original Vroom-Yetton model, the new model reflects the fact that the quality of decisions resulting from various levels of participation depends, in large part, upon the nature of the situation encountered.

## MODELING DECISION QUALITY

The literature comparing the quality of group versus individual decisions frequently cites three benefits when decisions are considered by a group (cf. Osborne, 1963; Maier, 1967; Davis, 1969; Kelley & Thibaut, 1969; Steiner, 1972):

- Greater knowledge and information brought to bear on the problem
- Greater number of approaches or perspectives on the problem
- Opportunities for "synergy"

The pooled information and expertise within a group is often greater than that possessed by any single individual within that group. (In the case of the various survival simulations, this pooled information leads to a more thorough list of potential uses for each survival item.) Additionally, if members of a group bring different perspectives to a problem, the group is less likely to pursue only a single line of reasoning or a rutlike "one-track" approach to a problem. A manufacturing manager is likely to view a problem from a manufacturing perspective, a marketing manager is likely to view the same problem from a marketing perspective, and so forth. Bringing them together encourages a fuller exploration of the problem and avoids the possibility of falling victim to the tunnel vision of specialization. Groups also provide the potential, if not always the reality, of a synergistic effect. The most common type of synergy is when a member of a group produces an idea that he or she would not have thought of alone but rather was triggered by something that someone else had said. Osborne calls this "idea hitchhiking."

The implications of the various decision-making methods for decision quality are reflected in the model's equation for this criterion (Appendix B). This equation operates on six of the model's twelve problem attributes: quality requirement (QR), leader information (LI), subordinate information (SI), problem structure (ST), goal congruence (GC), and subordinate conflict (CO). In the remainder of this chapter, we will describe how the model reacts to each of these variables (other things held constant) and provide some illustrations of its overall operation.

## IMPORTANCE OF DECISION QUALITY

The term *quality requirement* (QR) stands for the degree of importance that the manager attaches to attaining a decision of high technical quality. Setting aside any issues of subordinate commitment, the term represents the degree to which the decision must achieve some external set of objectives. Decisions about what products to produce, what markets to enter, how products are to be advertised, and so forth are clearly critical matters for which some alternative courses of action will be superior to others. Other situations, like the parking lot problem we encountered in Chapter 4, possess no quality requirement. No organizational goal or objective, external to the manager and his or her work group, is at stake, and any alternative that meets the constraints imposed by the problem will be effective providing it is successfully implemented.

Contributing to a quality requirement is the degree to which a decision problem possesses an analytic or technical component. If a codified body of knowledge (such as an existing science or technology) exists that can be applied to the analysis of the external consequences of the problem, this fact signals the presence of some level of quality requirement. If, for example, mathematics, engineering, or market research can be applied to the problem, the situation is one in which some alternatives are likely to be technically superior to others. The applicable body of knowledge, whatever it may be, helps one in determining where that superiority can be found.

The absence of such knowledge, however, does not also signal the absence of a quality requirement. Some of the most important strategic decisions that an organization may face are decisions for which scientific procedures may offer little help. Nonetheless, these situations contain an analytical component. Information, no matter how fuzzy and unreliable, must be processed and integrated if the decision is to succeed. The decision-making process may be more intuitive than scientific, but the alternative chosen will ultimately be judged against some criterion or goal.

Although most managerial decisions may contain some degree of a quality requirement, the variable QR and its treatment in the model reflect the fact that organizational decisions will vary in the need they impose on the manager to find the "technically best" or "optimal" or "wisest" alternative.

## LEADER INFORMATION AND DECISION QUALITY

A faulty decision can be produced in even the simplest of situations if a mechanism does not exist to relay required information to the decisionmaker (Shaw, 1964). AI provides no such mechanism and is therefore an inadequate alternative in circumstances in which leader information is incomplete.

The revised model imposes a penalty on the use of AI as leader information becomes more uncertain, that is, as it becomes increasingly apparent that a piece of the puzzle is missing. This can be illustrated (Figure 9-1) by plotting values, produced by the decision quality equation, as answers to the question "Does the leader have sufficient information to make a high-quality decision?" change from "no" to "yes" while holding other attributes of the situation constant. (Introduced in Chapter 8, such figures will be used throughout this

DECISION QUALITY

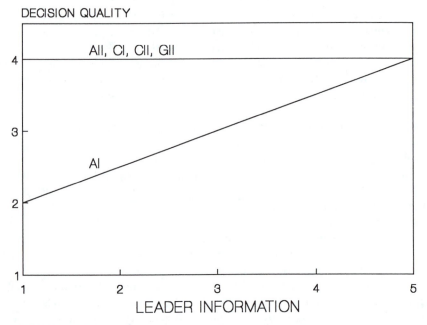

FIGURE 9–1    Relationship Between Decision Quality and Leader Information

chapter to illustrate the effects of each critical variable in the decision quality equation. Chapters 10 and 11 employ the same method to illustrate the effects of critical variables in the remaining equations in the model.)

The following situation is an example of the type of situation depicted in Figure 9–1:

> You must schedule a critical meeting with representatives of one of your most important clients. The client has informed you of the days and times convenient for these representatives. It is imperative, however, that at least four of your seven subordinates also attend the meeting. To schedule a time when one or more of the four was unavailable would render the conference worthless and, because of the importance of the meeting, would jeopardize your goodwill with the client. The four subordinates recognize the importance of the meeting. Fortunately, the client has given you enough alternatives that you are sure at least one will accommodate the existing commitments of your people.

The importance of having the four subordinates at the meeting makes this scheduling decision critical (QR = 5). The situation is highly structured (ST = 5) because you have a known and finite list of alternatives from the client. Collectively, subordinates have sufficient information to make a high-quality decision because each knows his or her schedule for the coming weeks (SI = 5). You are sure that there is a time that can accommodate everyone. More importantly, this is not a situation that involves any substantive conflict among subordinates over the issues that are involved (CO = 1). Moreover, they recognize the importance of the meeting, thereby sharing your goals that an accommodating schedule be found (GC = 5).

What is not conveyed in this short scenario is whether or not *you* have sufficient knowledge of your subordinates' schedules to choose a specific time that will accommodate all four of them. As Figure 9–1 suggests, the quality of an AI decision hinges on this important element of the situation. If you have complete information, an autocratic decision produces a date and time in which you are sure all subordinates can attend. It is a simple matter of comparing schedules, selecting an accommodating alternative, and issuing a memo. As you become more uncertain about your subordinates' schedules, the likelihood that you will make the right choice declines. If you know little or nothing about your subordinates' commitments, decision quality is severely threatened when an AI decision is made.

Figure 9–1 also suggests, however, that a decision made by any other process (that is, AII, CI, CII, or GII) will be of high quality regardless of the level of information that you possess. Each of these processes permits relevant information to be shared and a mutually convenient time arranged that meets the client's requirements. Nonetheless, some of these decision processes may be preferable to others for reasons other than decision quality (for example, AII is more time-efficient). Such considerations are the subject of subsequent chapters.

## SUBORDINATE INFORMATION AND DECISION QUALITY

What if the situation is reversed and the leader possesses all the relevant information to make a high-quality decision but subordinates do not? In this case, GII (consensus group decision making) replaces AI as the process threatening the ultimate quality of the decision (Figure 9–2).

A group decision that involves subordinates who are inexperienced in the issues at hand and collectively do not have the information to make a high-quality decision runs the risk of being less than optimal. In such a case, subordinates may add little in the way of additional technical expertise, yet they are given tremendous control in the selection of an alternative to solve the problem. Experiences in these types of decisions may have contributed to the belief, held by many, that *all* group decisions are ineffective—that "a camel is a horse designed by committee." However, such a generalization is unwarranted. A camel is a horse designed by a committee whose members know little about designing horses.

Of course, a knowledgeable leader can prevent a group from reaching the wrong decision. GII is defined as a consensus decision—one that each member of the group, including the leader, can stand behind and support. Because the leader is not abdicating responsibility to a poorly prepared group,

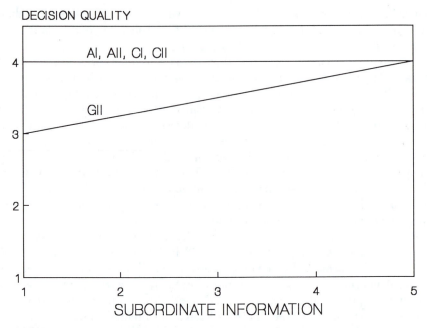

**FIGURE 9–2**    Relationship Between Decision Quality and Subordinate Information

the expected consequences of GII under such circumstances are less severe than those likely from other inappropriate decision processes in other circumstances. Making a decision by yourself when you do not have the necessary facts invites disaster. Making a group decision when you have the facts but your subordinates do not is less likely to be a disaster. You have the opportunity to share the knowledge and expertise you have and to persuade the subordinates of the technical merits of alternatives. (Compare the predicted decision quality for AI under inadequate leader information in Figure 9–1 with that of GII under inadequate subordinate information in Figure 9–2.)

A larger problem than either inadequate leader or subordinate information occurs when both happen simultaneously. This may be an indication that responsibility for the decision should properly reside with another organizational unit and the decision should be "bumped" up, down, or horizontally to another manager. However, on the assumption that the decision is properly located in the organizational hierarchy—an assumption made in the original Vroom-Yetton model and in our revision—then both AI and GII are deemed less appropriate than other alternatives. The leader must collect additional information from outside the group. AII, CI, and CII provide this opportunity if the definition of those consulted is expanded to include those individuals possessing the necessary information. This amounts to an expansion of what we referred to in Chapter 4 as the "information set" of people who have knowledge and expertise that bear on the problem.

## PROBLEM STRUCTURE AND DECISION QUALITY

A problem is well structured if the present state, the alternative courses of action, and the goals and criteria by which they are to be evaluated are all known. Elements of novelty, unfamiliarity, and uncertainty contribute to a lack of structure in a situation. The uncertainty may involve the present state, the desired state, or the ways in which the former may be transformed into the latter. As in the previous model, unstructured situations favor a group process (CII or GII) providing for a free and open exchange of ideas in an atmosphere encouraging exploration of the problem from multiple perspectives.

Because unstructured problems frequently require alternatives to be generated, AI and AII are deemed inappropriate ways of handling these situations. Any number of studies support the common sense notion that "two heads are better than one" in generating potential solutions to problems (see, for example, Taylor, Berry, & Block, 1958; Dunnette, Campbell, & Justaad, 1963; Vroom, Grant, & Cotton, 1969). The evidence suggests that combining the efforts of several individuals is particularly useful in generating *creative* alternatives for consideration, alternatives that any single individual working alone may overlook. Because novel problems frequently require novel solutions, the active participation of others increases the likelihood that a full range of potential alternatives will be considered.

CI (one-on-one consultation with others) is also unattractive because of the complexity of ill-structured situations. The literature on "communication networks," studies of the effects of constraining information flow through certain designated channels within a group, suggests that CI will overload the leader with information in a nonroutine situation. Shaw (1964) describes the leader in a CI-type network dealing with a complex problem as being information "saturated" and making poor decisions as a result. CII or GII opens more communication channels, reducing the concentration of information flow through a single person. A school official may be able to use CI in the relatively simple task of identifying candidates for a scholarship program that he or she administers. However, the same official may find CI inadequate in dealing with the complex problem of an unexpected sharp decline in standardized student test scores.

Figure 9–3 describes the effect of changes in problem structure holding constant other elements of the situation. If the situation is well structured, AII, CI, and CII are all equally likely to be effective. (AI and GII are less acceptable because both leader and subordinate information are low in the

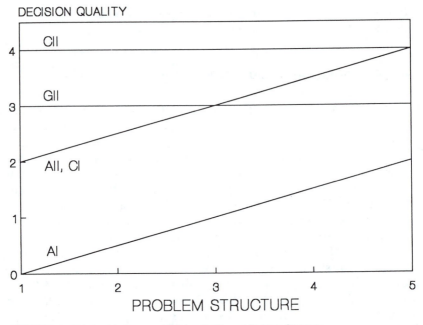

**FIGURE 9–3**   Relationship Between Decision Quality and Problem Structure

depicted situation.) On the other hand, if the situation is unstructured, AII and CI also become poor choices, and AI becomes even less acceptable.

## GOAL CONGRUENCE AND DECISION QUALITY

This model and its predecessor view decision quality as threatened by GII when subordinate goals and organizational goals differ. When the leader and subordinates share a common goal and mutual interests, the circumstance can be characterized as a "win–win" situation. If the problem is solved, everyone benefits and everyone wins. The manager and the work group are "all in the same boat" with a common objective. When goals conflict, the situation is "win–lose" and only one set of objectives can prevail. The use of GII in circumstances in which subordinates cannot be expected to pursue organizational goals runs the risk that they will win and the leader, representing organizational interests, will lose.

Goal congruence really deals with the *motivation* of subordinates, specifically the motivation to devote their resources and expertise toward a common organizational objective. However, the lack of such motivation does not necessarily imply that the manager has disloyal or uncommitted subordinates. Specific decision situations create goal incongruence in otherwise highly motivated and dedicated employees. The incompatibility of goals is inherent in the nature of some specific decisions. Promotions, salary increases, disciplinary and termination decisions, and performance appraisals are examples of decisions typically made by someone other than the affected employee because of the difficulty of overcoming the conflicting self-interest produced by the nature of the situation.

Vroom and Yetton (1973, pp. 73–78) report that the vast majority of situations are ones in which goal congruence can be assumed to exist. In one study of 342 actual decisions encountered by managers, less than 3 percent were situations in which the manager reported that subordinate goals and organizational goals were incongruent.

The behavior of the model in response to changes in the level of goal congruence is shown in Figure 9–4. As the incompatibility of subordinate and organizational goals becomes more evident, the effectiveness of GII declines. (Differences in the relative effectiveness of AI through CII as goal congruence changes are explained in the next section.)

## SUBORDINATE CONFLICT AND DECISION QUALITY

As noted in the original model, subordinate conflict can signal a need for participative processes to ensure subordinate commitment. Failure to resolve conflict could lead to some subordinates having less than the necessary commitment to the adopted course of action.

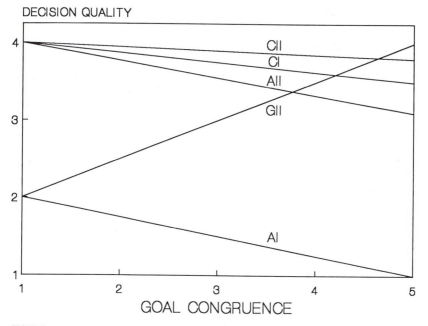

**FIGURE 9–4**  Relationship Between Decision Quality and Goal Congruence

Conflict also plays a role in decision quality. Conflict can be constructive to the extent that it causes people on different sides of an issue to articulate and defend their positions. The inferences and assumptions that survive such an evaluation and critique have been found to be more valid than those that do not survive (Mitroff & Mason, 1981; Mitroff, 1982). Constructive conflict may also produce new alternatives to consider:

> . . . through active, heated, and intense debate between and among inter-
> ested parties . . . [they] came to discover and to invent entirely new
> alternatives as well as elaborate on old ones. (Mitroff, 1982, p. 222)

Although conventional wisdom may suggest that the expression of conflict is always "bad" or "destructive," the accumulated research suggests just the opposite.

Unlike the original, the new model recognizes the benefits of more partici-pative processes in the expression of constructive conflict. Under one set of conditions, Figure 9–5 illustrates the model's response to changes in subordinate conflict. When conflict is low, AII, CI, CII, and GII are all predicted to lead to the same level of decision quality. As conflict becomes more likely, differences emerge among these processes. GII provides for the full expression of conflict and for its resolution. CII provides for the same level of debate as GII but does not guarantee the same level of conflict resolution. (CII does not require that conflicting parties reach some form of agreement.) CI guarantees that

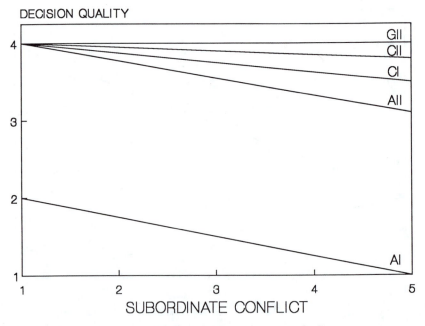

FIGURE 9–5   Relationship Between Decision Quality and Subordinate Conflict

the leader will be exposed to alternative positions and the rationales for those views, but debate among those in conflict is precluded. AII exposes the leader to some information that is the source of the conflict, but provides no opportunity for subordinates to take or defend a position.

It is important to note that these responses to conflict occur only when leader information (attribute LI) is low and subordinate goal congruence is high (attribute GC). Conflict is not expected to have a benefit if the leader is sure that he or she has all the necessary information to make a high-quality decision. Similarly, no benefit from conflict is expected if goal congruence does not exist. Subordinates must share a common goal that is organizationally relevant. The source of the conflict must be the means to obtain this goal, not the goal itself.

These interactions with conflict are not evident in Figure 9–5 because leader information and goal congruence are held constant. However, the interaction with goal congruence is evident if we return to Figure 9–4. The effect displayed by GII as goal congruence changes has been explained in the previous section. However, the effects that the other decision processes display are due to the model's response to the conflict assumed to exist. As goal congruence increases, the model recognizes the benefits of conflict we have discussed in *this* section. Figure 9–4 provides an excellent example of how the problem attributes can operate in conjunction with one another.

### A Caveat on Conflict

The model operates on the presence or absence of problem attributes, including subordinate conflict. Unlike the other attributes, however, subordinate conflict is, at least to some degree, under the control of the leader. Specifically, a leader can introduce conflict into a situation in which it otherwise does not exist. Given the benefits of constructive conflict, the leader may choose to conduct group meetings in ways that encourage differences of opinion to develop and emerge.

Within a CII or GII meeting, the leader can introduce conflict in either of two ways. The method of "devil's advocacy" (Cosier, 1981) requires a subgroup of participants to devote its energy to finding fault with the recommendations produced by the remaining group members:

> The devil's advocacy approach develops a solid argument for a reasonable recommendation, then subjects that recommendation to an in-depth, formal critique. The critique calls into question the assumptions and recommendations presented to the devil's advocate, and attempts to show why the recommendations should not be adopted. Through repeated criticism and revision, the approach leads to mutual acceptance of a recommendation. (Schweiger, Sandberg, & Ragan, 1986, p. 58)

A somewhat different technique has been labeled "dialectical inquiry" (Mitroff & Mason, 1981). It also requires that the group be divided into subgroups:

In the dialectical inquiry approach two different recommendations, based on contrary assumptions, are developed from the same data. The two recommendations and their respective assumptions are subjected to an in-depth, critical evaluation through a debate between two advocate subgroups. Using the same data, the debaters attempt to spell out the implications of each decision, reveal its underlying assumptions, and challenge (or defend) those assumptions as effectively as possible. In other words, each side is trying to win the debate. Following the debate the two advocate subgroups should settle on which assumptions survived the scrutiny of debate and attempt to develop a recommendation based on them. (Schweiger, Sandberg, & Ragan, 1986, pp. 57–58)

Some evidence suggests that either devil's advocacy or dialectical inquiry can produce higher-quality decisions than a simple GII meeting without these additional features (Schweiger, Sandberg, & Ragan, 1986).

The introduction of conflict may have an additional benefit. As we first mentioned in Chapter 3, Janis (1982) provides examples of how highly cohesive groups can replace the primary goal of reaching high-quality decisions with a goal of maintaining the harmony of the group, a mode of behavior he labels "groupthink." In such groups, the desire for unanimity can override a realistic appraisal of the alternatives that are available and can prevent the selection of one that is likely to best achieve overall goals and objectives. Simply stated, such groups desire a harmonious "group atmosphere" whatever the cost. The result is self-censorship within group discussions, widespread rationalizations, and the insulation of the group from challenging information. Janis analyzes several policy-making fiascoes that may have proven disastrous because of this type of goal displacement: the invasion of the Cuban Bay of Pigs, the decision to cross the 38th parallel in the Korean War, the decision not to place Pearl Harbor on alert prior to the Japanese attack, and the escalation of the Vietnam War during the Johnson administration. More recently, a director of NASA, in testimony before Congress, blamed the 1986 tragedy of the Challenger space shuttle explosion on groupthink.

Many of Janis's recommendations for preventing groupthink involve the introduction of conflict to prevent premature adoption of a particular position and to maintain the goal of thorough appraisal of all the options available. The introduction of task-based conflict can ensure the integrity of the group's purpose, challenge group rationalizations, and legitimize the existence of differences of opinion.

There are, therefore, persuasive arguments that the absence of conflict should signal the leader that the group may reach premature agreement on a course of action. Unanimity of view does not guarantee that the prevailing sentiment is correct. However, what is certain is that conflict must be managed. Whether conflict preexists due to the circumstances of the situation, or whether it is introduced by one of the above techniques, the successful leader is one who uses conflict to ensure that all perspectives on a problem are explored, keeps the conflict focused on the issues at hand (and not the personalities involved), and ultimately achieves its resolution.

## APPLICATION TO TWO EXAMPLES

To summarize, the ability of different decision processes to deliver the required level of decision quality depends upon : (1) leader information, (2) subordinate information, (3) problem structure, (4) congruence of organizational and subordinate goals, and (5) likelihood of subordinate conflict. Each variable is represented in at least one term in the equation predicting decision quality, and each of these terms operates in the manner we have described in the preceding sections. The entire equation can now be applied to two example situations that were first presented in Chapter 4.

The first example is the New Machines Decision Problem (the complete text of which can be found on page 43). In the following case, we have provided an analysis of this situation using the six problem attributes relevant to decision quality:

---

### CASE 3    NEW MACHINES DECISION PROBLEM

*Synopsis*

Although you do not know why, the expected productivity of newly installed machines has not been realized despite their operation at peak efficiency. The first-line supervisors reporting to you have different views about the likely source of the problem.

*Analysis*

| | | |
|---|---|---|
| Quality Requirement | Critical Importance | (QR = 5) |
| Leader Information | Probably No | (LI = 2) |
| Problem Structure | No | (ST = 1) |
| Goal Congruence | Probably Yes | (GC = 4) |
| Subordinate Conflict | Yes | (CO = 5) |
| Subordinate Information | Maybe | (SI = 3) |

*Synthesis*

*Highest Decision Quality:* **CII**

---

Figure 9–6 displays the relative decision quality that is likely to emerge if the leader approached this situation with each of the five available decision processes. AI is expected to produce the lowest-quality decision because of the lack of adequate leader information to properly handle the problem without input from subordinates. AII and CI are not expected to do much better because of the lack of structure in the situation and the inferiority of these decision processes in exploring all dimensions of the problem. CII and GII are both expected to produce high-quality decisions, CII having an edge over GII because of the lack of certainty that subordinates collectively have sufficient information and expertise to address the issue of declining productivity. On the basis of decision quality alone, CII is the model's choice for handling this situation.

The second example is the R & D Projects Decision Problem (the complete text of which is found on page 44):

---

## CASE 4   R & D Projects Decision Problem

*Synopsis*

**You must choose which projects an R & D team will be assigned. Current projects are appealing to the team; proposed projects will be profitable but are devoid of scientific interest.**

*Analysis*

| | | |
|---|---|---|
| **Quality Requirement** | **High Importance** | **(QR = 4)** |
| **Leader Information** | **Probably Yes** | **(LI  = 4)** |
| **Problem Structure** | **Yes** | **(ST  = 5)** |
| **Goal Congruence** | **Probably No** | **(GC = 2)** |
| **Subordinate Conflict** | **Probably No** | **(CO = 2)** |
| **Subordinate Information** | **No** | **(SI  = 1)** |

*Synthesis*

> *Highest Decision Quality:* **CII**

---

Figure 9–7 displays the relative decision quality that is likely to emerge if the leader approached this second situation with each of the five available decision processes. GII is expected to produce the lowest-quality decision because the motivation of the scientists to pursue projects of "academic" interest represents a threat to their approach to the problem with the organizational goal of profitability in mind. The remaining decision processes are expected to produce decisions of near-equal quality. AI is expected to be at a slight disadvantage to AII, CI, and CII because the leader is not completely certain of the information that is possessed. (That the two areas of research will be more profitable is described in the written case as being a personal judgment in an area that is often not clear.)

As these examples illustrate, the operation of the equation for decision quality provides a relative prediction for the suitability of the five decision processes. However, it would be inappropriate to make comparisons of the relative decision quality of different processes *across* problems or situations.

## Case #3: New Machines Problem

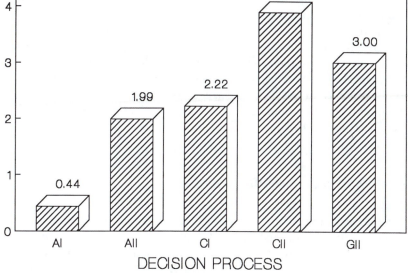

FIGURE 9–6 Predicted Quality: New Machines Decision Problem

## Case #4: R & D Projects Problem

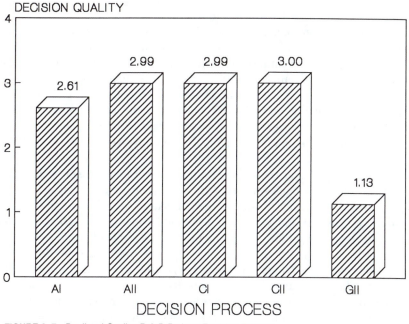

FIGURE 9–7 Predicted Quality: R & D Projects Decision Problem

For example, it would be wrong to conclude that CII is a better choice in the new machines problem (Figure 9–6) than in the R & D problem (Figure 9–7) because the projected score is higher in the former when compared to the latter. The maximum decision quality that a process can produce is limited to the amount of decision quality that is desired (that is, the answer to the diagnostic question, "How important is the technical quality of this decision?"). One can only compare the predicted decision quality of the different processes as they pertain *within* a particular decision. It also deserves emphasis that these illustrations do not include considerations of any necessary subordinate commitment, considerations of time, or considerations of subordinate development. These are issues addressed in later chapters.

## EXTENSION TO THE INDIVIDUAL MODEL

Considerations of quality are equally relevant to the involvement of individual subordinates in decision making. In Chapter 4 we discussed the concept of individual problems. It will be recalled that such situations permit five degrees of participation, ranging from the familiar AI, AII, and CI—also applicable to group problems—and two additional processes, GI and DI. GI involves a discussion between the manager and the subordinate concluded only by consensus between the two about the plan to be adopted. DI has the manager delegating the decision to the subordinate, hence providing maximum participation on the subordinate's part.

When goal congruence is low, DI is considered a threat to decision quality in much the same way that GII is a threat in the group model. Additionally, when subordinate commitment is not required, or when such commitment can be obtained with an autocratic decision, GI (joint decision making) is also considered to be a similar threat. Its use runs the risk of leading to a stalemate between the leader and subordinate, the two hoping to achieve different objectives. However, when commitment is required and not certain to result from an autocratic decision, the risk involved in GI is deemed a reasonable one to take.

It may be recalled that conflict among subordinates (CO) was deemed to have an effect on decision quality in the group model. The existence of conflict, combined with goal congruence, increased the relative value of group methods such as CII and GII. In the individual model, conflict is redefined to refer to the potential for disagreement *between the leader and subordinate* over the alternatives that they may initially prefer. Under conditions of low leader information and high goal congruence, the expression and resolution of such conflict can have the same benefits to the quality of an individual decision that the expression and resolution of group conflict can have in situations affecting a larger number of people. We have argued that constructive conflict can exist in a group. There is no reason to believe that it cannot also be found in the dyad.

As we did for the group model, the equation for decision quality in the individual model can be applied to a sample problem first presented in Chapter 4 (the complete text of the case appears on page 45):

---

### CASE 6    CLIENT COMPLAINT DECISION PROBLEM

*Synopsis*

A major client has complained about one of your most competent subordinates, who recently has seemed indifferent about his work. The client was not very clear about the problem, but it is clear your goodwill with the client is at stake.

*Analysis*

| | | |
|---|---|---|
| Quality Requirement | High Importance | (QR = 4) |
| Commitment Requirement | Average Importance | (CR = 3) |
| Leader Information | No | (LI = 1) |
| Problem Structure | Probably No | (ST = 2) |
| Commitment Probability | No | (CP = 1) |
| Goal Congruence | No | (GC = 1) |
| Subordinate Conflict | Yes | (CO = 5) |
| Subordinate Information | Probably Yes | (SI = 4) |

*Synthesis*

*Highest Decision Quality:* CI

---

Both quality and commitment are required, but it is assumed that reaching a high-quality decision is more important than reaching one acceptable to the subordinate. One alternative available to the manager is to terminate the subordinate, which would not require any acceptance at all!

Figure 9–8 displays the relative decision quality that is likely to emerge if the leader approached this situation with each of the five available decision processes. Considering only the criterion of decision quality, CI is deemed the best method of getting to the root of this problem. DI is considered inappropriate because the situation may require a disciplinary action for which goal congruence is assumed to be low. AI is considered inappropriate because you lack the necessary information regarding the specific nature of the subordinate's problem. AII and GI may produce a high-quality decision, but remain inferior to CI. AII prevents a thorough and frank discussion with the problem

## Case #6: Client Complaint Problem

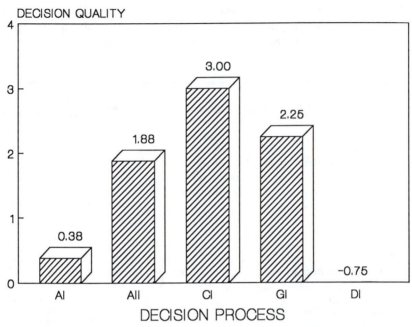

FIGURE 9–8   Predicted Quality: Client Complaint Decision Problem

subordinate. GI represents somewhat of a threat to decision quality because full agreement with the subordinate on a course of action may be difficult under the conditions of low goal congruence.

### SUMMARY

Employing decision quality as the criterion, the model's behavior in response to each problem attribute has been graphically illustrated in figures throughout this chapter. The model's logic can be condensed, with a necessary sacrifice in precision, to the following:

---

**FOR GROUP PROBLEMS, TO IMPROVE DECISION QUALITY:**

**1.    AVOID the use of AI when:**

    a.   the leader lacks the necessary information.

**2.    AVOID the use of GII when:**

    a.    subordinates do not share the organizational goals, *and/or*
    b.    subordinates do not have the necessary information.

**3.    AVOID the use of AII and CI when:**

    a.    the leader lacks the necessary information, *and*
    b.    the problem is unstructured.

**4.    MOVE toward GII when:**

    a.    the leader lacks the necessary information, *and*
    b.    subordinates share the organizational goals, *and*
    c.    there is conflict among subordinates over preferred solutions.

---

**FOR INDIVIDUAL PROBLEMS, TO IMPROVE DECISION QUALITY:**

**1.    AVOID the use of AI when:**

    a.    the leader lacks the necessary information.

**2.    AVOID the use of DI when:**

    a.    the subordinate does not share the organizational goals, *and/or*
    b.    the subordinate does not have the necessary information.

**3.    AVOID the use of GI when:**

    a.    the subordinate does not share the organizational goals, *and*
    b.    subordinate commitment is not required, or the subordinate will commit to the leader's decision.

**4.    AVOID the use of AII when:**

    a.    the leader lacks the necessary information, *and*
    b.    the problem is unstructured.

**5.    MOVE toward GI when:**

    a.    the leader lacks the necessary information, *and*
    b.    the subordinate shares the organizational goals, *and*
    c.    there is conflict between the leader and subordinate over preferred solutions.

These considerations would be irrelevant if decision quality were of no importance. They should play an increasing role in one's thinking and one's choices as the importance of decision quality increases.

# CHAPTER TEN

# MOTIVATIONAL OUTCOMES IN DECISION MAKING

## *Subordinate Commitment*

In the previous chapter we addressed the implications of participation for the quality of decisions. Under what circumstances can we expect a manager's involvement of others to enhance or to detract from the informational base of the decision?

This chapter examines the consequences of participation for the building of commitment to decisions. Our basic thesis is that a manager can gain not only more information and better integration of information from the use of participation, but also increased support and cooperation from those affected by the decision.

### MODELING DECISION COMMITMENT

The motivational consequences of power sharing have long been recognized by social scientists. Coch and French (1948) argued that participation developed "own forces" within the person to implement the decision; Maier (1963) discussed the role of participation in securing decision acceptance; Likert (1961) saw participative management in work teams as a core ingredient in his motivational theory of management; McGregor (1960) viewed power sharing both with groups and with individuals as a means for linking individual and organizational goals. Social science has not overlooked the fact that people support what they help to build!

Receiving somewhat less attention have been the circumstances in which the effects of participation on commitment are large as well as the circumstances in which they are minimal or even reversed. Do all people support what they help to build? Are there situations in which people would resist the opportunity to participate, preferring to have decisions made for them? Such questions lie at the root of a situational or contingency approach to leadership.

The evidence is quite strong and compelling that the effects of participation on commitment do depend on other factors. In their classic study of the effects of autocratic, democratic, and laissez-faire leadership styles in children's groups, Lewin, Lippitt, and White (1939) reported that one child, the son of an army officer, did not respond enthusiastically, as did others, to democratic leadership, preferring instead to have decisions made authoritatively. Later, Vroom (1960) identified two personality characteristics—*authoritarianism* and *need for independence*—that affected the responses of first- and second-level managers to participative methods. Those responding most favorably to participation scored low on a test of authoritarianism and high on a test of their need for independence.

In Chapter 3 we cited evidence pointing to cultural differences in reactions to participation. One of the studies was conducted by French, Israel, and Ås (1960), who failed to replicate, in a Norwegian factory, a study done earlier in the United States showing the beneficial effects of participation in changing work methods. We also described the resistance reported by Marrow to attempts to involve rank and file workers in decision making in Puerto Rico.

In developing a normative model one seeks situational variables that are consistent with the available research evidence and that can be expressed in a form in which a manager can reasonably be expected to make judgments prior to decision making. The Vroom-Yetton model, summarized in Chapter 5, included three attributes bearing on the likelihood that participation would generate commitment. These three attributes have proven their value over the years and are among those most critical to the validity of that model. Accordingly, they have been retained with only minor modifications and should be of even greater value in the more powerful framework of the new model.

The implications of the various decision-making methods for decision commitment are reflected in the model's equation for this criterion (Appendix B). The three attributes this equation operates upon are: commitment requirement (CR), commitment probability (CP), and subordinate conflict (CO). In the remainder of this chapter, we will describe how the model reacts to each of these variables (other things held constant) and provide some illustrations of its overall operation.

## IMPORTANCE OF COMMITMENT TO THE DECISION

Commitment requirement (CR) stands for the degree of importance that the manager attaches to attaining commitment from subordinates in a particular decision. Commitment to a decision by subordinates may be important for two different reasons. In the original model (Vroom & Yetton, 1973), we focused on only one of these—the fact that the subordinates would be involved in implementing the decision. Leaders do not need subordinate commitment for decisions that they intend to carry out themselves or that are contracted for execution by outside agencies. However, autocratic methods are likely to encounter problems when the implementation of a decision requires the support and cooperation of others within the organization. An autocratic academic administrator is likely to be more successful in building bricks and mortar than in restructuring the way in which classes are taught by the faculty. Similarly, an autocratic chief executive officer may be more successful in trimming corporate staff than in engendering market-consciousness throughout the organization. Finally, a human resources executive needs much more involvement of others in the line organization when designing a quality-control circle program than when establishing a day care center for employees.

The reason is an important one and we continue to subscribe to it. But we have come to see another reason for viewing commitment as important. Employees may not be involved in the implementation of a decision but may feel strongly about it for reasons both tangible and intangible. Employees may not be involved in the construction of a building but may have to work in it. They may not be responsible for implementing a particular policy but may be affected by that policy. Failure to consult and involve organization members in decision making can cause not only problems in the implementation of decisions, but also problems of alienation, disaffection, and departure of valued participants. Securing the commitment of an identified set of organization members to the decision can be important either because they have to carry out the decision or because it is somehow important to them and they, in turn, are important to the organization.

## COMMITMENT PROBABILITY AND ITS ACHIEVEMENT

Commitment probability (CP) refers to the likelihood that subordinates would commit themselves to a decision made autocratically by the leader. It would be a mistake to adopt the view that participation is always necessary to secure commitment. Leaders such as Winston Churchill, Martin Luther King, Adolf Hitler, and Ayatollah Ruhollah Khomenei of Iran are each reputed to have had an almost magnetic influence over many of their followers through methods that could hardly be described as consultative or participative.

Judgments of the likelihood of followers' commitment to decisions in which they have had little or no influence are complex ones and, from our limited research results cited earlier in this chapter, should consider the culture of the organization, the personality characteristics of the followers, and even the nature of their upbringing. We have all encountered people who seem to rebel against authority wherever it is manifest as well as others who seem to relish it. Even though the latter may be less common in this highly educated technological age, we cannot afford to ignore individual differences in reactions to the exercise of authority.

All the variance, however, cannot be explained in terms of individual differences among subordinates. Some leaders are more successful than others in gaining acceptance of their ideas.

In Chapter 5, we described a theory (French & Raven, 1959) suggesting that leaders are likely to be particularly successful in selling their ideas when they have achieved one or more of the following power bases: (1) *attraction power*—followers' respect, admiration, trust (or, in the extreme, their recognition of the leader as having charismatic qualities); (2) *expert power*—followers' belief that the leader has the credentials or a "track record" demonstrating the person's superior expertise in the area of knowledge in which the decision is to be made; or (3) *legitimate power*—followers' endorsement of the norms of the larger culture or the traditions of the immediate organization, attaching legitimacy to the exercise of authority by the leader and by occupants of the leaders' role.

Judgments of the likelihood that subordinates will commit to the leader's decision are also affected by the nature of the decision that the leader has made. Exploitative leaders gain less commitment and support than do benevolent and paternalistic ones. It is far easier to sell decisions that embody "good news" to organization members than those that foretell the cutting of budgets and the removal of cherished privileges.

We are left with one of the most complex judgments required by the model. Weighing each of the relevant factors—culture, nature of followers and of their relationship to the leader, and the nature of the decision—the leader must judge the likelihood that the autocratic decision that he or she would make would elicit the needed commitment. This judgment must be expressed on a five-point probability scale on which the extremes are a certain "yes" and a certain "no."

In Chapter 8, we introduced the structure of the new model by describing the operation of a hypothetical equation that predicted the amount of subordinate commitment produced by each of the five decision processes AI through GII. That equation reflected the joint effects of commitment requirement (CR) and commitment probability (CP) on the likely responses of subordinates. In reality, that illustration described the actual operation of the equation for decision commitment as it appears in Appendix B. (The only additional assumption is that subordinate conflict [CO] is absent, a variable to be discussed in the next section.)

Figure 8–2 (page 114) portrayed the model's response to varying levels of commitment probability (CP), assuming the requirement for commitment was critical. For this reason, the figure will not be repeated here. However, expressing the model's operation in words is quite simple. When commitment on the part of subordinates is of importance to the leader (CR), the greater the likelihood that subordinates will commit to the leader's own decision (CP) the less risk connected with the more autocratic decision processes. AI through GII are all equal (in terms of commitment) when subordinates are certain to commit to the leader's decision. As that certainty declines, the relative advantages of the more participative methods become apparent and reach a maximum when there is no chance that subordinates will commit to the leader's decision.

## CONFLICT AMONG SUBORDINATES AND DECISION COMMITMENT

We have described a situation in which the leader really requires the commitment of subordinates to the decision and also believes that there is little likelihood of their commitment to an autocratic decision. If we add to these two conditions the third ingredient of conflict among subordinates over the issues being decided, an additional argument can be made for the use of participative methods. If a "house is divided" but must function as a unity, it must be brought back together. Serious differences of opinion, in situations in which the support of all is necessary and not likely to be achieved by strong directive leadership, require methods for resolving the differences before the decision is made. While the resolution of such differences can take time (as those who have observed Japanese decision making have so often noted), these costs are typically recaptured in the implementation process.

Figure 10–1 illustrates the model's responses to conflict under conditions

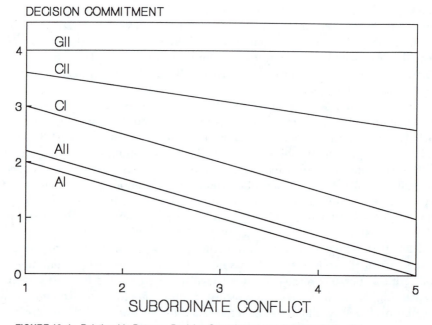

FIGURE 10–1    Relationship Between Decision Commitment and Subordinate Conflict

of a high requirement for commitment and no likelihood that it would be achieved from an autocratic decision. The presence of conflict favors decision-making processes such as CII and GII that permit subordinates to interact during the problem-solving process. When conflict is high, AI, AII, and CI are severely penalized because they provide little or no opportunity to resolve differences in advance of implementation of the decision. This effect is similar to one in the original model. The major difference lies in the recognition that GII has a somewhat higher likelihood of actually working through differences of opinion than does CII.

## APPLICATION TO TWO EXAMPLES

To summarize, the ability of different decision processes to deliver the required level of decision commitment depends upon both the probability that an autocratic decision will generate subordinate commitment and the likelihood that those subordinates will have differing views about what alternative should be chosen or how the problem should be handled. The equation can now be applied to the two situations, first encountered in Chapter 4, that were employed as examples in the discussion of decision quality in Chapter 9.

---

### CASE 3   NEW MACHINES DECISION PROBLEM

*Synopsis*

Although you do not know why, the expected productivity of newly installed machines has not been realized despite their operation at peak efficiency. The first-line supervisors reporting to you have different views about the likely source of the problem.

*Analysis*

| | | |
|---|---|---|
| Commitment Requirement | High Importance | (CR = 4) |
| Commitment Probability | Probably No | (CP = 2) |
| Subordinate Conflict | Yes | (CO = 5) |

*Synthesis*

*Highest Decision Commitment:* **GII**

---

Figure 10–2 displays the relative decision commitment that is likely to emerge if the leader approached this situation with each of the five available decision processes. The combination of a low probability that an autocratic decision would receive commitment and high conflict make both AI and AII very unattractive responses to this situation. CI fares little better. CII and

## Case #3: New Machines Problem

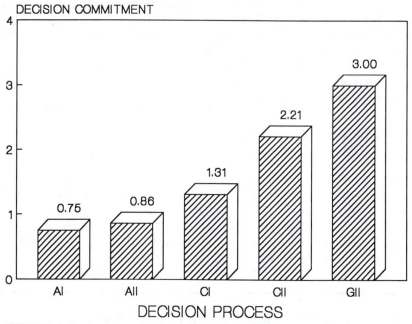

FIGURE 10–2   Predicted Commitment: New Machines Decision Problem

GII are both expected to perform better, but the decided advantage goes to GII. Ignoring any other considerations, GII provides a level of involvement that is expected to produce far greater commitment than would any other response to this situation.

---

### CASE 4   R & D Projects Decision Problem

*Synopsis*

You must choose which projects an R &D team will be assigned. Current projects are appealing to the team; proposed projects will be profitable but are devoid of scientific interest.

*Analysis*

| | | |
|---|---|---|
| Commitment Requirement | High Importance | (CR = 4) |
| Commitment Probability | No | (CP = 1) |
| Subordinate Conflict | Probably No | (CO = 2) |

*Synthesis*

*Highest Decision Commitment:* **GII**

Figure 10–3 displays the relative decision commitment that is likely to emerge if the leader approached this second situation with each of the five available decision processes. The figure looks much like that produced for the previous problem, but AI, AII, and CI are now closer to CII and GII. This occurs largely because of the absence of subordinate conflict.

## Case #4:  R & D Projects Problem

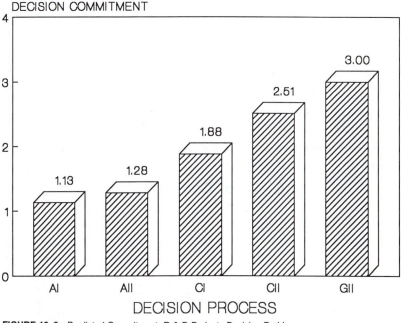

FIGURE 10–3   Predicted Commitment: R & D Projects Decision Problem

## EXTENSION TO THE INDIVIDUAL MODEL

Considerations of commitment are equally relevant to the involvement of individual subordinates in decision making. Consequently, the model for individual problems is similar to that governing group problems when the criterion is subordinate commitment. An exception, however, lies in how the models treat conflict. Conflict among subordinates plays a large role in group problems. In the individual model, however, conflict is conceptualized as differences of view between the leader and the subordinate. The reasons for employing participation to resolve conflicting preferences among subordinates no longer apply, and the dimension is therefore not critical to the model's treatment of individual problems.

Applying the model to our sample individual problem yields the following:

---

### CASE 6   CLIENT COMPLAINT DECISION PROBLEM

*Synopsis*

**A major client has complained about one of your most competent subordinates, who recently has seemed indifferent about his work. The client was not very clear about the problem, but it is clear your goodwill with the client is at stake.**

*Analysis*

| | | |
|---|---|---|
| **Commitment Requirement** | **Average Importance** | **(CR = 3)** |
| **Commitment Probability** | **No** | **(CP = 1)** |

*Synthesis*

*Highest Decision Commitment:* **DI**

---

## Case #6:   Client Complaint Problem

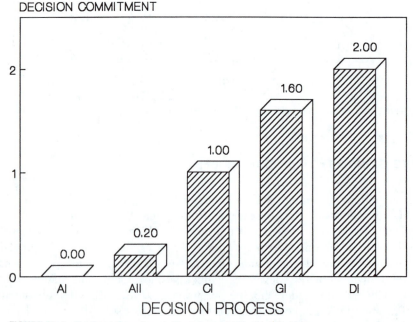

FIGURE 10–4   Predicted Commitment: Client Complaint Decision Problem

Figure 10–4 displays the expected subordinate commitment emerging if the leader approached this situation with each of the five available decision processes. There is a near linear progression in the degree of commitment produced by AI through DI. When all other considerations are set aside, this situation provides the quintessential example of "greater participation breeding greater commitment."

### SUMMARY

Employing subordinate commitment as the criterion, the model's behavior in response to relevant problem attributes has been graphically illustrated. The model's prescriptions can be condensed, with a necessary sacrifice in precision, to the following:

---

**FOR GROUP PROBLEMS, TO IMPROVE DECISION COMMITMENT:**

1. **MOVE toward GII when:**
   a.   subordinates are not likely to become committed to the leader's decision.

2. **MOVE toward GII when:**
   a.   subordinates are not likely to become committed to the leader's decision, *and*
   b.   there is conflict among subordinates over preferred solutions.

---

**FOR INDIVIDUAL PROBLEMS, TO IMPROVE DECISION COMMITMENT:**

1. **MOVE toward DI when:**
   a.   subordinates are not likely to become committed to the leader's decision.

These considerations would be irrelevant if decision commitment were of no importance. They should play an increasing role in one's thinking and one's choices as the importance of decision commitment increases.

---

In the next chapter we turn to the treatment in the new model of the two other criteria for evaluating decision effectiveness—the costs of making the decision and the degree to which subordinates are provided developmental opportunities by the decision-making process.

# CHAPTER ELEVEN

# PARTICIPATION
# AND HUMAN CAPITAL

Imagine a chief executive officer faced with a difficult capital budgeting problem. A maximum of $40 million is available for investment, but the demands of the three division presidents equal three times that amount. Furthermore, each division president fervently believes that his or her request is the minimum amount necessary.

Let us also assume that our chief executive officer elects to use GII to deal with this important but difficult decision. Several long meetings result. During the first, the focus of attention is on defining criteria for making the decision; during the second, they seek to apply the criteria to the initial proposals. Three meetings later, each proposal has been modified, and various combinations, which meet the $40 million constraint, have been proposed and evaluated. It is not, however, until the sixth meeting that consensus is reached and a final decision made.

In the two previous chapters we have examined two criteria by which this decision could be evaluated. To what extent did it represent sound analytic thinking on the part of the four executives? Was it consistent with both long- and short-term needs of the business? Was the package of investments chosen the one with the highest expected return? Was decision quality ($D_{Qual}$) maximized?

Complementing these indicators of decision quality, one might ask how committed the group was to their plan. Were they firmly behind it and did they jointly concur that it was the best course for the entire management? Was decision commitment ($D_{Comm}$) maximized?

We have argued that the effectiveness of the decision is influenced both by its quality and by issues of commitment. However, the effectiveness of a decision is not the only criterion by which decision processes are to be judged. There are other outcomes of making decisions—some costs and some benefits—that must also enter into our framework for estimating the relative value of different decision processes.

Arguing by analogy to economic models, we maintain that the making of a decision both depletes human capital and contributes to it. Let us analyze each of these in turn, beginning with the costs of decision making.

## DECISION COSTS

Decision making uses capital by consuming the time of organization members. In the example with which we began this chapter, resolution of the capital budgeting problem required six meetings, each of which occupied the time of four executives. Assuming that the average meeting took two hours, the GII process used up a total of forty-eight hours of valuable time in making this decision.

The magnitude of the investment hinges on the opportunity costs of this time. What other activities were neglected as a consequence of these meetings? Since time is finite, hours spent in one activity are unavailable for other activities.

To attach a specific economic value to the time used up is a difficult matter. Experienced management consultants may charge clients as much as $500 an hour, a figure that probably understates the marginal costs of time to the presidents in our example. While costs may be difficult to estimate with any degree of precision, to ignore the value of time in a prescriptive model of decision processes would be foolhardy.

In the new model, like its predecessor, time spent increases with the degree of participation. However, the new model also takes cognizance of four situational variables that influence the relative cost of different degrees of participation: motivation–time (MT), problem structure (ST), subordinate conflict (CO), and geographical dispersion (GD). In the sections to follow, we will describe how the model responds to each of these variables (other things being constant).

### Motivation–Time (MT)

Every manager experiences some periods of relative calm and tranquility during which the demands on his or her time and that of subordinates are not excessive and there seems to be enough time to go around to meet all demands. However, on other occasions the opposite is true. One crisis situation follows another and only the barest essentials can be attended to.

Many factors contribute to the importance of time. Industry differences, budgetary cycles, staffing levels, and illnesses of key participants are among them. It should be noted that the value of time does not depend on the particular decision being made but rather with other ongoing events impinging upon the manager.

The significance of this factor to the use of participative methods is obvious. If time has great importance, the costs incurred from the use of participative processes increase.

### Problem Structure (ST)

The length of and the associated costs of group meetings depends, in part, on the complexity of the problem and the cognitive demands it imposes. Decision problems require more time if efforts must be exerted in figuring out the nature of the problem, identifying its boundaries, searching for alternatives, and formulating goals—in short, time spent in structuring it.

The model imposes a greater time cost on participative processes as the problem becomes unstructured. This is illustrated in Figure 11–1. Under conditions of a high motivation to conserve time (that is, MT = 5), we see that GII is always expected to be more time consuming than CII which, in turn, is always more time consuming than CI, and so forth. (At the extreme, AI imposes no penalty regardless of the degree of structure.) The lines in Figure 11–1 do not cross. However, the "spread" between AI and GII is larger if the problem is unstructured than if it is well structured. In terms of time, participative processes become increasing costly as the degree of structure declines.

### Conflict Among Subordinates (CO)

If one sees a person confronted with a choice but apparently unable to make it, a reasonable conjecture is that the person is in a state of conflict. Whether poised at the top of a ski slope and unable to decide whether to walk away or venture down the mountain, or on the verge of an intimate relationship with another person and vacillating between commitment or non-commitment, the lack of action may reflect conflict.

A similar hypothesis is plausible for extended discussions within groups. Conflict and disagreement over solutions to problems among group members prolongs the time required to make decisions.

This increase in decision time presents a problem for participative decisions. The time costs of resolving differences are directly related to the magnitude of the conflict. Accordingly, the greater the magnitude of the conflict, the greater the costs associated with participative methods. Figure 11–2 illus-

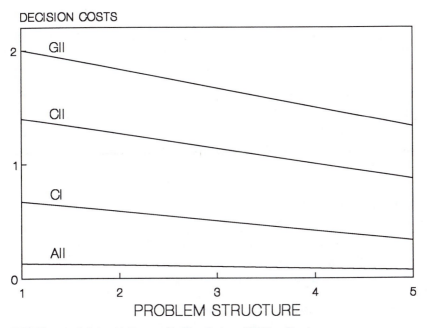

**FIGURE 11–1**    Relationship Between Decision Costs and Problem Structure

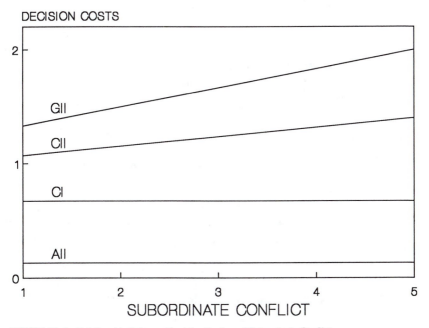

**FIGURE 11–2**    Relationship Between Decision Costs and Subordinate Conflict

trates the precise nature of this relationship as reflected in the model. Again, greater costs are associated with greater participation at any level of subordinate conflict. However, the spread between AI and GII increases with the probability of conflict.

Noteworthy are the constant costs associated with AII and CI across all levels of conflict. Only CII and GII are expected to become more costly as conflict increases (these two processes accounting for the overall spread). Only when a group meeting is held and the conflict is brought "out onto the table" does it have its impact on the length of discussion and therefore decision time.

### Geographical Dispersion (GD)

Geographical dispersion deals not with the cost of conducting the meeting but rather with the cost of *convening* that meeting. If subordinates are scattered geographically, the costs of decision-making methods involving face-to-face interaction among those subordinates increase dramatically because of the time and expense of getting people to and from the meeting. Teleconferencing may be possible to provide a "long-distance" CII or GII meeting, but its costs may be prohibitive both in its actual expense and the time necessary to set up the conference call itself. If geographical dispersion of subordinates exists, and travel and teleconferencing are both impractical, the model imposes a large penalty on both CII and GII.

No penalty is imposed on CI. Although teleconferencing can be an awkward and impractical alternative to "face-to-face" GII or CII, individual telephone calls to isolated subordinates have become an everyday occurrence in organizations of every type. If time permits, telex messages and mail service provide alternatives to the telephone in sharing the problem with individual subordinates and eliciting their ideas.

### Summary

With regard to time, the model's prescriptions can be condensed to the following:

---

### FOR GROUP PROBLEMS, TO REDUCE DECISION COSTS (TIME):

### 1.    MOVE toward AI, especially if:
   a.   a severe time constraint exists, *and/or*
   b.   the problem is unstructured.

## 2.     AVOID use of CII and GII if:

    a.    subordinates are geographically dispersed, *or*
    b.    there is conflict among subordinates over preferred solutions.

These considerations would be irrelevant if time were of no importance and if there were no severe time constraints on the making of the decision. They should play an increasing role in one's thinking and one's choices as the importance of time increases.

---

### SUBORDINATE DEVELOPMENT

So far we have dealt only with the debit side of the human capital equation. Now we turn to the potential "value added" of alternative decision-making processes. In the capital budgeting example with which we began this chapter, is it not possible that the successful application of GII could bring with it some future "dividends" stemming from its developmental consequences? Involvement in decision making can change people, sometimes in ways that make them more valuable to their organizations.

"Practice makes perfect" is an adage with which we have all been familiar since grade school. Its applicability is not just restricted to the learning of arithmetic or a foreign language, but also applies to decision-making skills. One learns less from carrying out the decisions of others than from playing an active and direct role in the making of decisions. The use of GII in the capital budgeting decision afforded the three division presidents a potentially valuable learning experience as they thought through the multiple issues involved in the budget allocations.

Development is not restricted to individual decision-making capabilities. It is also possible that the three presidents learned something about working together as a team. Likert was among the first management theorists to point out that one-on-one supervisory methods, such as CI in our model, may foster competitive relations among subordinates. He recommended instead the use of group methods (such as CII and GII) for the purpose of developing teamwork, collegiality, and of minimizing dysfunctional competition. Such methods offer the opportunity for subordinates to share information and perspectives. By providing a more open forum in which issues are discussed and resolved, they also prevent any divisive suspicion, sometimes possible in CI, that the leader is making "deals" with certain subordinates but not with others.

There is still another by-product of decision-making processes that is relevant to development. The investment of time in the group meetings to decide the capital budgets may have increased the identification of the division presidents with the larger organization of which they are a part. It is a reasonable conjecture that the loyalty that most Japanese workers and managers feel for their company is attributable, in part, to their feelings of involvement in decision making.

In the Vroom-Yetton model, the treatment of development was overly simplified. Participative methods were always seen as more developmental regardless of the nature of the decision or of the group. Clearly, a case can be made for this "main effect," but it is only a starting point. The new model provides a more complex, but more accurate, treatment of the developmental consequences of participation. It suggests that the likely benefits hinge on four key variables: motivation–development (MD), quality requirement (QR), subordinate conflict (CO), and goal congruence (GC).

### Motivation–Development (MD)

This attribute is similar to the importance of time discussed earlier in this chapter. It plays a pivotal role in controlling the effects of each of the other attributes.

There are undoubtedly circumstances under which development of one's subordinates is of little or no value to the organization. The development of temporary workers or of those who are likely to be victims of corporate downsizing is of much less significance than is the development of those who are being groomed for advancement or to whom the organization has made a lifetime commitment.

As was the case with motivation–time, this attribute is unlikely to vary from one decision to another and is likely to vary only slowly with changes in the specific subordinates and their relevance to future plans and organizational interests.

### Quality Requirement (QR)

Development and growth of subordinates is more likely to occur through their involvement in decisions with a substantial analytic component. The capital budgeting decision, through its importance and analytical complexity, is likely to have more developmental value than would, for example, group meetings concerning the company Christmas party or policies concerning coffee breaks.

The effect of a quality requirement is illustrated in Figure 11–3. None of the decision processes produces a developmental benefit if the decision is trivial or inconsequential. On the other hand, as the importance of the problem increases, so do the presumed developmental opportunities for those involved in participative decisions. Benefits accrue faster for GII and CII as the importance of quality increases, because these methods permit the type of interaction most likely to educate those involved, develop their teamwork, and build their identification with organizational goals and objectives.

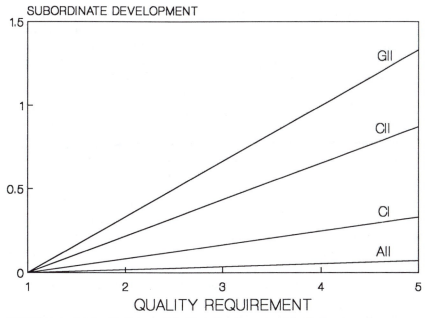

**FIGURE 11-3**   Relationship Between Subordinate Development and Quality Requirement

### Conflict Among Subordinates (CO)

One of the developmental benefits of participative group processes identified earlier was the reduction of conflict and its potential replacement by teamwork and collaboration. In our capital budgeting example this outcome could be of considerable value to the future viability of the entire organization.

What are the signs that conflict reduction might be a by-product of participation? The first such sign is the existence of conflict. Without at least some minimal level of conflict, it is hard to imagine conflict reduction taking place. Thus, the degree of existing conflict or disagreement sets an upper bound on the amount of conflict reduction that can be realized. But not all group meetings effect a reduction in the level of differences. We have all experienced meetings that seem to raise the level of hostilities among "warring factions" rather than ameliorate them.

Our predictions of this developmental benefit of participative group approaches to decision making depends not only on the level of conflict but also on the next attribute, the presence of which influences the likelihood of conflict reduction.

### Goal Congruence (GC)

Those who write about productive negotiations stress the importance of identifying common goals or respects in which both parties can benefit. "Superordinate" or shared goals make differences potentially manageable.

In a work group or task force within an organization, the common goal of successfully challenging the competition in the marketplace often provides the shared objective that makes the nature of the conflict one of means rather than ends. Differences that exist among people in how to get to a shared goal are potentially resolvable through analysis and problem solving.

In Chapter 9 we argued that participation increases decision quality when subordinates disagree but share a common goal. Participative methods provide an opportunity for divergent views to be pitted against each other thereby ensuring that all perspectives on an issue are considered.

Under the same conditions of conflict and high goal congruence, participative processes also offer a developmental benefit. CII and GII provide an opportunity for those in disagreement to learn from each other and to gain a broader perspective. With trends toward increasing specialization in organizations, members more and more often approach problems from the "tunnel vision" of their own area of expertise. Group processes are capable of bringing together people having unique perspectives, resulting in all achieving a greater appreciation for the "bigger picture." To emphasize, however, these outcomes (and those associated with building teamwork through conflict reduction) can only be expected if the relevant organizational goals are shared by all involved.

Figure 11–4 illustrates the expected developmental consequences of each decision-making method under varying amounts of subordinate conflict *assum-*

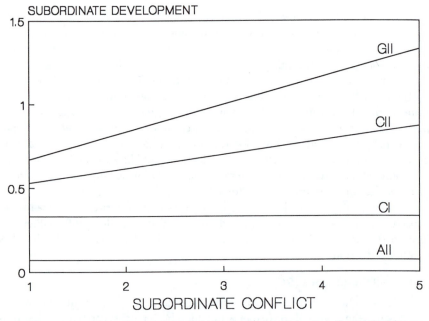

FIGURE 11–4    Relationship Between Subordinate Development and Subordinate Conflict (Goal Congruence High)

*ing subordinate goals and organizational goals to be congruent* (GC = 5). Under these conditions, the developmental benefits of CII and GII are predicted to increase with the likelihood of conflict. Notice, however, that the presumed benefits of CI remain constant across levels of conflict. Although CI can increase the quality of decisions under conditions of conflict by exposing the leader to different views and positions, if it fails to make the team members aware of that conflict it offers few developmental benefits above and beyond those expected under conditions of no conflict.

We also argued in Chapter 9 that, under conditions of low goal congruence, conflict offered no particular benefit to decision quality. The source of the conflict must be over means and not ends. With regard to subordinate development, not only is there no additional benefit to participation under these conditions, there is a potential liability. Without a shared organizational purpose, conflict in a group setting can be *destructure* rather than *instructive*. For example, "turf battles" waged in the conference room are likely to do little to help participants appreciate another's viewpoint or to help build teamwork. More likely, they can intensify the conflict and broaden it from the task to an interpersonal level. Positions become more entrenched; often, participants leave with a personal dislike for each other.

Figure 11–5 illustrates the expected developmental consequences of each decision-making method under varying levels of subordinate conflict *assuming*

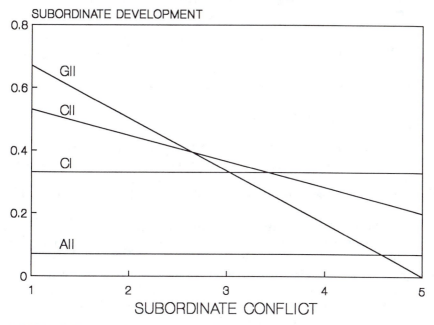

**FIGURE 11–5**    Relationship Between Subordinate Development and Subordinate Conflict (Goal Congruence Low)

*subordinate goals and organizational goals not to be congruent (GC = 1)*. As the likelihood of conflict increases, we see that CII and GII become increasingly unattractive choices. In fact, when conflict becomes either probable or certain, CI (offering no direct interaction among subordinates) becomes the choice on developmental grounds.

### Summary

The model's prescriptions regarding subordinate development can be condensed as follows:

---

**FOR GROUP PROBLEMS, TO INCREASE SUBORDINATE DEVELOPMENT:**

1. **MOVE toward GII when:**
   a. the problem possesses a quality requirement.

2. **MOVE toward CII and GII when:**
   a. subordinates share organizational goals, *and*
   b. there is conflict among subordinates over preferred solutions.

3. **MOVE away from CII and GII when:**
   a. subordinates *do not* share organizational goals, *and*
   b. there is conflict among subordinates over preferred solutions.

These considerations would be irrelevant if development of subordinates is of no importance. They should play an increasing role in one's thinking and one's choices as the importance of development increases.

---

### TIME AND DEVELOPMENT COMPARED

We have likened time and development to depletion and enhancement of the human capital account. The metaphor is not a perfect one, however, since the two cannot be directly exchanged for one another. Deposits occur in a different currency than withdrawals, and, although both have economic value, there is no direct mechanism of exchange.

The costs that we have attributed to the use of time cannot be recaptured through developmental benefits. In fact, the costs from time are immediately realizable, while the returns from development are liable to be felt over a longer term. It was this different property of the two classes of outcomes that led Vroom and Yetton to refer to Model A (which placed a high premium on time) as a short-term model, and Model B (which placed a high premium on development) as a long-term model.

While we have sought to attach numbers to time costs and to development benefits, the numbers are akin to apples and oranges with no exchange mechanism between these two commodities! In fact, we pay for participative processes in terms of immediately consumable apples, and the benefits are received in oranges, the value of which won't be realized until some future date. The widely recognized tendency of people to prefer present rewards to future ones—and hence to avoid delay of gratification—may account for our frequent observation that most managers' choices of decision processes come closer to the Time-Driven model than to the Development-Driven model.

## EXTENSION TO THE INDIVIDUAL MODEL

It should be apparent that similar considerations of time costs and developmental benefits can also apply to "individual problems," those affecting only a single subordinate. The model governing such problems is a direct extension of the model governing group problems, with two notable exceptions.

The first concerns what happens to the amount of time consumed as we move from autocratic to highly participative processes. For group processes the answer was fairly simple, and the relationship was argued to be linear. The more participation, the more time consumed. But such a simple formulation does not apply to individual problems. The most participative process—delegation—is probably one of the most time efficient and in fact has been recommended by "time management" experts as a solution to many an overworked manager.

While precise estimates are not possible, we shall treat time costs as greatest for GI, followed by CI, AII, DI, and AI in that order. DI, the most participative process, is considered only slightly more time consuming than AI. It involves a shift in assuming the burden of the time cost from the manager to the subordinate. In some situations this may involve a lower rate at which the opportunity cost is "charged" (for example, legal research by a law clerk is less "expensive" than the same research performed by a judge). We will assume, however, that these differences in most circumstances are relatively minor. When compared with AI, however, DI involves some additional communication with the subordinate, as the circumstances of the decision situation are conveyed to the person, and the ultimate decision is conveyed back to the leader. For this reason, DI is treated as slightly more costly than AI.

The other difference between the group and individual models is the absence in the latter's cost equation of a term dealing with geographical dispersion (GD). We have argued in this chapter that, for group problems, CI is unaffected by geographical dispersion of subordinates because it is always possible for one-to-one interaction to occur by telephone, letter, or telex. For individual problems, this argument extends to the availability of GI and DI. (By way of personal example, our telephone bills for the period during which we prepared this book, from a distance of 1000 miles from each other, provide ample evidence of the availability of GI.) Because geographical dispersion enters no other equation, its absence from the cost equation in the individual model has the effect of making this attribute irrelevant to such problems. The model for individual problems therefore operates on eleven problem attributes rather than on the twelve contained in the group model.

### Summary

With regard to time and development, the model's prescriptions for individual problems can be condensed to the following:

---

**FOR INDIVIDUAL PROBLEMS, TO REDUCE DECISION COSTS (TIME):**

1. **MOVE toward AI (in the order AI, DI, AII, CI, GI), especially if:**
    a.   a severe time constraint exists, *and/or*
    b.   the problem is unstructured.

2. **AVOID the use of GI if:**
    a.   there is conflict between the leader and subordinate over preferred solutions.

---

**FOR INDIVIDUAL PROBLEMS, TO INCREASE SUBORDINATE DEVELOPMENT:**

1. **MOVE toward DI (in the order AI, AII, CI, GI, DI) when:**
    a.   the problem possesses a quality requirement.

2. **MOVE toward GI when:**
    a.   the subordinate shares organizational goals, *and*
    b.   there is conflict between the leader and subordinate over preferred solutions.

3. **MOVE away from GI when:**
    a.   the subordinate *does not* share organizational goals, *and*
    b.   there is conflict between the leader and subordinate over preferred solutions.

These considerations would be irrelevant if the particular criterion (time or development) were of no importance and if there were no severe time constraints on the making of the decision. They should play an increasing role in one's thinking and one's choices as the importance of the criterion increases.

In Chapters 9 and 10 we illustrated the operation of the model on criteria of decision quality and decision commitment by applying it to three specific examples. In the next chapter we will return to these (and other) examples as we examine how the model operates when all criteria for effectiveness are jointly considered, including those of time and development.

# Chapter Twelve

# APPLYING the NEW MODEL

## *Putting It All Together*

The last three chapters have described our efforts to model the effects of degrees of participation on decision quality, subordinate commitment, decision costs, and subordinate development. Each of these criteria correspond to a subsystem of the model. It is now possible to combine these subsystems and see how the model operates when all criteria are considered together. In the first portion of this chapter we will revisit some of the cases that were first introduced in Chapter 4. We will then use the method of computer simulation to explore what the implementation of the model may mean to the typical manager. Additionally, we will describe the first empirical evaluation of the model and compare its validity to the original Vroom-Yetton formulation. Finally, we will describe two ways in which the model can be represented to facilitate its application to real managerial decision problems.

### APPLICATION TO ILLUSTRATIVE CASES

As we have seen, the model predicts the overall effectiveness of different decision strategies by first estimating decision effectiveness—composed of quality ($D_{Qual}$), commitment ($D_{Comm}$), and time penalties ($D_{TP}$)—then adding to this the implications for human capital, specifically the costs associated with different decision processes (Cost) and the developmental opportunities they afford subordinates (Devpt). In Chapter 5 we illustrated the earlier model by applying it to several concrete situations. We now return to several of these problems to see how the new model can be applied:

---

## CASE 2   COAST GUARD CUTTER DECISION PROBLEM

You are the captain of a 210 ft. medium-endurance coast guard cutter, with a crew of nine officers and sixty-five enlisted personnel. Your mission is general at-sea law enforcement and search and rescue. At 2:00 A.M. this morning, while en route to your home port after a routine two-week patrol, you received word from the New York Rescue Coordination Center that a small plane had ditched 70 miles offshore. You obtained all the available information concerning the location of the crash, informed your crew of the mission, and set a new course at maximum speed for the scene to commence a search for survivors and wreckage.

You have now been searching for 20 hours. Your search operation has been increasingly impaired by rough seas, and there is evidence of a severe storm building to the southwest. The atmospherics associated with the deteriorating weather have made communications with the New York Rescue Center impossible. A decision must be made shortly about whether to abandon the search and place your vessel on a northeasterly course to ride out the storm (thereby protecting the vessel and your crew, but relegating any possible survivors to almost certain death from exposure) or to continue a potentially futile search and the risks it would entail.

You have contacted the weather bureau for up-to-date information concerning the severity and duration of the storm. While your crew are extremely conscientious about their responsibility, you believe that they would be divided on the decision of leaving or staying.

### Analysis

| | | |
|---|---|---|
| Quality Requirement | Critical Importance | (QR = 5) |
| Commitment Requirement | High Importance | (CR = 4) |
| Leader Information | Yes | (LI = 5) |
| Problem Structure | Yes | (ST = 5) |
| Commitment Probability | Yes | (CP = 5) |
| Goal Congruence | Yes | (GC = 5) |
| Subordinate Conflict | Yes | (CO = 5) |
| Subordinate Information | Maybe | (SI = 3) |
| Time Constraints | No | (TC = 1) |
| Geographical Dispersion | No | (GD = 1) |
| Motivation–Time | High Importance | (MT = 4) |
| Motivation–Development | No Importance | (MD = 1) |

### Synthesis

*Highest Overall Effectiveness:*    **AI**

The critical factors in this situation are the motivation to conserve time versus the motivation to develop subordinates. In the analysis above, we have assumed a motivation consistent with time conservation, that is MT = 4 and MD = 1. If, however, the captain truly desired to provide opportunities for the nine officers to develop their command skills, there is no better opportunity than to involve them in this kind of very difficult decision. Setting MT = 1 and MD = 5 provides a recommendation of CII rather than AI.

Clearly the situation requires prompt action. It does not, however, possess a severe time constraint as we have defined that term. If this had been the case then the analysis would be different. In this case, TC = 5 and the model would impose severe penalties on all the decision processes other than AI. The captain may be motivated to provide developmental opportunities for subordinates, but the press of time would dictate that this not be one of those opportunities.

Figure 12–1 illustrates the model's predictions with the original situational analysis (that is, MT = 4, MD = 1, and TC = 1). The closeness of the predictions is the reason for the sensitivity in this case to changes in MT and MD. (In the examples to follow we will be using different values for MT and MD to illustrate their operation. Remember, however, that for any given manager and organizational climate these values will be relatively stable across decision situations.)

## Case #2: Coast Guard Problem

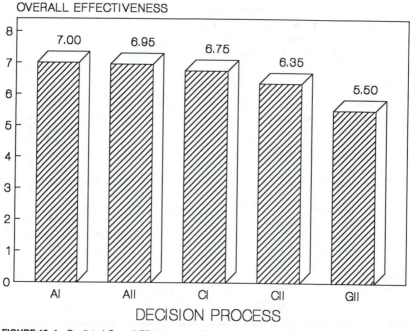

**FIGURE 12–1**   Predicted Overall Effectiveness: Coast Guard Decision Problem

## CASE 3  NEW MACHINES DECISION PROBLEM

You are a manufacturing manager in a large electronics plant. The company's management has always been searching for ways of increasing efficiency. The company has recently installed new machines and put in a new simplified work system, but to the surprise of everyone, including yourself, the expected increase in productivity was not realized. In fact, production has begun to drop, quality has fallen off, and the number of employee separations has risen.

You do not believe that there is anything wrong with the machines. You have had reports from other companies that are using them, and the reports confirm this opinion. You have also had representatives from the firm that built the machines go over them, and they report that the machines are operating at peak efficiency.

You suspect that some parts of the new work system may be responsible for the change, but this view is not widely shared among your immediate subordinates, who are four first-level supervisors, each in charge of a section, and your supply manager. The drop in production has been variously attributed to poor training of the operators, lack of an adequate system of financial incentives, and poor morale. Clearly, this is an issue about which there is considerable depth of feeling within individuals and potential disagreement among your subordinates.

This morning you received a phone call from your division manager. He had just received your production figures for the last six months and was calling to express his concern. He indicated that the problem was yours to solve in any way that you thought best but that he would like to know within a week what steps you plan to take.

You share your division manager's concern with the falling productivity and know that your people are also concerned. The problem is to decide what steps to take to rectify the situation.

*Analysis*

| | | |
|---|---|---|
| Quality Requirement | Critical Importance | (QR = 5) |
| Commitment Requirement | High Importance | (CR = 4) |
| Leader Information | Probably No | (LI = 2) |
| Problem Structure | No | (ST = 1) |
| Commitment Probability | Probably No | (CP = 2) |
| Goal Congruence | Probably Yes | (GC = 4) |
| Subordinate Conflict | Yes | (CO = 5) |
| Subordinate Information | Maybe | (SI = 3) |
| Time Constraints | No | (TC = 1) |
| Geographical Dispersion | No | (GD = 1) |
| Motivation–Time | Average Importance | (MT = 3) |
| Motivation–Development | Average Importance | (MD = 3) |

*Synthesis*

*Highest Overall Effectiveness:*     **CII**

## Case #3:  New Machines Problem

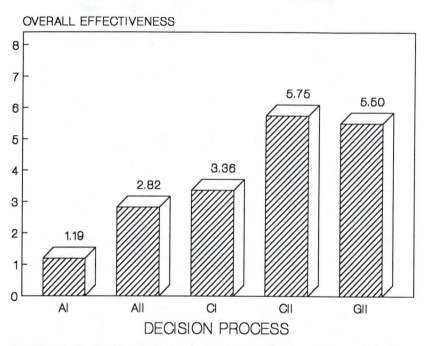

**FIGURE 12–2**  Predicted Overall Effectiveness: New Machines Decision Problem

As Figure 12–2 illustrates, the model's predictions for this situation are quite unlike those for the Coast Guard problem. There are substantially greater differences among the decision processes in their predicted effectiveness. As we saw in Chapter 9 (Figure 9–6), CII and, to a lesser extent, GII are superior to AI, AII, and CI when only issues of decision quality are considered. Add to this the need to generate subordinate commitment (Figure 10–2), and the clear choice becomes CII.

---

### CASE 4   R & D PROJECTS DECISION PROBLEM

You are the head of a research and development laboratory in the nuclear reactor division of a large corporation. Often it is not clear whether a particular piece of research is potentially of commercial interest or merely of "academic" interest to the researchers. In your judgment, one major area of research has advanced well beyond the level at which operating divisions pertinent to the area could possibly assimilate or make use of the data being generated.

Recently, two new areas with potentially high returns for commercial development have been proposed by one of the operating divisions. The team working in the area referred to in the previous paragraph is ideally qualified to research these new areas. Unfortunately, both the new areas are relatively devoid of scientific interest, while the project on which the team is currently engaged is of great scientific interest to all members.

At the moment, this is, or is close to being, your best research team. The team is very cohesive, has a high level of morale, and has been very productive. You are concerned not only that they would not want to switch their effort to these new areas, but also that forcing them to concentrate on these two new projects could adversely affect their morale, their good intragroup working relations, and their future productivity both as individuals and as a team.

You have to respond to the operating division within the next two weeks indicating what resources, if any, can be devoted to working on these projects. It would be possible for the team to work on more than one project but each project would need the combined skills of all the members of the team, so no fragmentation of the team is technically feasible. This fact, coupled with the fact that the team is very cohesive, means that a solution that satisfies any team member would very probably go a long way to satisfying everyone on the team.

### Analysis

| | | |
|---|---|---|
| Quality Requirement | High Importance | (QR = 4) |
| Commitment Requirement | High Importance | (CR = 4) |
| Leader Information | Probably Yes | (LI = 4) |
| Problem Structure | Yes | (ST = 5) |
| Commitment Probability | No | (CP = 1) |
| Goal Congruence | Probably No | (GC = 2) |
| Subordinate Conflict | Probably No | (CO = 2) |
| Subordinate Information | No | (SI = 1) |
| Time Constraints | No | (TC = 1) |
| Geographical Dispersion | No | (GD = 1) |
| Motivation–Time | No Importance | (MT = 1) |
| Motivation–Development | Critical Importance | (MD = 5) |

### Synthesis

*Highest Overall Effectiveness:*     **CII**

---

This is another problem we highlighted in Chapters 9 and 10 when discussing decision quality and commitment. The model showed that AII, CI, and CII were about equally likely to produce a high-quality decision. When a high commitment requirement is added, CII becomes the model's clear choice (Figure 12–3).

It may be noteworthy that CII remains the model's choice even if a time-driven motivation is considered (that is, MT = 5 and MD = 1). This is a situation in which considerations of quality and commitment outweigh any considerations of time or development.

## Case #4:  R & D Projects Problem

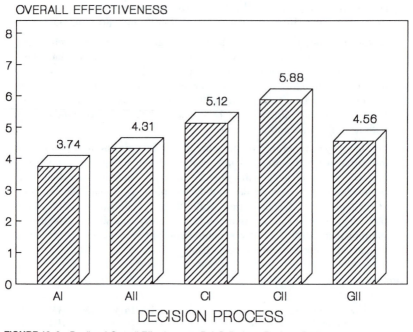

**FIGURE 12–3**   Predicted Overall Effectiveness: R & D Projects Decision Problem

---

### CASE 5   PURCHASING DECISION PROBLEM

You have recently been appointed vice president in charge of purchasing for a large manufacturing company. The company has twenty plants all located in the Midwest. Historically, the company has operated in a highly decentralized fashion with each of the plant managers encouraged to operate with only minimal control and direction from the corporate office. In the area of purchasing, each of the purchasing executives who report to the plant manager does the purchasing for his/her plant. There seems to be little or no coordination among them, and the relationships that do exist are largely ones of competition.

Your position was created when it began to appear to the president that the company was likely to face increasing difficulty in securing certain essential raw materials. In order to protect the company against this possibility, the present haphazard decentralized arrangement must be abandoned or at least modified to meet the current problems.

You were chosen for the position because of your extensive background in corporate purchasing with another firm that operated in a much more centralized fashion. Your appointment was announced in the last issue of the company house organ. You are anxious to get started, particularly since the peak buying season is now only three weeks away. A procedure must be established that will minimize the likelihood of serious shortages and secondarily achieve the economies associated with the added power of centralized purchasing.

*Analysis*

| | | |
|---|---|---|
| Quality Requirement | High Importance | (QR = 4) |
| Commitment Requirement | Critical Importance | (CR = 5) |
| Leader Information | Probably No | (LI = 2) |
| Problem Structure | Maybe | (ST = 3) |
| Commitment Probability | Probably No | (CP = 2) |
| Goal Congruence | Probably No | (GC = 2) |
| Subordinate Conflict | Probably Yes | (CO = 4) |
| Subordinate Information | Probably Yes | (SI = 4) |
| Time Constraints | No | (TC = 1) |
| Geographical Dispersion | No | (GD = 1) |
| Motivation–Time | Average Importance | (MT = 3) |
| Motivation–Development | Average Importance | (MD = 3) |

*Synthesis*

*Highest Overall Effectiveness:*     **CII**

As we pointed out in Chapter 5, this is our version of a popular Harvard Business School case called *The Dashman Company*. In the case, the situation is handled with an AI directive that proves to be completely and totally ineffective. From Figure 12–4, we see why. The model predicts AI to be the least effective mechanism for handling this situation.

Notice that in the description of this circumstance, the subordinate purchasing managers are physically isolated in twenty different manufacturing facilities, but in the analysis of the situation we have coded geographical dispersion (GD) as "no." This is because the definition of geographical dispersion (Appendix A) requires a "no" response if the decision is important enough to warrant the cost of travel if it is necessary. In this case it does. If the situation were less critical, or the subordinates were located around the world instead of around the Midwest, then GD might be "yes." In that case, the suitability of CII and GII would drop and CI would become the model's choice. In lieu

## Case #5: Purchasing Problem

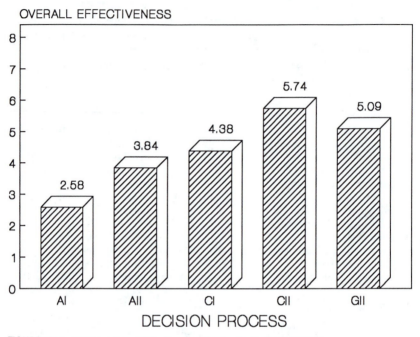

FIGURE 12–4   Predicted Overall Effectiveness: Purchasing Decision Problem

of a meeting, the manager individually consults with each subordinate by means of telephone, telex, or letter.

The remaining three situations from Chapter 4 represent "individual problems" affecting a single subordinate:

---

### CASE 6   CLIENT COMPLAINT DECISION PROBLEM

You are regional manager of an international management consulting company. You have a staff of six consultants reporting to you, each of whom enjoys a considerable amount of autonomy with clients in the field.

Yesterday you received a complaint from one of your major clients regarding the effectiveness of the job being done by one of your people. The nature of the problem was not made very explicit, but it was clear that the client was dissatisfied and that something would have to be done if you were to restore the client's faith in the company.

The consultant assigned to work on that contract has been with the company for six years. Trained in systems analysis and one of the best in that profession, this person is capable of superb performance and for the first four or five years was a model for the more junior consultants. More recently, however, there has been a marked change in attitude. What used to be identification with the company now seems to be replaced with an arrogant indifference. This change in interest has been noticed by other consultants.

This is not the first complaint that you have had from a client. Several months ago another client told you that the consultant had seemed to him at times to be under the influence of drugs.

It is important to get to the root of the problem quickly if your major client is to be retained. Your consultant has invaluable skill and experience and would be almost impossible to replace. Your instincts tell you that this person must be "salvageable," but how?

*Analysis*

| | | |
|---|---:|---|
| Quality Requirement | High Importance | (QR = 4) |
| Commitment Requirement | Average Importance | (CR = 3) |
| Leader Information | No | (LI = 1) |
| Problem Structure | Probably No | (ST = 2) |
| Commitment Probability | No | (CP = 1) |
| Goal Congruence | No | (GC = 1) |
| Subordinate Conflict | Yes | (CO = 5) |
| Subordinate Information | Probably Yes | (SI = 4) |
| Time Constraints | No | (TC = 1) |
| Motivation–Time | No Importance | (MT = 1) |
| Motivation–Development | High Importance | (MD = 5) |

*Synthesis*

*Highest Overall Effectiveness:*     **CI**

---

The model's choice is CI. Although GI approaches the effectiveness of CI (Figure 12–5), the latter is nonetheless recommended because of the lack of goal congruence and the potential for conflict. Defensiveness on the part of the troubled subordinate may produce a stalemate if a GI meeting were held and could threaten whatever relationship existed between the subordinate and the manager. The situation may require that the subordinate be relieved of the account, and this is a decision that the subordinate may be reluctant to make.

## Case #6:  Client Complaint Problem

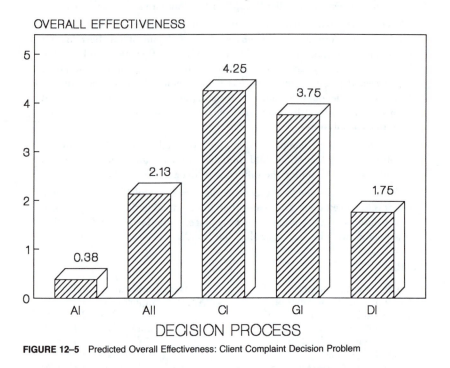

OVERALL EFFECTIVENESS

DECISION PROCESS

**FIGURE 12–5**   Predicted Overall Effectiveness: Client Complaint Decision Problem

---

### CASE 7   LIBRARY SPACE DECISION PROBLEM

You are the head librarian in corporate headquarters of a large multibillion dollar company. Your library maintains most business periodicals, reference works, and textbooks dealing with various facets of business management. Recently, you have acquired a small collection of works of fiction and "best sellers" that can be borrowed by employees for their personal reading. To take on this additional function it was necessary to acquire additional space and to hire an assistant librarian, with whom you have developed a close working relationship.

The new space was previously used for storage and is in substantial need of redecoration before it can be of much use. As a first step it must be painted, and you have made arrangements with the maintenance department to do that next week. You have just received a color chart showing available colors, any one of which would be acceptable. You must notify maintenance of your choice by late afternoon.

*Analysis*

| | |
|---|---|
| **Quality Requirement** | No Importance  (QR = 1) |
| **Commitment Requirement** | Maybe  (CR = 3) |

| Leader Information | Yes | (LI  = 5) |
| Problem Structure | Yes | (ST  = 5) |
| Commitment Probability | Yes | (CP  = 5) |
| Goal Congruence | Yes | (GC  = 5) |
| Subordinate Conflict | Probably No | (CO  = 2) |
| Subordinate Information | Yes | (SI  = 5) |
| Time Constraints | No | (TC  = 1) |
| Motivation–Time | Average Importance | (MT = 3) |
| Motivation–Development | Average Importance | (MD = 3) |

*Synthesis*

*Highest Overall Effectiveness:*    **AI**

This situation is trivial and possesses no quality requirement. Commitment may be an issue, but certainly this is not the type of situation that engenders strong feelings. AI is the appropriate choice; DI is a close second since it is also quite time efficient (Figure 12–6).

## Case #7: Library Space Problem

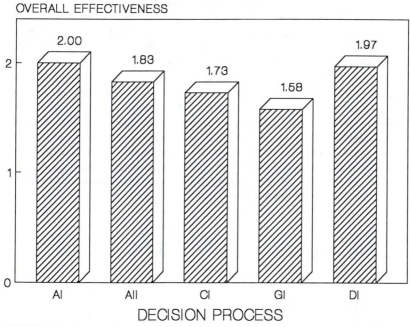

**FIGURE 12–6**  Predicted Overall Effectiveness: Library Space Decision Problem

## CASE 8   HIRING DECISION PROBLEM

Six months ago you were brought in as manager of research and development of a large pulp and paper firm. Your appointment was brought about by a policy decision to phase out the long-range basic research program on which the company had embarked ten years ago and to develop a research program that was more immediately applicable to the company's needs. You realized that your assignment would be a difficult one—the total budget was to be cut 25 percent over that under which your predecessor operated—but it was a challenge and a significant increase in responsibility over your previous job.

Your previous reputation as a hard-nosed cost-conscious manager was not helped when you had to let several of your subordinates know that they had six months in which to find new employment. One of the others, a specialist in data analysis whom you did not want to lose, found a better job and resigned, giving only two-weeks notice. You tried to persuade this person to rethink the matter, but it was clear to you that this individual was very unhappy over the changed mission of the R & D function and with the "arbitrary dismissal" of several close friends. This departure will be a loss. The individual's superb technical skills more than compensated for deficiencies in other areas.

You began a search for a successor immediately, hoping to find someone who could start work before the month was up. The requirements for the position are quite clear-cut. You need a person who is competent in multivariate analysis and experimental design, who is experienced in working with computers, and who is knowledgeable, concerned, and interested in solving applied problems in an industry such as yours.

A phone call to your previous employer produced a couple of candidates, and you have interviewed both of them, checked out their recommendations, and made an assessment of their qualifications. You have also learned of a potential candidate in your present organization. This candidate appears to have the kind of educational background that you require, but you don't know anything about the person's familiarity with computer programming. The individual most knowledgeable about this should be your present data analysis specialist. You hope to reach a decision among the three candidates by next week.

*Analysis*

| | | |
|---|---|---|
| Quality Requirement | High Importance | (QR = 4) |
| Commitment Requirement | No Importance | (CR = 1) |
| Leader Information | No | (LI = 1) |
| Problem Structure | Yes | (ST = 5) |
| Commitment Probability | Yes | (CP = 5) |
| Goal Congruence | No | (GC = 1) |
| Subordinate Conflict | Maybe | (CO = 3) |

| | | |
|---|---|---|
| Subordinate Information | No | (SI  = 1) |
| Time Constraints | No | (TC  = 1) |
| Motivation–Time | Low Importance | (MT = 2) |
| Motivation–Development | No Importance | (MD = 1) |

*Synthesis*

*Highest Overall Effectiveness:*     **AII**

In this final example, AII is the prescribed choice under conditions in which time is a greater consideration than subordinate development. If the reverse were true, CI becomes the model's choice (Figure 12–7).

## Case #8:  Hiring Decision Problem

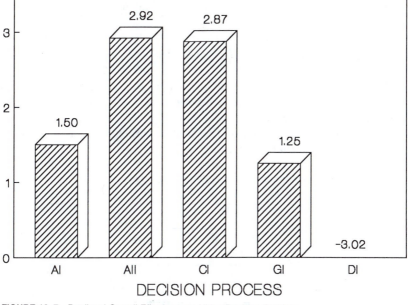

FIGURE 12–7   Predicted Overall Effectiveness: Hiring Decision Problem

### COMPARING THE NEW AND FORMER MODELS

In Chapter 5 the original Vroom-Yetton model was applied to these same seven situations. (An eighth situation, the parking lot problem, has been omitted here.) It is therefore possible to compare the behavior of the new model against its predecessor to see what differences emerge in its predictions.

The former model applied seven rules to produce the feasible set for a given decision problem. An analogous set does not exit for the new model. The reader will recall, however, that we introduced the labels *Time Driven* and *Development Driven* in Chapter 8 to describe the operation of the model under conditions in which maximum weight is given to considerations of time or development respectively. In application, the time-driven operation of the model sets motivation–time (MT) to 5 and motivation–development (MD) to 1. Alternatively, the development-driven operation of the model reverses these weights. When the weights are set to reflect these alternative motivations, the new model provides prescriptions analogous to the choices of extremes in the former feasible set—choices labeled Model A (Time-Efficient) and Model B (Time-Investment) back in Chapter 5. These can be directly compared.

The lower portion of Table 12–1 contains the former model's choices for all eight cases as they were reported in Chapter 5. The top portion of the table contains the new model's prescriptions when the managerial motivations are adjusted to reflect either MT = 5 and MD = 1 or, alternatively, MT = 1 and MD = 5. (For purposes of comparison, the parking lot problem, Case 1, is included in Table 12–1. As can be seen, all models prescribe GII for this circumstance.)

There are only three of the eight cases where the two models make identical prescriptions (Cases 1, 5, and 8). In the remaining five situations, either the Time-Driven model fails to match the original Model A or the Development-Driven model fails to match the original Model B. Of some interest, however, is the fact that at least one of these two possible matches exists in each example case.

There are three reasons for the lack of agreement between the new model and its older brother, reasons that should be apparent from our discussion

**TABLE 12–1    Comparison of New and Former Models: Sample Cases**

| | NEW MODEL | | | | | | | |
| --- | --- | --- | --- | --- | --- | --- | --- | --- |
| | | | | (Cases) | | | | |
| | 1 | 2 | 3 | 4 | 5 | 6 | 7 | 8 |
| *Time-Driven* | GII | AI | CII | CII | CII | CI | AI | AII |
| *Development-Driven* | GII | CII | GII | CII | CII | CI | AI | CI |
| | FORMER MODEL | | | | | | | |
| | | | | (Cases) | | | | |
| | 1 | 2 | 3 | 4 | 5 | 6 | 7 | 8 |
| *Model A* | GII | AI | GII | CI | CII | CI | AI | AII |
| *Model B* | GII | GII | GII | CII | CII | GI | DI | CI |

*Note*: Time-Driven: MT = 5, MD = 1. Development-Driven: MT = 1, MD = 5.

of the considerations that went into the new model's design. The first is that the new model allows more sensitive analyses of the status of problem attributes by substituting five-point scales for dichotomous yes–no scales. The second is that considerations of time and development are given a somewhat smaller role in governing behavior in the new model. (Notice that the time-driven and development-driven prescriptions are identical in Cases 4, 6, and 7, while Models A and B prescribe different processes in these cases when the former model is applied.) The third reason is that the new model considers additional relevant features of the situation beyond those of its predecessor. Subordinate information (SI) is now considered a factor relevant to the analysis of group problems; subordinate conflict (CO) is now considered a factor relevant to the analysis of individual problems.

Of course, we must be careful not to draw any broad conclusions from these comparisons of the two models. Eight situations represent far too few opportunities for similarities and differences to be accurately documented. We will try to correct this, however, by examining the new model's behavior across a wider array of circumstances.

## MODEL BEHAVIOR ACROSS SITUATIONS

It is possible to examine how the model behaves across a large number of situations by aggregating its prescriptions to summarize what its use would mean to the typical manager. What would the behavior of the leader look like if the model were used across the spectrum of problems and decisions that the typical leader encountered?

The question is difficult to answer because there is no "typical" manager with a set of "typical problems." The mix of situations that one is likely to encounter depends upon one's organizational mission, managerial function, hierarchical level, and specific managerial assignments and responsibilities. We can, however, get some idea of the behavior of the model in the aggregate if we assume the widest distribution of situations possible. This would involve varying the problem attributes in all possible combinations.

With the help of a computer simulation, we have studied the model across this range of possible circumstances. The simulation produced the model's behavior as each attribute was varied from 1 to 5 in all possible combinations (such as, no, probably no, maybe, probably yes, and yes). However, time constraints (TC) and geographical dispersion (GD) were held constant. The occurrence of either is infrequent, and to assume that half of the situations possess a time constraint (or involve geographically isolated subordinates) would drive the model to a level of autocracy that would definitely be unrepresentative of the behavior required of any manager.

Actually, two simulations were conducted. Motivation–time (MT) and motivation–development (MD) were varied *between* simulations but held constant *within* each simulation. One simulation studied the behavior of the model when it was time driven (MT = 5, MD = 1) and a second simulation studied its behavior when it was development driven (MT = 1, MD = 5).

Within each of these motivations (time-driven and development-driven), the remaining attributes can be combined in $5^8$ or 390,625 ways. These possibilities were further reduced by eliminating unreasonable or unrepresentative combinations of attributes (such as, the combination of "no commitment requirement" but a "low probability that an autocratic decision will receive subordinate commitment").[1] This reduced the number of situations to 220,605. Table 12–2 describes the operation of the model across these circumstances.

The distribution of decision processes for the time-driven operation of the model suggests that it avoids the extremes, both AI and GII. This is indeed so when all possible combinations of the problem attributes are considered because so many of these circumstances have one or more of these attributes that are less than definitive (that is, responses of 2, 3, or 4). Nonetheless, there are 7,190 unique decision problems in which the model prescribes AI and 10,842 unique decision problems in which it prescribes GII. The frequencies with which these decision problems occur in the reader's organizational role are, of course, unknown.

As the motivation to conserve time is replaced with a motivation to develop subordinates, the model substantially reduces the use of AI and AII (from a combined total of 48 percent to less than 1 percent) and increases its use of CII and GII (from a combined total of 51 percent to 99 percent). ("Mean level of participation" in Table 12–2 employs the same scale values described in Chapter 7 to construct a 0 to 10 index of overall participativeness.)

These simulations reflect the model's operation when maximum weight is given to considerations of either time or development. Of course, other combinations of MT and MD are possible (for example, MT = 4, MD = 2). Under any of these other circumstances, the prescribed level of participation would fall between that of the Time-Driven and the Development-Driven models in Table 12–2. This is also true if time and development are given no weight at all and the criterion becomes decision effectiveness rather than overall effectiveness (that is, MT = 1 and MD = 1).

**TABLE 12–2    Model Behavior Across 220,605 Group Problems**

|  | AI | AII | CI | CII | GII | MLP |
|---|---|---|---|---|---|---|
| *Time-Driven* | 3% | 45% | 1% | 46% | 5% | 4.65 |
| *Development-Driven* | <1 | 0 | 1 | 76 | 23 | 8.45 |

*Note*: Time-Driven: MT = 5, MD = 1. Development-Driven: MT = 1, MD = 5. MLP = Mean Level of Participation.

[1] When QR = 1, the retained situations were LI = ST = SI = GC = 5. When LI = 5, the retained situations were ST = 5. When CR = 1, the retained situations were CP = 5.

TABLE 12–3    Model Behavior Across
185,325 Individual Problems

|  | AI | AII | CI | GI | DI | MLP |
|---|---|---|---|---|---|---|
| *Time-Driven* | 13% | 6% | 44% | 10% | 27% | 5.75 |
| *Development-Driven* | <1 | 0 | 37 | 59 | 4 | 6.99 |

Table 12–3 reports the results of a similar analysis for individual (as opposed to group) problems.[2] Although CI plays little role in either the Time-Driven or Development-Driven group model, it can be seen that it plays a prominent role when the model is applied to situations affecting a single subordinate.

What these simulations do not convey is how the new model compares to its predecessor. Of course, the original Vroom-Yetton model, requiring clear yes–no responses to the problem attributes, was not designed to apply to such a wide spectrum of situations. However, the two models can be compared if we restrict our attention only to those situations where both models apply. For group problems, this set of decision problems numbers seventy-eight unique combinations of yes–no attributes.

Table 12–4 describes how the two models behave when applied to these situations. In this comparison, the time-driven operation of the new model is more participative than the Model A version of the original. Additionally, the development-driven operation of the new model is more autocratic than the Model B version of the original. Alternatively stated, on a scale of participation the span between the time-driven and development-driven versions of the model is shorter and falls entirely within the span representing the distance

TABLE 12–4    Model Behavior Across Seventy-Eight
Group Problems

| | NEW MODEL | | | | | |
|---|---|---|---|---|---|---|
| | AI | AII | CI | CII | GII | MLP |
| *Time-Driven* | 26% | 15% | 5% | 42% | 12% | 4.95 |
| *Development-Driven* | 5 | 0 | 10 | 55 | 29 | 7.87 |
| | FORMER MODEL | | | | | |
| | AI | AII | CI | CII | GII | MLP |
| *Model A* | 26% | 21% | 5% | 31% | 18% | 4.72 |
| *Model B* | 0 | 0 | 0 | 46 | 54 | 9.08 |

[2] In this simulation, an additional combination of attributes was eliminated from consideration. When GC = 1, only situations of CO = 5 were retained. When combined with the other assumptions, 185,325 distinct situations were analyzed.

**TABLE 12–5    Model Behavior Across Sixty**
**Individual Problems**

| | NEW MODEL | | | | | |
|---|---|---|---|---|---|---|
| | AI | AII | CI | GI | DI | MLP |
| Time-Driven | 27% | 10% | 20% | 20% | 23% | 5.03 |
| Development-Driven | 7 | 0 | 20 | 53 | 20 | 7.27 |

| | FORMER MODEL | | | | | |
|---|---|---|---|---|---|---|
| | AI | AII | CI | GI | DI | MLP |
| Model A | 27% | 13% | 23% | 10% | 27% | 4.77 |
| Model B | 0 | 0 | 20 | 40 | 40 | 8.20 |

Note: Model behavior of the original Vroom-Yetton model reflects the changes to the individual model made by Vroom and Jago (1974).

between the former Model A and Model B. Table 12–5 displays a similar pattern in a comparison of the two models' behavior on the set of sixty comparable "individual" decision problems.

One of our objectives in revising the original model was to increase its specificity in responding to the circumstances of a decision. As we noted in Chapter 6, the original model often produced large feasible sets, leaving much of the choice of a decision process to the inclinations and motivations of the individual manager. The distance between Model A and Model B in Tables 12–4 and 12–5 reflects the degree of discretion that remains with the manager after the model has been employed. However, the distance between the time-driven and development-driven operations of the new model is smaller, indicating that these motivations now do less of the "work" of the model. To be sure, they remain important to the application of the model, but their role is now in a more proper proportion to the role played by more important considerations.

## ON THE VALIDITY OF THE NEW MODEL

As was the case with the original Vroom-Yetton model in 1973, the new model is published without complete empirical evidence establishing its validity. Certainly, the model is thought to be consistent with what we now know about the benefits and costs of participation. Moreover, it represents a direct extension of the original 1973 model for which ample validation evidence now does exist (see Chapter 6). Nonetheless, without extensive evidence that the use of the new model can improve decision effectiveness—and, by extension, leadership success—its value as a theoretical contribution and as a practical tool remains an open question.

Although but one example of the type of evidence that must be accumulated, we have (with Jenny Ettling) conducted an experiment to test the ability of the new model to correctly predict the success of the different decision strategies. For present purposes we will only summarize the study. Details of the scientific controls, procedures, and precautions that were employed are available elsewhere.[3]

Four of the five decision processes in the group model were examined in the study. (AII was eliminated because of the difficulty of distinguishing it from CI under laboratory conditions.) The decision task was a survival exercise of the type we have described in the beginning of Chapter 9. Four hundred subjects, in eighty groups of five each, participated in the study. In twenty of the eighty groups, the leader made the decision using AI. In another set of twenty groups, the leader made the decision using CI. In a third set of twenty groups, the leader made the decision using CII. In the final set of twenty groups, a consensus decision was reached (GII). Independent and objective numerical measures of decision quality and subordinate commitment were obtained and were summed to produce the index of decision effectiveness.

An independent panel of seven people, trained in the use of the situational variables employed in the new model, diagnosed the situation on the five-point scales representing these variables. Their collective judgments provided the basis for determining the model's predictions of decision quality, subordinate commitment, and decision effectiveness. For purposes of comparison, the original Vroom-Yetton feasible set provided alternative predictions.

Figure 12–8 summarizes the results of the study. The values that are graphed are correlation coefficients between the predictions of the models and the actual outcomes produced in the 80 decisions. (A correlation of 1.00 would indicate that the model could perfectly predict, without exception or error, the numerical outcomes of all 80 decisions.)

The results reveal the clear superiority of the revised model over its predecessor. In terms of decision effectiveness, the new model accurately predicts decision success ($r = 0.75$) at a rate over two and one-half times that of the former model ($r = 0.29$). Figure 12–8 also reveals that both models are much better at predicting decision commitment than decision quality. This lends further support to our speculation that the decision process plays the major role in determining subordinate commitment to a course of action. The decision process also contributes to decision quality, but we are less able to predict differences in quality than those in commitment because the former are also affected by factors other than the decision process used, especially the knowledge and information available to those involved.

We must caution, however, not to overinterpret the results from this single study. The experiment tested the predictive ability of the revised model in only a single situation, one of a million and a half possible combinations of

[3] A complete discussion of this research, based on a preliminary and therefore somewhat different version of our revised model, is reported by Jago, Ettling, and Vroom (1985).

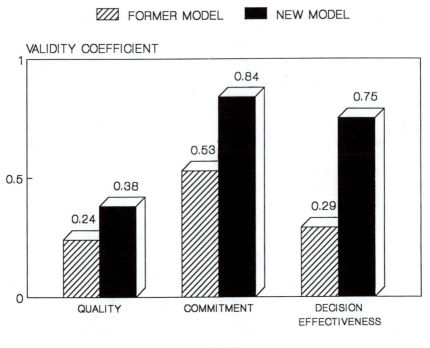

**FIGURE 12–8**  A Comparison of Model Validity

the relevant problem attributes. Complete confirmation of the model will certainly require years of testing. Nonetheless, these initial results are quite encouraging.

## A TECHNOLOGY FOR IMPLEMENTATION: FROM EQUATIONS TO EXPERT SYSTEMS

When the new model was introduced in Chapter 8, we noted that, as a practical matter, its use required an adaptation to some sort of computer or programmable calculator. Like the transmission of an automobile, these devices efficiently convert the power of the model's "engine"—the equations—into something of benefit. Without them, to continue the analogy, the advanced horsepower of the new model goes unused and a return to the horse and carriage is required.

With a bit of programming knowledge and a little time we have successfully programmed the model on an IBM PC and the Apple II Plus, as well as on less advanced equipment like the Texas Instrument's 99/4A home computer, the handheld Radio Shack TRS-80 PC-2 computer, and the Hewlett-Packard

41 programmable calculator. The programs differ somewhat from each other depending upon the programming language of the device and its display capabilities. However, each performs the necessary calculations with reliability, precision, and speed. For the reader interested in programming his or her own device, Appendix B contains a complete set of equations, and the various examples and figures in this chapter provide a standard against which the accuracy of the programming can be verified.

For those interested in the model but who have no programming experience—or, perhaps, no inclination to use one's experience—a commercially available, but modestly priced, program for the IBM PC and fully compatible computers (for example, COMPAQ, AT&T) is available.[4] Once one becomes familiar with this program, a decision problem can be analyzed extremely quickly. For the novice user, however, extensive "Help" screens are available. Each diagnostic question appears on the screen along with the range of possible responses available to the decisionmaker. Upon request, further help is available that explains the meaning of the question and the types of situations for which each response is appropriate. When all questions have been answered, the screen indicates the model's choice of a decision process and its choice if each of the underlying criteria (quality, commitment, time, and development) is considered alone.

Additional output is available after the model's choice is displayed. Upon request, the complete definition of the chosen process appears on the screen. Bar graphs of the predicted success of each process, similar to those graphs used to illustrate application of the model in this chapter, are available on demand. In addition, one can summon to the screen a display of the numerical values on which these predictions are based and a display of the effects of a tradeoff between the two elements of human capital, time and development, can be requested. (This tradeoff compares the model's behavior if the time-driven $MT = 5$ and $MD = 1$ were to be changed to the development-driven $MT = 1$ and $MD = 5$). Finally, the program will compare the new model's behavior with that prescribed by the previous model, complete with the "rule violations" (Chapter 5) applicable to the situation. Figure 12–9 depicts one of the output screens produced by the program.

Before proceeding to the analysis of another situation the user can save both the diagnosis of the situation and the predictions of the model. If a record of decisions is to be maintained, the output can be directed to a printer or, alternatively, to a disk file.

It has been our experience that the software facilitates an explanation

[4] Besides IBM compatibility, the program—"Managing Participation in Organizations— MPO™"—requires a minimum of 256K of memory, DOS 2.0 or greater, a minimum of one disk drive, and either a monochrome or color monitor. Two versions of the program are available, one copy-protected (requiring the original disk to be kept in the disk drive during execution) and one not copy-protected (and thereby fully hard-disk compatible). For information regarding the availability of this software, please write: **Leadership Software, Inc., P.O. Box 271848, Houston, Texas 77277–1848.**

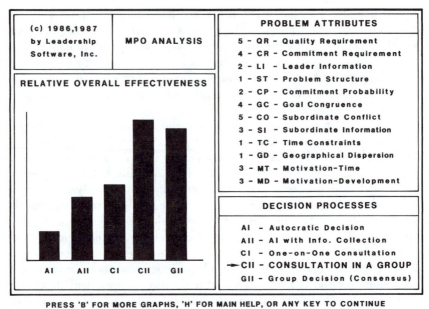

| (c) 1986,1987 by Leadership Software, Inc. | MPO ANALYSIS | PROBLEM ATTRIBUTES |
|---|---|---|

**PROBLEM ATTRIBUTES**

5 – QR – Quality Requirement
4 – CR – Commitment Requirement
2 – LI – Leader Information
1 – ST – Problem Structure
2 – CP – Commitment Probability
4 – GC – Goal Congruence
5 – CO – Subordinate Conflict
3 – SI – Subordinate Information
1 – TC – Time Constraints
1 – GD – Geographical Dispersion
3 – MT – Motivation-Time
3 – MD – Motivation-Development

**RELATIVE OVERALL EFFECTIVENESS**

(bar chart: AI, AII, CI, CII, GII)

**DECISION PROCESSES**

AI  – Autocratic Decision
AII – AI with Info. Collection
CI  – One-on-One Consultation
➤CII – CONSULTATION IN A GROUP
GII – Group Decision (Consensus)

PRESS 'B' FOR MORE GRAPHS, 'H' FOR MAIN HELP, OR ANY KEY TO CONTINUE

**FIGURE 12–9** Sample Output Screen from *Managing Participation in Organizations—MPO* (1987)
Source: Leadership Software, Inc.

of the new model to a managerial audience. It is engaging, "user-friendly," and provides a wealth of information without the burdensome task of solving each equation with pencil and paper (or, more often, chalk and board). However, it is not designed to replace a thorough discussion of the underlying psychological and managerial principles governing the effectiveness of participation that we attempt in this book. Like computer programs designed to represent the original Vroom-Yetton model (to be briefly discussed in the next chapter), this program remains a "black box" that transforms input (a situational diagnosis) into output (a prescription) without revealing much about the transformation process itself (the logic or rationale of the equations).

Nor is the program the type of managerial tool that we would expect a leader to consult and follow each and every time the person encountered a decision. To do so would result in programming the manager rather than the computer. Instead, the program, like the model itself, is intended to provide nothing more than a standard against which one's choices or intended choices can be compared. Sometimes such a standard is not required. An awareness of the benefits and liabilities of participation and an understanding of the contingencies involved are often enough to help the manager select which decision process to use.

Nonetheless, there are three distinct purposes that the computer program can serve. First, in situations in which the manager recognizes competing benefits and liabilities of different decision processes, the program provides a degree of precision greater than otherwise available. Just as there are occasions in which a precise yardstick is required for a physical measurement, there are difficult leadership situations that will require the degree of precision that the program provides. Second, the program is useful in answering "what if" questions when the critical features of a situation are ambiguous, unknown, or subject to change. Sensitivity analyses of the model's behavior can be performed rapidly by changing the value of one input variable while the others are held constant. Finally, the program can be used as a tool to develop and calibrate the internal "rules" that govern our habitual responses to situations. Just as a flight simulator trains the pilot in the proper responses to a variety of situations, the computer program can help the leader internalize the basic contingencies reflected in the model.

## A LESS-SOPHISTICATED TECHNOLOGY
## FOR IMPLEMENTATION: BACK TO DECISION TREES

Of course, not everyone has access to a computer. Moreover, there are some situations where one may be physically separated from a computer to which one does have access (for example, the professor in a college classroom). If the model can only be represented by a complex set of equations or by magnetic impulses on a 5¼-inch disk, its use is naturally restricted to a small number of contexts. Many readers may share in a refrain that we have heard from several of our colleagues during the development of this book: "Please don't abandon the decision trees!"

A decision tree representation of the new model is possible if two simplifying assumptions are made. Both of these assumptions were made implicitly in the original Vroom-Yetton model. Here the implicit becomes explicit.

The first assumption is that there are no "shades of gray." The decision tree can only be used when the status of attributes is clear cut and only yes-no answers exist. This is an acceptable assumption in some circumstances (such as, the diagnosis of hypothetical decisions in the college classroom), but is clearly a liability for "online" use.

The second assumption is that there are no critically severe time constraints and that subordinates are not geographically dispersed. This assumption restricts the applicability of the model by eliminating its use in some clearly defined—but relatively infrequent—situations.

Figures 12–10 and 12–11 contain decision trees for group problems corresponding to the Time-Driven (MT = 5, MD = 1), and Development-Driven (MT = 1, MD = 5) models respectively.[5] Figures 12–12 and 12–13 contain decision trees corresponding to these two models for individual problems.

[5] These decision trees were constructed using the same assumptions regarding problem attributes reflected in footnotes 2 and 3 in this chapter. Tree structures have been created that eliminate unreasonable combinations of attributes.

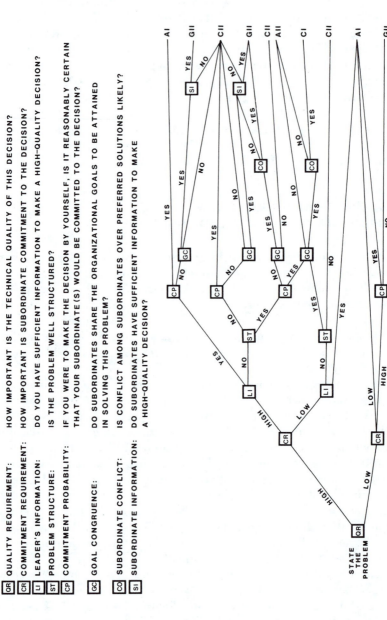

FIGURE 12–10  Time-Driven Decision Tree—Group Problems (Vroom & Jago, 1987)

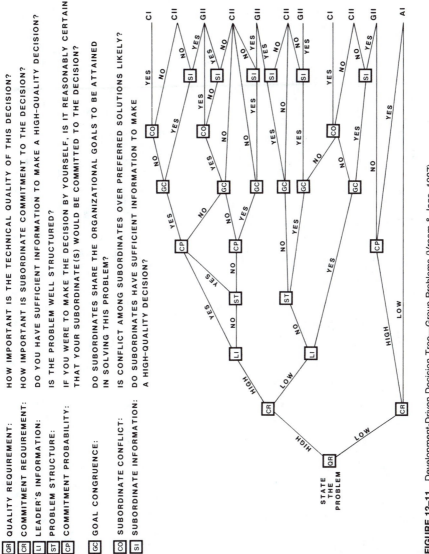

QR QUALITY REQUIREMENT: HOW IMPORTANT IS THE TECHNICAL QUALITY OF THIS DECISION?

CR COMMITMENT REQUIREMENT: HOW IMPORTANT IS SUBORDINATE COMMITMENT TO THE DECISION?

LI LEADER'S INFORMATION: DO YOU HAVE SUFFICIENT INFORMATION TO MAKE A HIGH-QUALITY DECISION?

ST PROBLEM STRUCTURE: IS THE PROBLEM WELL STRUCTURED?

CP COMMITMENT PROBABILITY: IF YOU WERE TO MAKE THE DECISION BY YOURSELF, IS IT REASONABLY CERTAIN THAT YOUR SUBORDINATE(S) WOULD BE COMMITTED TO THE DECISION?

GC GOAL CONGRUENCE: DO SUBORDINATES SHARE THE ORGANIZATIONAL GOALS TO BE ATTAINED IN SOLVING THIS PROBLEM?

CO SUBORDINATE CONFLICT: IS CONFLICT AMONG SUBORDINATES OVER PREFERRED SOLUTIONS LIKELY?

SI SUBORDINATE INFORMATION: DO SUBORDINATES HAVE SUFFICIENT INFORMATION TO MAKE A HIGH-QUALITY DECISION?

**FIGURE 12–11** Development-Driven Decision Tree—Group Problems (Vroom & Jago, 1987)

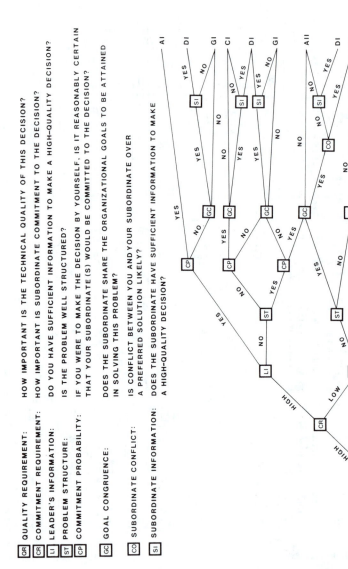

QR QUALITY REQUIREMENT: HOW IMPORTANT IS THE TECHNICAL QUALITY OF THIS DECISION?

CR COMMITMENT REQUIREMENT: HOW IMPORTANT IS SUBORDINATE COMMITMENT TO THE DECISION?

LI LEADER'S INFORMATION: DO YOU HAVE SUFFICIENT INFORMATION TO MAKE A HIGH-QUALITY DECISION?

ST PROBLEM STRUCTURE: IS THE PROBLEM WELL STRUCTURED?

CP COMMITMENT PROBABILITY: IF YOU WERE TO MAKE THE DECISION BY YOURSELF, IS IT REASONABLY CERTAIN THAT YOUR SUBORDINATE(S) WOULD BE COMMITTED TO THE DECISION?

GC GOAL CONGRUENCE: DOES THE SUBORDINATE SHARE THE ORGANIZATIONAL GOALS TO BE ATTAINED IN SOLVING THIS PROBLEM?

CO SUBORDINATE CONFLICT: IS CONFLICT BETWEEN YOU AND YOUR SUBORDINATE OVER A PREFERRED SOLUTION LIKELY?

SI SUBORDINATE INFORMATION: DOES THE SUBORDINATE HAVE SUFFICIENT INFORMATION TO MAKE A HIGH-QUALITY DECISION?

**FIGURE 12-12** Time-Driven Decision Tree—Individual Problems (Vroom & Jago, 1987)

QR QUALITY REQUIREMENT: HOW IMPORTANT IS THE TECHNICAL QUALITY OF THIS DECISION?

CR COMMITMENT REQUIREMENT: HOW IMPORTANT IS SUBORDINATE COMMITMENT TO THE DECISION?

LI LEADER'S INFORMATION: DO YOU HAVE SUFFICIENT INFORMATION TO MAKE A HIGH-QUALITY DECISION?

\* ST PROBLEM STRUCTURE: IS THE PROBLEM WELL STRUCTURED?

CP COMMITMENT PROBABILITY: IF YOU WERE TO MAKE THE DECISION BY YOURSELF, IS IT REASONABLY CERTAIN THAT YOUR SUBORDINATE(S) WOULD BE COMMITTED TO THE DECISION?

GC GOAL CONGRUENCE: DOES THE SUBORDINATE SHARE THE ORGANIZATIONAL GOALS TO BE ATTAINED IN SOLVING THIS PROBLEM?

CO SUBORDINATE CONFLICT: IS CONFLICT BETWEEN YOU AND YOUR SUBORDINATE OVER A PREFERRED SOLUTION LIKELY?

SI SUBORDINATE INFORMATION: DOES THE SUBORDINATE HAVE SUFFICIENT INFORMATION TO MAKE A HIGH-QUALITY DECISION?

\* ST IRRELEVANT IN THIS VARIANT OF THE MODEL

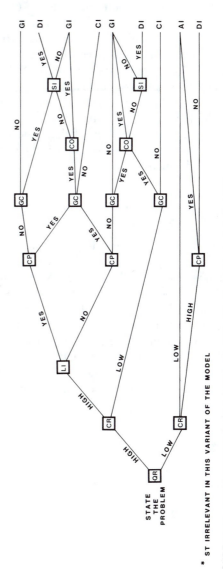

**FIGURE 12–13** Development-Driven Decison Tree—Individual Problems (Vroom & Jago, 1987)

187

They are not appreciably more complex than the previous trees used for Models A and B and for the feasible set in the former model described in Chapter 5.

These trees have all the virtues that have been associated with the previous model. They are simple to use, easy to understand, and easy to teach. There are also reasons for believing they are more accurate than those of the former model. The inclusion of the additional attribute of subordinate information, and the decreasing influence of managers' judgments of the importance of time and of development clearly make the recommendations more responsive to changes in situational demands.

The greatest virtue of the new decision trees is their perfect consistency with the new model for which they are but a special case. Having mastered the concepts and operation of that "special case," it is very simple to relax the limiting assumptions and to use the computer-based version that permits the finer distinctions.

## SUMMARY

The model's components, described in the previous four chapters, are brought together and applied to several concrete decision problems. The behavior of the model is examined in several specific situations and in the aggregate across hundreds of thousands of situations. The first evidence pertaining to the validity of the model is summarized, and the model is shown to be of potentially more value than its predecessor. Technologies for representing the model include a computer program and, if restricting assumptions are made, decision trees that have a familiar structure. In the next and concluding chapter we will review some of the ways in which managers have been exposed to the original model and will discuss a training format adapted for the new model.

# Chapter Thirteen

# Using the Models in Developing Managers and Organizations

The models that have been described in this book have been widely used in the education and training of managers and in the development of the organizations in which they work. Many hundreds of thousands of actual and aspiring managers in most of the developed countries of the world have been exposed to the model. The nature of this exposure has, of course, varied in intensity. We list some of the major forms below.

*Books* More than a hundred textbooks on management and organizational behavior have been published incorporating the essential components of the Vroom-Yetton model such as the taxonomy of decision processes, the decision trees, the rules, and the problem attributes. Through this medium, a minimum level of exposure to the existence of the Vroom-Yetton model and to its essential elements has become part of the education of many future managers.

*Computer programs* In the previous chapter we described a computer program for using the new model. There also exist several computer programs stored on floppy or hard disks that contain the elements of the Vroom-Yetton model.

The computer representations of the model differ from textbooks in an important way. They typically provide no explanation of the concepts used in the model or the rationale for the recommendations provided. While they are the functional equivalent of a decision tree, the tree structure is not revealed, making it more difficult for the user to see the effects of particular answers for the recommendations provided. Such programs enable one to efficiently "use" the model but not to understand it. For this reason, this technology is probably best viewed as a useful adjunct to other forms of training rather than as a method that can stand alone.

*Exercises*    While textbooks provide exposure to concepts and computer programs provide for efficient online use, neither are particularly good vehicles for changing attitudes or developing skills. Thus, many instructors have been complementing textbooks with books of experiential exercises, several of which provide opportunities for practice using the model. For example, Kolb, Rubin, and McIntyre (1984) include in their book of exercises one in which students analyze five cases (three group problems and two individual problems) and then compare their analyses with other group members. Then each person studies the model, after which they reconvene as a group and apply the model to the five cases. The model's answers and the individual choices are then compared and reasons for differences discussed. Sharing, as we do, John Dewey's dictum that people "learn by doing" we view experiential exercises as far more effective than reading a textbook in developing understanding and a modicum of experience.

*Cassettes*    Entitled *The Kepner-Tregoe Program for the New Leadership: Managing People and Change*, a set of six cassettes has been produced that explains in great detail the concepts used in the Vroom-Yetton model and illustrates these concepts by applying them to a number of cases. The pedagogy is similar to that employed by textbooks, although the depth of coverage is far greater than that to be found in any textbook. It also has the advantage of potentially being used in a variety of situations, such as while driving your car to and from work, when reading would be impossible.

*Expectation setting*    An announcement by a CEO about the introduction of participative management may create very different expectations among managers and among workers about how much participation is to be expected and in what kinds of decisions. Our taxonomy of decision processes and the problem attributes provide a common language that, once learned, can facilitate the development of shared expectations about how much participation is envisioned and in what kinds of decisions it will be used.

Confusion over the meaning of participation frequently occurs in new-design plants set up to be testbeds for participative ideas. Lawler (1986) discusses what may be the typical experience of the first-level supervisor in such a plant:

In almost all instances, first level supervisors and elected leaders have complained about a lack of role clarity and confusion about what decisions they can and cannot make. Typically, they are uncomfortable with ordering and directing people, because they feel things should be done on a participative basis. . . . They also have a great deal of difficulty in deciding which decisions should be made on a participative basis and which should not. (p. 183)

The language that we have developed for describing decision processes and situational demands is naturally suited to this "expectation setting" purpose. The concepts of AI, CII, GII, DI, and the like provide a language to enable managers and workers to talk about degrees of participation. The problem attributes and the normative model in which they are embedded provide a framework for talking about the kinds of situations in which various methods can be expected to be used.

Several organizations have begun training not only managers but also workers in the model for the purpose of establishing shared expectations about the roles of managers and of workers. Such training courses are short—usually one day—and are viewed as providing shared meanings and expectations for changing the culture of an entire plant.

*Residential courses devoted to the model*  The preceding activities are designed to provide varying degrees of exposure to the model. However, each falls short of providing the type and degree of exposure offered by management development courses devoted exclusively to the model. In such courses, managers come to a central location for a period of time—usually from three to five days—for the purpose not only of learning the model, but also of exploring avenues for improving their effectiveness in leadership roles.

The number of managers who have participated in such residential training programs can be conservatively estimated in six figures. Many of these programs have been conducted by the training staff of Kepner-Tregoe, Inc. or by leadership counselors trained and licensed by that firm. Called TELOS, or more recently MANAGING INVOLVEMENT, these courses are typically attended by managers from a single organization. Other courses have been conducted at universities in the United States, the United Kingdom, Austria, and Norway. Typically, these include managers from many different organizations.

These residential training programs vary in many respects. The length of program, the proportion of time devoted to didactic exposition as opposed to experiential exercises, and the size and composition of the group are among the major dimensions of variation. Let us examine the design of one fairly intensive and experiential four-day training program based exclusively on the Vroom-Yetton model.

## A FOUR-DAY RESIDENTIAL PROGRAM

### Preparatory Work

About two weeks in advance of the training, each participant is given two problem sets to complete. The first problem set consists of thirty group problems and was described earlier in Chapter 7. The second problem set is made up of twenty-four individual problems, examples of which were given in Chapter 4. Following is an excerpt from the instructions accompanying the cases:

> This exercise will be an integral part of our forthcoming sessions together. Not only will we refer to many of the cases and to the various ways of handling them, but also you will be provided with a very detailed analysis of your leadership style based on your responses to these cases. This analysis will be performed by computer and, from past experience with several thousand managers who have worked on this or comparable sets of cases, we believe that you will find it an informative and personally rewarding experience.

> It is important that you not regard this as a test or examination in which your objective is to get the "right" answer. Rather, you should look at this exercise as an opportunity to learn about your reactions to managerial situations. Accordingly, you and you alone will receive the analysis of your behavior. No copy or report will go to anyone else in your organization.

> There is space on the answer sheet for your name, but any other identifying code (mother's birthday, car license number, etc.) that you will be sure to remember would serve just as well. We just need some identification to make sure that we get the analysis back to the right person. The answer sheet also contains some factual questions which are not for identification purposes but rather to enable us to make selected group comparisons.

Most people describe the process of responding to the cases as an interesting one in its own right. They invariably note that they implicitly subscribe to a contingency or situational theory of leadership because they find themselves selecting autocratic methods for some situations, consultative methods for others, and consensus or delegation for still others. For many, the process of understanding the sources of this variation is already beginning.

We have found it highly desirable to have managers fill out the problem set in advance of entering the training environment. Not only does this provide more time for computer processing of data, but it also avoids the possibility that the highly participative climate of the training environment might affect people's responses to cases.

We have also found it useful to try to match the content of the case with the background of the participants. Ideally, managers should be able to think about how they have dealt with similar situations that they have encountered in the past instead of treating the cases purely as an intellectual exercise.

For example, managers in the private sector would be expected to have more difficulty in identifying with the content of an all-military problem set or one consisting solely of public sector or not-for-profit cases.

The matching of people to the cases they are given increases in difficulty as the heterogeneity of the training group increases. For this reason, the most commonly used problem sets are heterogeneous ones, including cases involving many different kinds of decisions set at different levels in many different kinds of organizations.

The processing of participants' responses to the prework cases typically occurs before the program begins, thereby permitting the staff to familiarize themselves both with group and individual profiles before the actual work sessions.

### Day 1: Team Building

Following in the tradition of Kurt Lewin, we have come to view small informal groups as useful, if not necessary, components of the change process. In the sample program that we are describing, about one-half of the total time is spent by participants interacting with other participants in groups of six to eight persons. Within these groups they discuss their ways of dealing with written cases, examine their own processes of working together, provide feedback to one another, consult with one another in how to solve real world problems, and generally provide emotional support in what can be a stressful learning situation.

The first day of the program is devoted to creating the groups that will perform these functions during the rest of the course. Participants are seated in a semicircle in a large room devoid of fixed furniture. After a brief discussion of the purpose of the day and its role in the entire program, each person is asked to identify another person with whom he or she is previously unacquainted and to sit down somewhere in the room and "spend ten minutes getting to know that person as well as you can." (To eliminate a tendency for people to follow the path of least resistance and to encourage use of all of the space within the rooms, a prohibition is usually placed on the choice of the person to their immediate right or left.)

After ten minutes the process is stopped by the instructor who "speculates" about the likely topics of conversation in the pursuit of the objective of "getting to know" the other person. Most typically, the things talked about are "safe" subjects—matters of public record such as one's job, one's career history, where one was born, where one went to school, and the like. After noting that safe topics are not likely to reveal much about many deeply felt attitudes and feelings on both sides, each person is given about sixty seconds to think of some alternative and more effective way of getting to know the other person. At the conclusion of this interval of "private thinking time," the pairs scattered about the room are asked to turn to one another and to do or say "whatever they are thinking about." The dialogue that then ensues is much more animated and far less superficial than that of the previous ten minutes. After about a quarter of an hour, each pair is asked to choose another pair and then to introduce their partner to that pair in such a way that they can get to know him or her really well.

The process continues in this fashion. The size of the group is gradually increased by combination of existing groups until the desired size of eight is achieved. The activities that people are asked to perform include sharing of first impressions of one another, sharing of hopes and fears regarding the program, and finally, when the group is at full size, choosing an appropriate name for their group.

In a typical program, the process that we have rather incompletely described would take three to five hours. Frequently, the last activity or two would be carried out by a group huddled around a table eating lunch.

The remainder of the day is also concerned with team building. However, it differs in the processes examined because the group is given an external problem to solve. The senior author has developed a survival exercise that is more complex but follows in the tradition of the survival exercises described in Chapter 9. Called the Hurricane Survival Problem, it concerns a group sailing in the Caribbean. The boat is destroyed by a violent hurricane, which smashes it against an uninhabited island.

After viewing a set of slides showing the boat, various aspects of the island, and its geographical relationship to other islands, each person is asked to rank order fifteen items in terms of their usefulness for survival. The judgments are complex ones and involve a knowledge not only of hurricanes and of the kinds of gear typically found in a sailboat, but also of medicine (the group includes a diabetic who has lost his insulin and a person with broken ribs).

Each of the groups is then asked to reach consensus on the relative value of the fifteen items—a process that typically occupies about an hour and is recorded on videotape. Following an exposition of the experts' answers and the rationale for them, differences are computed between individual and group judgments and those of the experts. The results typically show group decisions to be higher in quality than the average individual decision and, about 30 percent of the time, to exceed that of the most knowledgeable group member. However, the amount of this "synergy" varies markedly from group to group.

Exhilarated, intrigued, or occasionally disheartened by this evaluation of its performance, each group then returns to review its videotape, stopping it for discussion whenever any member notes anything in the group process that may aid in understanding how the group works and how it can improve. The day of team building concludes with a sharing of experiences across groups. In addition to its team-building outcomes, the exercise thereby generates shared evidence of the assets and liabilities of GII that can be referred to in later portions of the program.

### Day 2 Morning: Introducing the Normative Model

To set the stage for the exposition of the first of the models—dealing with group problems (see Chapter 5, pages 54–69)—each participant is asked to study five cases similar to, but not necessarily identical to, those contained in the thirty-case problem set. Then each of the groups formed the previous day is assigned the task of arriving at consensus concerning the most effective leadership style for each case.

This task is not an easy one for most groups. There are likely to be substantial differences in the positions taken by participants. Much of the time these differences can be reconciled through analysis of the facts of the case and sharing of experiences on similar situations. However, about one half of the groups find that they cannot resolve their differences in at least one case.

Once the decisions, consensual or by vote, are recorded by the instructor for each group on each case, the model is explained and then illustrated by applying it to each of the five cases.

### Day 2 Afternoon: Group Feedback

The afternoon begins with an exposition of the ten-point scale used to measure participation and a brief excursion into what is known about differences in leadership style among cultures, institutions, and organizations. This foray into descriptive research on leadership style includes many of the findings reported in Chapter 7 and highlights the fact that leadership styles are not "fixed." Instead, leaders seek, albeit imperfectly, to reshape their styles to fit the worlds that they encounter. Finally, the average mean level of participation (MLP) score for each training group and a frequency distribution of those scores is presented based on the precourse problem sets on which the groups all worked.

The frequency distribution typically shows considerable variance within the group. This fact inevitably promotes speculation about who is the most autocratic and the most participative within the group. Each person is then asked to record these speculations using a form specially designed for that purpose. Each person ranks the members of his or her small group in terms of their predicted leadership styles, describes the bases for these predictions, and then selects one positive and one potentially negative aspect of working for each other group member.

Once the form is completed, usually a thirty-minute task, groups reassemble and share their perceptions with one another. Each person, in turn, receives the benefit of the perceptions of his or her style held by each of the others and, most importantly, the bases of these perceptions. In addition each person hears what others feel would be the positive and negative features of working for him or her.

The time taken varies from a minimum of ten minutes to as much as forty-five minutes per group member. Although these sessions are typically approached with apprehension, the participants find they learn a great deal from them, and the bonds among group members are strengthened. The insights obtained from other participants are frequently viewed as one of the greatest benefits of the program. These benefits are not realized, however, unless an appropriate group climate has been established by the team-building events of the previous day.

### Day 3 Morning: Computer Feedback

This day begins with each person receiving a detailed computer analysis of his or her leadership style based on the responses to the thirty group problems (this feedback is described in detail in Vroom and Yetton [1973, pp. 163–73]). The computer analysis is accompanied by a twenty-four-page manual for later study. The instructor chooses one printout from the set and, using transparencies made from the original (with the name removed), projects the results so that they can be viewed by the entire group. This person then becomes a case study for discussion and analysis by the entire group. Since participants have their own results in front of them, the case study is immediately translated into inferences about the meaning of their own results. The small groups then reassemble for the purpose of comparing results, particularly with regard to prior predictions.

### Day 3 Afternoon: The Individual Model

This session begins with an exploration of the normative model for individual problems. The concepts and logic underlying this model are more quickly understood since they have many similarities to the model for group problems. The presentation of the model leads naturally into a discussion of the aggregate results for the entire group and then to the computer results prepared for each participant based on the twenty-four individual cases.

In a significant variant of the computer-generated feedback, we have sometimes added feedback from subordinates. Prior to the training, each participant asks at least four subordinates to complete the problem set(s), indicating how they think the leader would actually deal with each case. These subordinate predictions are then aggregated, and a computer program compares the participant's view of his or her style with that of subordinates.

### Day 4 Morning: Practice with the Model

Earlier in the program (or alternatively prior to the start of the program), participants are asked to generate one or more examples of personal decisions that they are about to make as a part of their managerial roles. These cases then become the basis for practicing using the model in the small groups formed on Day 1. Each person has the option of communicating the case(s) verbally or distributing written copies to other group members.

Other group members serve as consultants to the manager in the formulation of the problem and in the analysis of its status on the problem attributes. This process is what we have referred to throughout this book as CII. Jointly, they discuss the appropriateness of the model's prescriptions. Discussion is usually terminated by the manager when he or she indicates an intended method for resolving the problem. The discussion continues until each manager has had the opportunity to use the group as consultants on one or more situations of immediate and direct relevance and to make a more informed judgment concerning the applicability of the model to their own decision making.

### Day 4 Afternoon: Consolidation

In the course of the four days of training, each participant has received feedback from several different sources—from peers in the small informal group, sometimes from subordinates, and from two computer-based analyses of their choices. Most participants experience significant areas of convergence among these different types of feedback, but for others there may be tension between different feedback components, or between their prior self-image and the feedback they have received. The final component of the training is a personal counseling session between the participant and a staff member. The object of the counseling is to help the participant understand and integrate the components of the training and to identify several action steps or areas to "work on" back on the job. The action steps are typically much more specific than "following the prescription of the Time-Efficient model." They may include such things as: trying more group meetings on unstructured problems, not wasting so much time holding group meetings on issues of little organizational or personal concern, or more delegating to individual subordinates whose talents one seeks to develop. The action steps are invariably consistent with feedback concerning discrepancies between the person's choices and those of the model and are also consistent with the participants' views of their own capacities and of the nature of the organization in which they work.

## A STUDY OF TRAINING EFFECTIVENESS

A great deal of time, money, and effort goes into the conduct of management education programs. In comparison, relatively little attention is given to their evaluation. While it is customary for course participants to be asked to evaluate the course upon its conclusion, systematic efforts to assess long-term effects of the experience on the behavior of managers on the job are quite rare.

Several years ago, we set out to evaluate a residential course similar to the one just described. One hundred and fifty-nine managers from a single large international corporation participated in eight separate workshops on leadership and participation, centered around the Vroom-Yetton model. The managers were highly diverse and were working in twenty-three different countries. Two of the workshops were conducted in the United Kingdom, one in the Philippines, and five in the United States. Five of the workshops were three-and-one-half days in length, while three lasted five days.

The evaluation study began well after the last of the workshops had been conducted. For the most recent "graduates" the course had taken place one year earlier. For the earliest graduates the training had occurred three-and-a-half years earlier.

Three distinct but complementary methods were used to measure training effects:

*Problem set*   As described earlier in the section on course design, each participant worked on fifty-four cases prior to coming to the course. At the time of the followup, each participant was sent another problem set with different, but comparable, cases. With untrained managers, this new set was found to yield identical results to the previous problem set. A comparison of the problem set results before and after training could provide one type of evidence concerning training effects.

*Participant evaluation questionnaire*   Each participant was sent a nine-page questionnaire containing both structured and open-ended questions intended to solicit the participants' present evaluation of the program and the effects that they believed that it had on their behavior. In the design of questions, every effort was made to get concrete examples of things that they had tried to do differently as a result of the workshop, and the success or failure of these attempts was noted.

*Co-worker evaluation questionnaire*   Each participant was sent two questionnaires that he or she was asked to distribute to a co-worker (usually a superior or subordinate) who knew the person both before and after the training and might be in a position to provide useful information. These questionnaires were returned directly to the researcher and not to the participant.

While the methods are far from precise, the results are very encouraging. The fact that similar conclusions flow from each of the methods strengthens the confidence that can be placed in each. Following are some of the major findings.

### Participation in Decision Making

All three sources of evidence suggest that many of the participants changed their leadership styles toward a more participative direction. On the problem set, the mean score prior to training (on a scale of 0 to 10) was 4.54; after training it had increased to 5.61. This difference is highly significant statistically. Underlying this mean difference is a decrease in the frequency of use of autocratic methods and a marked increase in the frequency of use of participative methods.

Comparable results were obtained from identically structured questions asked of participants and of co-workers. Sixty-two percent of the participants and 58 percent of the co-workers saw an increase in the frequency with which the participant held meetings for the purpose of problem solving and decision making. Seventy-five percent of the participants and 65 percent of the co-workers saw an increase in the degree to which subordinates were involved in decision making.

Participants' written comments amplify this picture. Sixty-one percent of the participants provided qualitative descriptions of the way in which they had altered their managerial styles by providing greater opportunities for participation by subordinates and other affected individuals. Some sample comments follow:

> Company policy and the implementing procedures can be complex, confusing, or nonexistent! During our operational audits I have broadened the number of other Directors and Managers that I will "sound out" before deciding that a particular practice is acceptable or conforms to a good business practice criterion.

> \*       \*       \*

> After suitable digestion of the course material, I instigated regular weekly meetings with my peers and the relevant subordinates. This was in order to air problems and feelings both upwards and downwards and they proved fairly beneficial. I believe that working relationships, performance, job satisfaction, etc., were all improved as well as the hitherto unplumbed depths of several members of staff being revealed.

> \*       \*       \*

> A decision had to be made as to how a group of computer operators shift rota [rotation] would be changed due to changing work loads. The previous shift rota pattern had been originated by myself, and had worked well after a few teething troubles. I was tempted to act in a similar manner— nothing succeeds like success—but instead, threw the problem open to a meeting of operators. Results were, as expected, in that no agreement was reached. However, when I eventually proposed a new shift rota pattern, acceptance was almost universal, and initial troubles were trivial. In addition this regular chore is now handled by the senior operators in rotation. This is a situation, I believe, in which everybody won!

\*       \*       \*

We redesigned our office layout. I outlined the results we wanted to my director and my secretary and asked them to come up with a plan they both could agree upon and which would meet the needs of the department. It worked beautifully.

\*       \*       \*

I now use a different approach to problem solutions. Rather than give my position immediately, I wait for my subordinates to voice their recommendations without undue influence of my opinion. This, I feel, has helped to stimulate their job satisfaction and groom these employees for promotions within the department. Surprisingly, I have found that some of their solutions were immensely better than I would have proposed.

\*       \*       \*

I have held more meetings with my senior staff covering matters for which previously meetings were not held. These meetings proved to be very useful as the decisions made have been more accepted by participants and therefore were carried out more effectively.

Not all of the efforts to apply new decision-making processes turned out to be successful. Three of the managers described what could be termed "failure" experiences. These comments appear as follows:

I tried on one occasion to delegate to one of my subordinates a complete project to be carried out without my supervision but I also did not brief him as to what was required to be done. The result was disastrous.

\*       \*       \*

[I] attempted group meetings [but] find them time consuming. [I also] attempted to have subordinates make decisions but they missed the greater picture. Instead [I now] have them feed input and [I] attempt to explain why I arrived at my conclusion.

\*       \*       \*

[I] delegated more authority for decisions to people under me. . . . [I] found this risky and discovered that people to whom authority was delegated were themselves not tuned into the benefits of a participative management style. Some wrong decisions were made as a result.

Comparable evidence of greater efforts to involve subordinates in decision making is to be found in comments made by co-workers. Subordinates were unequivocally enthusiastic about the success of these efforts as revealed in the following comments:

Certainly [he] has improved his management ability since taking the workshop. He is willing to discuss problems and their solutions. He certainly has developed an ability to make subordinates at ease.

*      *      *

[He] is delegating more since participating in the workshop. He is also very alert to any innovative idea which can be used for the benefit of the organization.

*      *      *

I believe his desire to involve his subordinates in decision making via group and personal meetings is the most noticeable change in his managerial behavior which could be attributed to his participation in the workshop.

*      *      *

[He] can delegate responsibility much easier without having the feeling of "I can do it better myself." He also organizes his work much better and is therefore more useful to his superiors.

*      *      *

I noted that for the two last campaigns [he] gave me a lot more freedom to select new contractors, new spots, move series from one city to another city in order to obtain the most valuable accommodations or rates. As long as my reasons were valid, my suggestions were either adopted or fully supported.

*      *      *

The most obvious change is [his] desire to add ideas of others to departmental responses; his willingness to listen; and his care to hold back [the] decision until all parties are heard from.

*      *      *

He has been holding more group meetings for problem solving and encourages us to make more suggestions regarding improvements within the office.

*      *      *

[He] has changed since the workshop by being able to delegate the workload better than before. Also involving subordinates in decision making.

\*        \*        \*

He was much better organized following the seminar. He carried out an extensive reorganization in his division and involved key subordinates in decision making which he rarely did before.

### Flexibility in Leadership Styles

The purpose of the workshop was, in no sense, to inculcate an indiscriminate use of participative methods but rather to encourage an examination of situational requirements and a matching of leadership styles to differences in situations. The evidence collected reveals some degree of success in this endeavor. A comparison of results in the problem sets worked on before and after the workshop shows a significant increase in the number of choices in agreement with the model from twenty cases to almost twenty-two cases out of thirty. Significant reductions occurred in the frequency of violations of five of the seven rules underlying the original model (Rules 1, 3, 5, 6, and 7). The greater flexibility in leadership styles is reflected in the fact that 93 percent of the participants agreed with the statement that "The program has helped me to know when and where to involve my subordinates in decision making."

A large number of the participants noted such changes in their written comments including the following:

> Through this training I have become more aware of the fact that, for those problems where a decision can be made by myself it is not necessary to share these with others. . . . Previously, I used to discuss some of these problems with others just to convince myself that my decision was correct.

\*        \*        \*

> One of the things I have tried to do, after attending this program, was to put more thought into how I would make a decision (i.e., individually, group discussions, etc.) based on the particular situation at hand. I have found that, in the majority of cases, choosing the right approach in arriving at a final decision greatly helped to insure the support and follow through of all concerned parties.

\*        \*        \*

> I no longer involve subordinates in decision making when they are not really affected by the decision. [I] let more decisions be truly made by subordinates.

\*        \*        \*

> I think that I got most out of the fact that on the problem set I used a participative method on unimportant items. I have tried to apply it to more difficult assignments where I need others' information and knowledge.

*     *     *

I take under consideration the following before making a decision: the problem, how to procure a workable solution, the people involved, and the effect it will have on both immediate and future developments. This formula I have employed since the workshop, and I feel that it has improved my management skills.

### Development of Subordinates

One of the consequences of greater feedback and more frequent use of delegation and participation is likely to be the development of the talents and job-related skills of subordinates. Eighty-seven percent of the participants indicated either strong or moderate agreement with the statement "The program has helped me to do a better job of developing the talents and skills of those who report to me." Further evidence of a change in participants' leadership styles in a direction consistent with subordinate development comes from an examination of problem set responses before and after the workshop. In the terminology of the normative model, Model A was that alternative that would be most time efficient and Model B was that alternative that would be most developmental. The number of cases in which participants indicated that they would employ the Model B solution increased from 22 percent before training to 32 percent at the time of the followup. It should be noted that this increase was not at the expense of time efficiency since the number of Model A choices remained constant at 38 percent.

Several comments from participants further reflect these efforts, most of them successful but one unsuccessful.

I have been able to recognize subordinates' weaknesses and to develop them [the subordinates] further for their own progress and for the Company's benefit.

*     *     *

[The workshop] helped me to identify autocratic behavior in one of my managers and [I] was able to correct problems resulting from his behavior.

*     *     *

[I] tried to get key subordinates to be more aware of their management styles and how it was affecting their ability favorably or unfavorably to achieve planned goals. Results were mixed and in those cases where early beneficial results were achieved there was a quick relapse to old habits or styles.

One of the superiors supplied the following observation:

[He] has always maintained a rapport with his staff. Since the workshop I have noticed an improvement in his development of subordinate managers.

These results are indeed encouraging. Particularly gratifying is the fact that there is no evidence of a decline in effects with the passage of time. Those who had been trained three-and-a-half years earlier were indistinguishable on all quantitative measures from those who had been through the course in the previous year.

The results of our study are largely confirmed by three additional studies that have independently evaluated the effectiveness of similar training designs. Zimmer (1978) compared problem set responses collected six weeks after training with responses from a parallel form of the set collected prior to training. The results revealed that managers became more participative as a consequence of the training design. More importantly, their violations of five of the seven underlying rules declined.

Using materials developed for training in Austria and Germany, Böhnisch (1987) also reports successful results. When trained managers are compared to untrained managers, the former are found to be more participative. They exhibit significantly fewer violations of three of the seven underlying rules that form the basis of the model. Smith (1979) summarizes posttraining attitudes about the program of 216 managers from 13 different organizations. In general, these attitudes reflect patterns similar to those we have reported from our study.

## USING THE NEW MODEL IN TRAINING

The training program that we have described in depth, and evaluated in the study just reported, used the original Vroom-Yetton model. What modifications are necessary to incorporate in training the revised model that we have introduced in this book?

Our earliest efforts were predicated on a view of the new model as a potential instrument to be "used" back on the job but not something to be "taught" in its own right. Accordingly, managers would continue to be taught the older model but would be encouraged to use the more powerful one for online analysis of decisions when they return to the job.

In support of this position, we have found that managers who understand the Vroom-Yetton model can readily adapt to the new model without significant additional training. During the later phases of the training program that we have described, managers have been given the software described in the previous chapter. Practice in using this model on one's own decision problems and comparing experiences with others typically lead to both an understanding of and an appreciation for the greater power and complexity of the new model.

More recently we have designed a complete training program that makes no reference to the Vroom-Yetton model, but instead relies exclusively on the greater predictive power of the new model. This new program follows the lines of the one described earlier in this chapter. The principal differences are to be found in terminology. The concept of the feasible set and of the rules that generate it are replaced by the heuristics that constitute the summaries of Chapters 9 through 11. The new decision trees shown in Chapter 12 replace those of the earlier model, and the terms *time driven* and *development driven* replace Models A and B.

The new training program required the development of new problem sets containing cases systematically varying eight problem attributes (subordinate information being added to the seven varied in previous designs).

Geographical dispersion of subordinates and time constraints are absent in all thirty cases. As was true in the previous problem sets, no information is provided within any of the cases on either motivation–time or motivation–development. This permits managers to attach whatever values they customarily give to these criteria.

In addition, the new approach to training required the development of new computer programs to compare managers' choices with the recommendations of newer models. The feedback permitted by the new problem set includes much that was of value in the previous printouts. However, the relevance to the manager is enhanced by the greater validity of the new model and the more precise estimates it provides of the likely consequences of the manager's choices. The first page of the feedback actually received by a manager whom we shall call John Doe appears in Figure 13–1.

The number of times each of the five alternatives has been chosen appears in the first row of the table in the upper left; for comparison, the second row shows the average results for the manager's peer group. This is usually the group trained in the same executive education program but could be any group for which data are available. From the comparison of these two rows, John Doe can see which methods he uses more frequently and less frequently than the comparison group. He makes more use of AI and CI and less use of CII and GII than does the comparison group.

The remaining rows in the first table provide other bases for comparison— how the models behave across the thirty cases. The third row provides results for the *Time-Driven* model when applied to the set of cases. This is the distribution of choices when the criterion for choice is the highest overall effectiveness in the special case in which maximum weight is placed on time and no weight is placed on development (MT = 5, MD = 1). The fourth and final row shows the distribution for the *Development-Driven* model (MT = 1, MD = 5).

These last two rows contain values that are dependent solely on the configuration of the problem set and are the same for all managers responding to the same problem set. They represent what would result from strict adherence to the model under two distinct managerial motivations. As such, they provide managers with benchmarks against which their results can be compared. John Doe's pattern of choices is somewhat more similar to that of the Time-Driven model than to its development-driven counterpart, although in fact it does not correspond very closely with either.

In the upper righthand corner of Figure 13–1, mean level of participation (MLP) scores for John Doe, the peer group, and the two variants of the normative

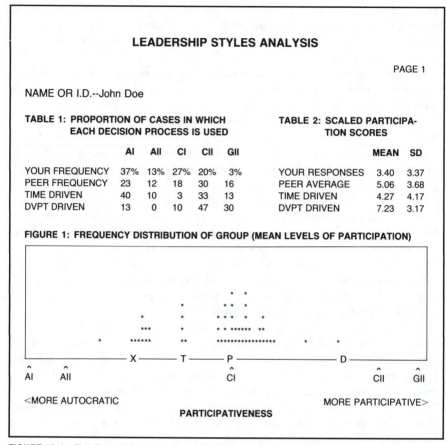

FIGURE 13-1   First Page of Computer-based Feedback

model are presented. (As explained in Chapter 7, these means are obtained by multiplying numbers of choices by the values 0, 1, 5, 8, and 10 for AI, AII, CI, CII, and GII respectively.) John's mean score is more autocratic overall than the mean for the peer group as well as the two models. As is true for most groups of U.S. managers, the peer group mean is between those of the Time-Driven and Development-Driven models and somewhat closer to the Time-Driven model.

The column marked "SD" to the right of the mean scores shows the standard deviations corresponding to each mean. This score is an index of the degree of variability around each mean and is computed using the following formula:

$$SD = \sqrt{\frac{\Sigma(X_i - MLP)^2}{30}}$$   (Equation 13-1)

where $X_i$ is a manager's (or a model's) behavior on the $i^{th}$ case. The maximum standard deviation is 5 and occurs when AI and GII are each chosen 50 percent of the time. The minimum standard deviation is 0 and occurs if the same process is chosen in each of the cases. SD corresponds roughly to a measure of the leader's flexibility or responsiveness to the changing circumstances represented within the problem set.

It is interesting to note that the standard deviation is greatest for the Time-Driven model and least for the Development-Driven model. In using the entire range of decision processes, particularly the extremes of AI and GII, the Time-Driven model is highly responsive to differences among situations. On the other hand, the Development-Driven model emphasizes the use of participative processes and exhibits less flexibility. John Doe is slightly less variable than the peer group and closer in that respect to the Development-Driven model.

At the bottom of Figure 13–1 is a frequency distribution of mean scores. Each asterisk denotes a particular person's mean score within the training group. The symbol "X" is printed directly below the manager's score (thereby identifying him or her within the distribution), the symbol "P" is printed below the peer average, and the symbols "T" and "D" below the Time-Driven and Development-Driven models respectively. John Doe can see that of the fifty-five managers in the training group, only one has a more autocratic mean.

Figure 13–2 shows the second page of the computer feedback. This page presents analyses that relate not to mean scores or distributions, but to the degrees of correspondence with the respective models. On the top of the page, John Doe can see a table containing a listing of his choices, problem by problem, and the corresponding choices made by the Time-Driven and Development-Driven models. This permits John to check that his choices have been entered into the computer accurately and, more importantly, to see in which cases his choices conformed to the prescriptions of each model.

The evaluation of the consequences of the manager's choices in terms of each of the four criteria employed by the model is presented in the middle of the page. For each criterion two measures are employed. The first (PERCENT "HITS") is the percent of cases in which John Doe's choices corresponded to the optimum choice for that criterion. The second is the *degree* to which each criterion is predicted to be achieved by John's choices on the problem set. It is also expressed in percentage terms. A value of 100 percent would signify that, in each case, the choice was optimal. A value of 0 percent would signify that, in each case, the choice was the poorest on that criterion. Because the second measure considers the magnitude, not just the frequency, of departures from optimal choices, it is far more precise and deserves much greater attention.

Comparison values for peers are shown for both measures and the comparative levels of achievement of the two models are also given. John Doe does exceptionally well on two criteria—quality and time—but comparatively poorly

# LEADERSHIP STYLES ANALYSIS

PAGE 2
John Doe

## TABLE 3: CHOICES BY PROBLEM

| PROBLEM NUMBER | YOUR CHOICE | TIME DRIVEN | DVPT DRIVEN | PROBLEM NUMBER | YOUR CHOICE | TIME DRIVEN | DVPT DRIVEN |
|---|---|---|---|---|---|---|---|
| 1 | AI | CII | CII | 16 | CI | CII | CII |
| 2 | CI | AI | GII | 17 | AI | AI | AI |
| 3 | CII | GII | GII | 18 | CI | CII | CII |
| 4 | CII | CII | CII | 19 | CI | CI | GII |
| 5 | AI | GII | GII | 20 | AI | CII | CII |
| 6 | CII | CII | CII | 21 | CII | AII | CI |
| 7 | GII | GII | GII | 22 | AI | AI | GII |
| 8 | AII | GII | GII | 23 | CII | AII | CII |
| 9 | CII | CII | CII | 24 | CI | AII | CII |
| 10 | AII | CII | CII | 25 | CI | AI | CII |
| 11 | AI | CII | CII | 26 | AI | AI | CI |
| 12 | AII | AI | CII | 27 | CI | AI | GII |
| 13 | CI | CII | GII | 28 | AII | AI | AI |
| 14 | AI | AI | AI | 29 | AI | AI | CI |
| 15 | AI | AI | AI | 30 | AI | AI | CII |

\*         \*         \*

## TABLE 4: PREDICTED CONSEQUENCES OF CHOICES

| CRITERIA | PERCENT "HITS" | | DEGREE OF ACHIEVEMENT | | | |
|---|---|---|---|---|---|---|
| | SELF | PEERS | SELF | PEERS | TIME DRIVEN | DVPT DRIVEN |
| QUALITY: | 80% | 70% | 92% | 82% | 99% | 99% |
| COMMITMENT: | 10 | 26 | 27 | 59 | 84 | 87 |
| TIME: | 37 | 23 | 70 | 54 | 60 | 32 |
| DEVELOPMENT: | 8 | 19 | 36 | 50 | 41 | 85 |

\*         \*         \*

## TABLE 5: CASES FOR RESTUDY

| | | DEVIATIONS FROM OPTIMAL | |
|---|---|---|---|
| CASE NO | TOTAL | QUALITY | COMMITMENT |
| 13 | −4.50 | −1.50 | −3.00 |
| 5 | −4.00 | 0.00 | −4.00 |
| 8 | −3.80 | 0.00 | −3.80 |
| 18 | −2.60 | −2.00 | −0.60 |
| 1 | −2.60 | 0.00 | −2.60 |
| 10 | −2.40 | 0.00 | −2.40 |
| 16 | −2.00 | −2.00 | 0.00 |
| 20 | −1.60 | 0.00 | −1.60 |

FIGURE 13–2    Second Page of Computer-based Feedback

on the other two—commitment and development. The good results on time and relatively poor attention to development are characteristics generally associated with the overall mean score (3.40) he exhibits. However, the results for quality and commitment are much less predictable from a manager's mean score and reflect the circumstances under which different methods are employed as much as their overall frequencies. John Doe, with a 3.40 mean score, has a much higher level of achievement on quality than most managers but a much poorer level of achievement on commitment than most managers with this mean. The reasons for this state of affairs will be apparent later when we examine the third page of the printout.

An inspection of the performance of the Time-Driven and Development-Driven models at the extreme right is instructive. Both models do well in comparison to most managers—an event that should not be surprising since the standards used in assessing achievement are identical to those controlling the models. The Time-Driven model does significantly better on time while the Development-Driven model achieves significantly more on development. Neither model achieves 100 percent on quality and commitment—a fact attributable to the existence of tradeoffs among these two outcomes. Frequently the process that provides the highest quality will not provide the highest commitment, and vice versa. The tradeoff is even greater for the other two criteria—time and development. On average, the better one does on time the more poorly one does on development, and vice versa.

The final section of Figure 13–2 indicates cases for restudy. They are selected on the basis of departures from optimal effectiveness. A maximum of eight cases are selected, each having at least a one-point deviation from optimal when the likely effects of the manager's choices are considered. They are listed in descending order of departures from optimal. For each case the manager can see the deviation from optimal decision effectiveness and the amounts of deviation attributable to the two components of decision effectiveness—quality and commitment.

The deviations for quality and commitment sum to the total deviation for decision effectiveness. If these two deviations differ in sign, the case involved a tradeoff between the two, and the manager's choice favored the criterion with the positive sign.

As might be expected, more of John Doe's problematic choices arise from inattention to matters of commitment than from inattention to matters of quality. Seven of the eight cases exhibit deviations on commitment and only three show deviations on quality.

For each case singled out in this way, the feedback recipient is encouraged to read the situation again and to consider the likely consequences of her or his choices and those of the model (all listed above on the same page). Sometimes the manager cannot understand the basis for her or his previous choice and attributes it to not having attended to key factors in the case. More frequently, the manager can understand the reasons for making the earlier choices but can now see the designated risks and believes the models' answer(s) would be better. In that case the manager is encouraged to think of decisions recently made, or those about to be made, in his or her managerial role that are similar to the decision described in the case. The manager is then asked to consider what the model would recommend in that situation and what the likely consequences of that choice would be.

There are some occasions in which rereading cases results in people continuing to believe their own choice to be better than that of the model. They believe that there are attributes of the situation, perhaps but not necessarily restricted to their own skills, that the model has not considered adequately. Such disagreement is fine since our purpose is reflection and thoughtfulness rather than conformity.

The last part of the feedback appears in Figures 13–3 and 13–4. It is generally regarded as the most interesting and valuable of the computer-based results. Not only does it describe the conditions under which one utilizes autocratic and participative methods, but it also helps explain degrees of achievement scores on the previous page of the feedback.

This table capitalizes on the fact, discussed at length in Chapter 7, that a problem set is not a random assortment of cases but is constructed in accordance with a strict set of principles corresponding to a multifactorial experimental design. This means that not only are the eight problem attributes varied across the cases but that each attribute is statistically independent of the other attributes. This latter feature makes it possible for the feedback to portray the role of each attribute in each manager's choices and provide answers to questions such as: Which attributes are most influential in the decision to involve others in decision making? Which attributes appear to play no part whatsoever in the person's choices? Are there any respects in which the manager is responding in the "wrong way" to situational demands?

John Doe's superior performance on quality and inferior performance on commitment provides us with some clues of what we might find. It is likely that he successfully discriminates situations in which participation by subordinates may be expected to enhance decision quality, but does less well at identifying situations in which participation may be required to create commitment.

Beneath each of the eight attribute headings, one finds two lines each of which represents a 0 to 10 scale of participation. These two scales are used to depict mean scores on subsets of cases. The existence of a large difference between those means is an indication that the attribute played a role in that person's choices. Furthermore, the direction of the difference signifies the nature of that role, for example, whether the presence of the attribute causes the person to become more participative or more autocratic.

The actual mean scores for subsets of problems are shown just below each scale and are represented on the scale by the symbol "X." By comparing the values for X where the attribute is present with the values for X where it is absent, one can see the influence of that attribute on the person's choices. For example, on problems for which there was a quality requirement, John Doe had a mean score of 3.88, compared with a mean of 1.50 when there was no quality requirement. Clearly he is much more likely to involve direct reports in the solution of important problems.

The same result can be shown graphically by drawing a line connecting the Xs on the upper and lower lines. The positive slope of that line (upward

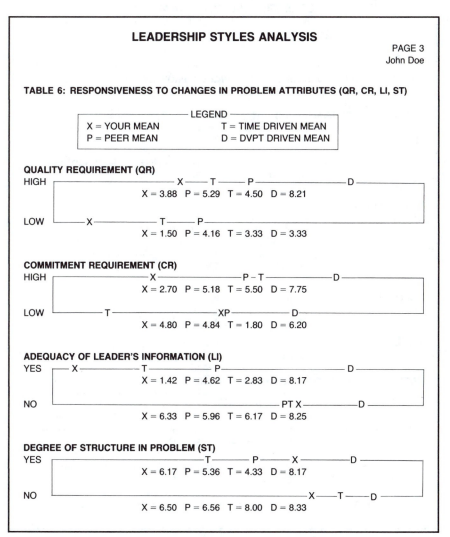

**FIGURE 13–3**  Third Page of Computer-based Feedback

and to the right) is indicative of the tendency to be more participative on problems with an analytic component.

For comparison purposes, managers can also see the main effect of this attribute for their peer group, represented by the points marked "P" on the two scales and by the mean scores beside the symbol "P." A manager can also see the role that each of the attributes plays in the models. "T" and "D" stand for the Time-Driven and Development-Driven models respectively. The

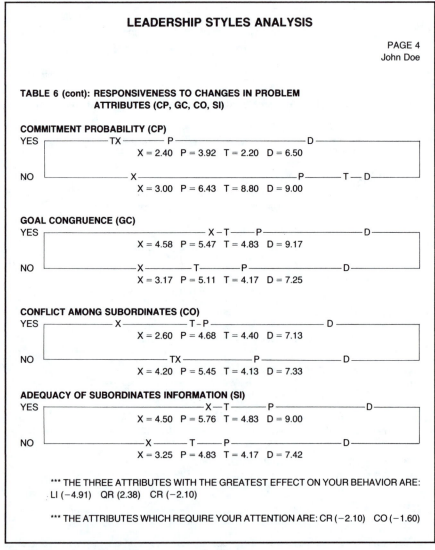

FIGURE 13–4    Fourth Page of Computer-based Feedback

slopes for both models are also positive, indicating that in this respect the manager (and, in fact, most of the peer group) is responding sensibly to this situational demand.

While the relative values on the upper and lower lines are of most interest, one should not overlook the potential significance of differences on the same line. For example, the ordering of points X, T, P, and D on the lower line indicates that in low-quality requirement situations John Doe is more autocratic than either the Time-Driven or Development-Driven models. (T and D fall at the same location on this scale and only T is printed out.) By way of contrast, the average member of the peer group is slightly more participative than either model.

More of the picture begins to emerge as one examines the next seven attributes. In addition to quality, our manager's choices are strongly influenced by leader information, goal congruence, and subordinate information. In each of these respects, the slopes resemble those not only of the peer group but also those of the Time-Driven and Development-Driven models. John Doe is autocratic when the problem is unimportant, when he has all the needed information and his subordinates do not, and when the goals of subordinates do not coincide with those of the organization. On the other hand, he becomes more participative (usually CI or CII) on important problems that subordinates are motivated to solve, and when they have the information and he does not. It is clear that this manager is employing participative methods as a means of gaining information from subordinates in the interest of better decisions. Only one problem attribute relevant to decision quality, degree of problem structure (ST), has no significant effect on John Doe's choices. His achievement on quality would have been even higher if he were more participative on unstructured problems. In fact, three cases for restudy showing quality deviations involved the use of CI rather than CII on unstructured problems.

The remaining three attributes—commitment requirement (CR), commitment probability (CP), and conflict among subordinates (CO)—are relevant to commitment to decisions. It is here that we should look for some understanding of why John Doe does poorly in achieving commitment and for some specific suggestions about the behavioral changes he might make.

The problems are not hard to find. On commitment requirement, John Doe's slope is negative, not positive as is true for the peers, and the Time-Driven and Development-Driven models. He is more likely to seek participation in situations in which commitment is unnecessary. The problem is with his choices on the twenty problems in which there is a high commitment requirement. Here his mean score is 2.70 compared to 5.50 for the Time-Driven model and 7.75 for the Development-Driven model. John should pay more attention to the support and feeling of ownership over decisions that frequently result from participation. The need for such commitment should be a signal to him calling for more participative approaches such as CII and GII.

Comparisons on commitment probability (CP) are more subtle but also revealing. This attribute has a very large effect on the Time-Driven and Development-Driven models, as it does on the peer group. In each case the choices are more autocratic when the person has the power to sell his or her own decision than where he or she lacks that power. John Doe does not appear to make this discrimination. The mean difference of .60 is a very small fraction of the other differences.

A final problem in John Doe's style is shown in the attribute subordinate conflict (CO). He displays a negative slope on this attribute indicating a tendency to try to avoid conflict by using more autocratic methods in controversial situations. A similar although much weaker tendency is shown for the peer group. In contrast, the Time-Driven model shows a very slight positive slope and the Development-Driven model shows a very slight negative slope. A positive slope on conflict is based on the potentially constructive uses of conflict in avoiding "groupthink," as well as the desirability of resolving differences before decisions are made. John Doe was encouraged to reread the fifteen high conflict situations and to try to identify, in as many of those cases as possible, the benefits as well as the risks of using interactive processes to bring the differences out into the open.

The computer feedback concludes with two notes for John Doe. The first reads: THE THREE ATTRIBUTES WITH THE GREATEST EFFECT ON YOUR BEHAVIOR ARE: . . . . This is followed by letters signifying the three attributes (of the total set of eight) that show the largest mean differences, and hence, play the greatest role in his choice. Following each attribute is a numerical value corresponding to the mean difference for that attribute and a sign indicating the direction of that difference (or slope).

This message is useful in constructing the manager's own decision tree, or implicit set of criteria, used to determine when and where to share decision-making power. John Doe's choices are most affected by leader information (LI), quality requirement (QR), and commitment requirement (CR). He is most autocratic when he does have the necessary information, the problem has no technical component, and he needs commitment from subordinates.

The second message pertains to situational demands to which the manager appears to be responding incorrectly. The statement reads: THE ATTRIBUTES THAT REQUIRE YOUR ATTENTION ARE: . . . Here the manager is reminded of any attributes in which the slope (or mean difference) is opposite in direction to that of the Time-Driven model. To reduce the likelihood that the differences might be attributable to chance, we use .7 as the minimum mean difference for inclusion here. For John Doe there are two attributes mentioned—commitment requirement and conflict—both of which we have discussed above.

The preceding computer feedback has pertained to group problems. If the manager had also completed a problem set containing individual problems, a comparable computer analysis could have been produced pertinent to her or his behavior patterns in situations involving a single direct report.

## SOME CONCLUDING THOUGHTS ON TRAINING

Compared to its predecessor, the new model is a more powerful device for use after training and, with the aid of the kind of computer feedback we have described, provides a more accurate and more diagnostic framework during training for understanding managers' choices on a problem set. Although the model is not the final answer to the management of participation, we feel confident that it is the best answer available at this time.

The ultimate test of the worth of the ideas, including the applications to training, is the extent to which they encourage thought by the managers who are exposed to it. We do not envision a world in which managers cannot make a decision without referring to a decision tree, calculator, or personal computer. Rather, we see these pieces of technology as adjuncts and extensions to a learning process that emphasizes an awareness of alternatives and informed judgments about the consequences of those alternatives.

Although we have reviewed much evidence in these pages that has pointed to the adaptability of leadership style to situational demands, we believe that behavior can become a matter of habit rather than choice. Most managers have been making decisions for such long periods of time that the processes can become automatic. Methods and actions are selected without reflecting on their implications.

Habituation of action obviously has a function. Habits reduce the need to make choices and enable us to act quickly. We don't have to think when it is time to brush our teeth or to tie our shoes. However, habits have another property that can be somewhat troublesome. At best, they reflect the learning environment at the time the habit was formed. If the environment remains constant, they are likely to continue to be effective. But if the environment changes markedly, habit patterns have to be reevaluated.

Managers seldom live in an unchanging world. They change jobs, change organizations, move from one country to another, or from public sector to private, or vice versa. Such changes bring with them new challenges, new opportunities, and new situational demands on leadership. Old approaches need to be rethought and new habits substituted for old.

While mobility requires change, it is by no means its only cause. Deregulation, foreign competition, and new tax laws have brought with them massive changes in the way in which corporations have to be structured and managed. Managerial leadership is no longer maintaining the status quo. Old habits must be discarded if one is to respond to today's challenges and opportunities.

To meet these challenges, managers must have the capabilities of being both participative and autocratic and of knowing when to employ each. They must be capable of identifying situational demands, of selecting or designing appropriate methods of dealing with them, and they must have the skills necessary to implement their choices. The evidence cited in this chapter, along with our experience in working with managers over the last fifteen years, suggests that training focused on analytical models of participation contributes to these critical components of effective leadership.

## A LAST WORD

The last half of this book has been devoted to a new model that purports to guide managers' use of participation in decision making. We have examined each of the model's subsystems and then put them together to show how the model works in its entirety. Finally, we have examined its applications in training and development.

We believe the model to be a significant advance over its much publicized predecessor. Managers faced with the task of solving the enormous challenges of today's organizations should find its prescriptions much more specific and of greater value than those of its older brother. While the computer version undoubtedly provides the most information and is of greatest value, the decision trees provide potentially useful guidance on how effectively to match one's behavior with situational demands.

The greater precision of the new model should also be of benefit to the many hundreds of trainers who have tried to make the old model "come alive" to the managers they train. In fact, we have found the new model somewhat easier to teach than the old. It is totally unnecessary for managers to be exposed to the equations and formulae we have placed in a technical appendix. Managers *do* need to understand the model's four subcriteria (quality, commitment, time, and development) and the composite criteria of decision and overall effectiveness. They must also understand the problem attributes that provide the basis for selecting the process most likely to be effective and the heuristics or rules of thumb descriptive of this selection. However, these are easily mastered concepts that are sufficient for one to grasp the fundamental logic behind the decision trees or computer program.

While we believe that the new model will find immediate applications for managers and trainers, we also hope that our colleagues in the organizational behavior research community will find that the model stimulates ideas that will ultimately make it even better. More research is needed on the validity of the total model as well as research on the validity of its various component processes.

Fifteen years have passed since the publication of the Vroom-Yetton model. The research that we and others have carried out during this time has formed the basis for the improvements reported here. We sincerely hope that history repeats itself and that tomorrow's research will make possible further improvements in the model in the years to come.

# Appendix A

# DEFINITIONS OF THE PROBLEM ATTRIBUTES

**QR: QUALITY REQUIREMENT**

## HOW IMPORTANT IS THE TECHNICAL QUALITY OF THIS DECISION?

| 1 | 2 | 3 | 4 | 5 |
|---|---|---|---|---|
| No Import | Low Import | Average Import | High Import | Critical Import |

*Alternative Question:*

Given commitment, how important is it which course of action is adopted?

This attribute refers to the importance of finding a high-quality solution independent of the need to satisfy any acceptance criteria. There are some problems for which the nature of the solution reached is not at all critical. Within the constraints specified in the definition of the problem, you are (or should be) indifferent among possible solutions provided they are acceptable to those affected by them. In all such problems, there is no quality requirement and the question presented above should be answered *no importance*.

When a problem lacks a quality requirement, the solutions that meet the constraints specified are finite in number and obvious. Furthermore, there is no technical or rational basis for selecting among them in terms of their contribution to the attainment of external goals (for example, what color to paint the cafeteria walls). The only requirement is that one of these alternatives be successfully implemented.

The majority of managerial decision problems and decisions do possess some degree of a quality requirement in the sense that some solutions are more likely than others to attain external objectives (that is, less costly, more likely to succeed, and so forth). For example, decisions about what products to produce, what markets to enter, and how to advertise your products, are clearly critical matters about which some alternative courses of action would be superior to others. You may not know at the moment which course of action is best but you do know that it is going to make a difference which alternative is chosen and you should not be indifferent among them.

Problems with such a quality requirement can range from *low importance* for those relatively minor yet nontrivial situations to *critical importance* for the major strategic decisions that a manager might face. In making your assessment, think of the likely difference between the value to the organization of a "wise" versus an "unwise" decision.

## CR: COMMITMENT REQUIREMENT

### HOW IMPORTANT IS SUBORDINATE COMMITMENT TO THE DECISION?

| 1 | 2 | 3 | 4 | 5 |
|---|---|---|---|---|
| **No Import** | **Low Import** | **Average Import** | **High Import** | **Critical Import** |

*Alternative Questions*:

How much importance do your subordinates attach to this decision?

How critical is it that your subordinates "buy in" to this decision?

This attribute refers to the importance of getting acceptance or commitment to the solution or decision on the part of your immediate subordinate(s). There are some situations in which a course of action (even a "technically correct" one) can fail miserably because it is resisted or opposed by those who have to execute it. These are problems or decisions possessing a commitment requirement if the decision is to be successful. The success or failure of the decision hinges to an important degree on the enthusiastic support of one or more of your subordinates.

In judging the degree to which a problem possesses a commitment requirement, look for two things:

1.  Are your subordinates going to have to execute the decision under conditions in which their initiative, judgment, and thinking will be required in order to make the decision successful?

2.  Are your subordinates likely to "feel strongly" about the decision such that they might actively support some alternatives and actively oppose others? In an extreme case, would such opposition take the form of an overt or covert attempt to block the execution of a decision, or failing that, cause subordinates to leave the organization?

In judging the degree to which commitment is required, think of the likely result if your subordinates fail to support the decision. How might this affect implementation? How might this affect morale?

Do not confuse the need for commitment with the need for compliance. If you are able to specify exactly what you want people to do and have the control systems to insure that they do it, commitment may not be of importance. In addition, you should judge the importance of the commitment to the decision without regard to the importance of the technical quality of the decision (that is, your judgment should be independent of attribute QR).

## LI: LEADER INFORMATION

### DO YOU HAVE SUFFICIENT INFORMATION TO MAKE A HIGH-QUALITY DECISION?

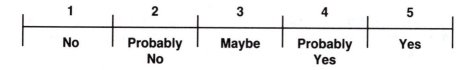

| 1 | 2 | 3 | 4 | 5 |
|---|---|---|---|---|
| No | Probably No | Maybe | Probably Yes | Yes |

*Alternative Question*:

Do you have the necessary expertise to deal with this decision?

This attribute refers to the degree to which you believe you have sufficient information and expertise to solve the problem or make the decision by yourself without the aid of your subordinate(s). The information referred to is information relevant to the technical or rational side of the problem, that is, you are asked if you have the information needed to achieve the external objectives of the decision, not the information as to what solution would most please your subordinate(s). Note that what is called for is a judgment about your knowledge in relation to the demands of the problem, not a relative judgment of your knowledge versus that of your subordinate(s).

## ST: PROBLEM STRUCTURE

### IS THE PROBLEM WELL STRUCTURED?

| 1 | 2 | 3 | 4 | 5 |
|---|---|---|---|---|
| No | Probably No | Maybe | Probably Yes | Yes |

*Alternative Questions*:

Are you familiar with problems of this kind?

Do you know the current situation, the goals, and the alternatives for achieving these objectives?

A problem is well structured if the current state, the desired state, and the methods of transforming the former into the latter are all known. A structured situation is potentially "programmable" in that a standard operating procedure could be devised for handling its recurrence. Often, optimization techniques are available for structured situations, sometimes in the form of a computer program.

Unstructured problems fail to lend themselves to standard responses. A problem is unstructured when the current situation is not fully understood, the goals and objectives to be obtained are "fuzzy" or unclear, and/or the mechanisms of transforming the current state to the desired state are unknown. Unstructured problems are often poorly defined and lack specificity. Sometimes the boundaries of the problem are unknown.

Clearly the same decision could be well structured for one person and relatively unstructured for another. Experience in dealing with problems of a given type is likely to contribute to the development of a structure or framework for dealing with future problems of that type. On the other hand, the elements of novelty, unfamiliarity, and uncertainty contribute to a lack of structure.

## CP: COMMITMENT PROBABILITY

### IF YOU WERE TO MAKE THE DECISION BY YOURSELF, IS IT REASONABLY CERTAIN THAT YOUR SUBORDINATE(S) WOULD BE COMMITTED TO THE DECISION?

| 1 | 2 | 3 | 4 | 5 |
|---|---|---|---|---|
| No | Probably No | Maybe | Probably Yes | Yes |

*Alternative Questions*:

Would your subordinates be likely to "buy in" to your decision?

Would it be a relatively simple matter for you to sell your own solution to the problem to subordinates?

If a problem possesses a commitment requirement (as defined in "CR") it is important to select a decision-making process that will generate that commitment. Increasing the amount of voice that subordinates have in the decision is one method of building commitment but is clearly not the only method. There are some circumstances under which the leader's own decision will be readily accepted by subordinates.

This attribute refers to the likelihood that subordinates would be committed to the leader's autocratic decision. The judgment called for is a complex one but the most critical factor is the "power" of the leader. There are at least three aspects of the relationship between the leader and followers (or subordinates) that affect the likelihood of their commitment to an autocratic decision. They can be thought of as "bases of power" from which a leader can operate:

1. *Legitimate power.* Do subordinates think that the leader should make the decision, that is, that it is his or her legitimate right or job to do so because of the formal authority vested in the leader's role by the organization?

2. *Expert power.* Do subordinates think that the leader is the expert on the matter in question, that is, that he or she has substantially greater wisdom or knowledge than they on the technical issues to be decided?

3. *Attraction (that is, charismatic) power.* Do the subordinates greatly admire the leader, value the leader's approval, and wish to model their behavior after the leader?

Leaders who, in the eyes of subordinates, possess one or more of these bases of power are more likely to get commitment to an autocratic decision than those who lack them.

It should be noted that the amount of power needed to produce required commitment may vary with the amount of commitment required (attribute CR). Differences exist in exactly how critical the cooperation and support are to the ultimate success of the decision. These differences may make it harder (or easier) for the manager to "sell" an autocratic decision and have it gain the required level of commitment. To put it more generally, this attribute deals not with an absolute judgment of the leader's qualities but with a judgment relative to the demands of the particular decision situation.

There are some situations in which the ability of the leader to sell a solution to subordinates, and thereby gain commitment, depends on the particular solution that he or she advocates. Some solutions would be highly palatable to, and easily accepted by, subordinates, whereas others would be openly opposed or subtly resisted. In such instances, consider the most rational, technically correct solution in making your estimate of the leader's ability to sell it to subordinates.

## GC: GOAL CONGRUENCE

### DO SUBORDINATES SHARE THE ORGANIZATIONAL GOALS TO BE ATTAINED IN SOLVING THIS PROBLEM?

| 1 | 2 | 3 | 4 | 5 |
|---|---|---|---|---|
| No | Probably No | Maybe | Probably Yes | Yes |

*Alternative Questions*:

Can you trust your subordinates to pursue the best solution to the problem, as judged from an organizational standpoint?

Does the situation involve a "mutual interest"?

This attribute refers to the extent to which you believe your immediate subordinate(s) would be motivated to pursue a solution to the problem which is rational from the standpoint of the goals of the organization, rather than their own self-interest. It involves the motivation of subordinates, rather than their level of information, knowledge, or expertise. (The used car salesperson might be most knowledgeable concerning the reliability of the cars on the lot, but one might be reluctant to delegate to that person the choice of car due to marked differences in goals). In responding to this question, search for evidence in the problem of a common goal or an area of mutual interest. When these conditions exist, you and your subordinates are in a win–win situation. In a sense you are all "in the same boat," having a common interest or objective.

Shared goals do not exist if, in the course of trying to solve the problem, solutions preferred by, and acceptable to, subordinates are likely to violate corporate interests or objectives. Subordinates are likely to prefer solutions that are "easy" or "comfortable" to them or that attain their own personal goals rather than those solutions that are most likely to attain the organizational objectives.

In some situations, you may not know exactly what goals your subordinates would be likely to pursue. For such decisions, an intermediate judgment (2, 3, or 4) on the preceding scale is appropriate. In other situations, the goals of subordinates may be known but they are neither totally congruent nor totally conflicting with those of the organization. These are "mixed-motive" situations in which there are aspects from which subordinates would benefit but also aspects from which they would suffer from the course of action that is most advantageous to the organization. For these situations, an intermediate scale value (2, 3, or 4) is also appropriate.

## CO: SUBORDINATE CONFLICT

### IS CONFLICT AMONG SUBORDINATES OVER PREFERRED SOLUTIONS LIKELY? (Group Problems Only)

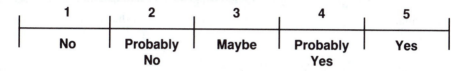

| 1 | 2 | 3 | 4 | 5 |
|---|---|---|---|---|
| No | Probably No | Maybe | Probably Yes | Yes |

*Alternative Questions:*

Is there likely to be substantial disagreement among your subordinates over which course to pursue?

Is the decision problem controversial and likely to evoke very different views among your subordinates?

This attribute refers to the likelihood of disagreement among subordinates over their solutions to the problem. At least initially, prior to any discussions aimed at resolving differences, are subordinates likely to have widely varying opinions about what should be done? These different opinions may have their origins in differences in training, expertise, opposing goals or interests, or they may be due to the fact that the problem or decision is, in itself, highly controversial.

In coding this attribute some people confuse it with goal congruence (GC). Situations involving conflict or disagreement are often seen as lacking in goal congruence and vice versa. Clearly, situations involving both elements exist but so do other alternatives. It is entirely possible for subordinates to share the organizational goal but differ widely in their opinions about how to attain it. Here there is agreement about the ends to be achieved and disagreement about the means for achieving it. It is also possible for subordinates to be unanimous and without any disagreement in their opposition to the organizational goal.

### IS CONFLICT BETWEEN YOU AND YOUR SUBORDINATE OVER A PREFERRED SOLUTION LIKELY? (Individual Problems Only)

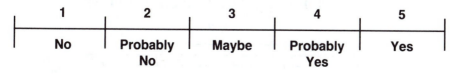

| 1 | 2 | 3 | 4 | 5 |
|---|---|---|---|---|
| No | Probably No | Maybe | Probably Yes | Yes |

*Alternative Questions*:

> Is there likely to be substantial disagreement between you and your subordinate over which course of action to pursue?

> Is the decision problem controversial and likely to evoke a view from your subordinate that is very different from your own?

This question replaces the preceding one if the problem is an "individual" problem, one affecting only a single subordinate. Disagreement among subordinates is not relevant in these situations. What is relevant is if *you* and that subordinate are likely to disagree over a course of action that is initially preferred.

## SI: SUBORDINATE INFORMATION

### DO SUBORDINATES HAVE SUFFICIENT INFORMATION TO MAKE A HIGH-QUALITY DECISION?

| 1 | 2 | 3 | 4 | 5 |
|---|---|---|---|---|
| No | Probably No | Maybe | Probably Yes | Yes |

*Alternative Question*:

> Do your subordinates have the necessary expertise to deal with the decision problem?

This attribute refers to the likelihood that subordinates *collectively* have sufficient information and expertise to solve the problem by themselves. (If the situation is an individual problem, however, the question refers only to the single subordinate.) What is called for is a judgment about their knowledge in relation to the demands of the problem, not a relative judgment of their knowledge versus yours.

Note that in evaluating this attribute you are making a judgment about the information and expertise of subordinates, not their motivation to use that information and expertise in the pursuit of organizational goals. The latter is dealt with in attribute GC.

## TC: TIME CONSTRAINT

### DOES A CRITICALLY SEVERE TIME CONSTRAINT LIMIT YOUR ABILITY TO INVOLVE SUBORDINATES?

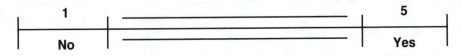

| 1 | | 5 |
|---|---|---|
| No | | Yes |

*Alternative Question:*

Is this an emergency that requires immediate attention to avert either a disaster or a missed opportunity?

Some decisions require quick thinking and immediate action if a crisis is to be handled or a problem prevented from growing into a crisis. In such circumstances it may be difficult, if not impossible, to meaningfully involve one's subordinates in the decision without losing precious time while the problem grows worse or the opportunity disappears. This attribute refers to the existence of such severe time constraints.

A time constraint exists if *both* of the following two conditions exist:

1. Virtually any apparently reasonable decision would be better than a decision that comes too late. In other words, doing something (and thereby meeting the deadline) would be better than doing nothing (and missing the deadline).
2. Involving subordinates, even if they were readily available, is likely to cause the decision to be too late.

The first condition exists in true emergencies and crises or when a firm, irrevocable deadline exists after which no decision would be effective. The second condition exists when time is in extremely short supply (such as, when a flash fire breaks out in a chemical plant).

Rarely do both conditions exist, even in some so-called crises. (Recall President Kennedy's Cuban missile crisis in which the situation nonetheless permitted 13 days of consultation with advisors before a naval blockade was ordered.) There are, however, certain circumstances in which the type of time constraint defined here would definitely exist. A football coach facing fourth down and inches would be wise to do anything other than face a delay of game penalty because he consulted with his team members.

Notice that, unlike the others, this question can only be answered either *yes* or *no*. When a severe time constraint exists, it is usually quite obvious to the manager. Little uncertainty exists and therefore an answer of *maybe* is highly unlikely. If a manager truly cannot decide if a time constraint, as defined above, exists, then in all probability it does not exist and the answer should be *no*.

## GD: GEOGRAPHICAL DISPERSION

### ARE THE COSTS INVOLVED IN BRINGING TOGETHER GEOGRAPHICALLY DISPERSED SUBORDINATES PROHIBITIVE? (Group Problems Only)

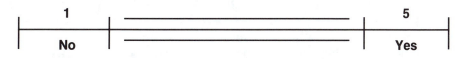

| 1 | | 5 |
|---|---|---|
| **No** | | **Yes** |

*Alternative Question*:

Are the people affected by this decision problem physically isolated and would getting them together be almost impossible?

Sometimes the subordinates affected by the decision are geographically dispersed and unavailable for a meeting with you and each other. For example, the subordinates of a marketing vice president may be regional managers each located in a different region or, worse yet, a different country. Bringing them together to discuss a problem may be impractical.

Of course, such a meeting is never impossible given the availability of air travel and the technology of teleconferencing. In judging this attribute, the manager must weigh the cost of such a meeting against the quality and acceptance requirements of the problem or decision. Important decisions may warrant the additional costs involved in bringing together subordinates no matter how high those costs may be.

This question should be answered *no* if *any* of the following conditions exist:

1. Relevant subordinates are available in the same building, complex, or general location.
2. A regularly scheduled meeting with subordinates is to occur before the decision deadline.
3. Teleconferencing is possible and the costs are not prohibitive.
4. The decision is important enough to warrant travel *if* a meeting is deemed necessary.

On the other hand, the question should be answered *yes* if *none* of the preceding conditions exist.

Like the preceding attribute, this question can only be answered *yes* or *no*. If subordinates are close by, the judgment is simple. If subordinates are dispersed, the judgment is more difficult because the costs of bringing them together must first be assessed. However, an answer of *maybe* in such a circumstance would be merely avoiding the issue. If one has difficulty making a clear *yes* or *no* choice, further analyses are required that weigh the costs of travel or teleconferencing against the quality and acceptance requirements of the problem.

## MT: MOTIVATION–TIME

### HOW IMPORTANT IS IT TO YOU TO MINIMIZE THE TIME IT TAKES TO MAKE THE DECISION?

| 1 | 2 | 3 | 4 | 5 |
|---|---|---|---|---|
| **No Import** | **Low Import** | **Average Import** | **High Import** | **Critical Import** |

*Alternative Question*:

How important is the press of time that you and your subordinates are experiencing?

All managerial decisions incur an "opportunity cost" reflected in the investment of human resources to solve the problem or reach the decision. Presumably, if the problem did not exist, the time and talents of those involved could be directed toward other objectives. Thus, the hours (or days) involved in the making of a decision reflect a very real cost attributable to that decision. The relevance of this point to the model stems from the fact that the amount of your time, and that of your subordinates, consumed in the making of a decision varies with the decision process that is employed.

This attribute refers to your motivation to reduce costs by minimizing the investment of time necessary to make effective decisions. Two considerations become relevant in answering this question. The first is your overall managerial style and the importance you personally attach to considerations of time. The second, perhaps more important, consideration is the press of work that currently exists in your organization. In relatively lax periods, the opportunity costs involved in making decisions may be quite low. Time, in essence, is a free (or nearly free) commodity. In relatively busy periods, however, the same opportunity costs may be quite high. Time becomes a highly valued commodity.

Because these two considerations will be relatively stable from one day to the next, your answer to this attribute will also be relatively stable. Your answer would change only with: (1) an effort on your part to change your overall managerial style, or (2) a changing workload affecting you and your subordinates.

As a characteristic of you and the organizational situation rather than the immediate decision, remember that your answer to this question should not be affected by answers to any previous attributes. If, for example, you are not particularly motivated to conserve time (for example, attribute MT = 1), this answer should not change simply because of the existence of a time constraint (attribute TC) or because your subordinates are unavailable (attribute GD).

## MD: MOTIVATION–DEVELOPMENT

### HOW IMPORTANT IS IT TO YOU TO MAXIMIZE THE OPPORTUNITIES FOR SUBORDINATE DEVELOPMENT?

| 1 | 2 | 3 | 4 | 5 |
|---|---|---|---|---|
| **No Import** | **Low Import** | **Average Import** | **High Import** | **Critical Import** |

*Alternative Question*:

> How much importance do you attach to the broadening of your subordi-nates' problem-solving and technical skills?

Being involved in decisions can further develop the managerial and techni-cal skills of participants. Such involvement may also help develop teamwork, facilitate the effective working relationships among subordinates, and increase their understanding of, and commitment to, overall organizational goals. In a sense, the "human capital" of the organization may be increased by the appropri-ate use of participation in decision making. It should be noted that these benefits do not occur as a consequence of involvement in all decisions but they tend to be most evident when those who participate are exposed to new information, different approaches, and novel ideas.

This attribute refers to the importance to *you* of such benefits. In some countries, such as Japan with its history of lifetime employment, development of employees tends to be of much greater importance than in other countries where the relationships between employers and employees may be more tran-sient. However, not all of the differences are cultural. Like attribute MT, this attribute also reflects considerations of individual managerial style and organizational requirements. Some managers personally attach high importance to providing opportunities for subordinate growth and development. Alterna-tively, organizational needs may dictate such importance. Consider, for exam-ple, a manager facing promotion or transfer within the next six months. If a replacement is to be considered from the ranks of his or her subordinates, providing opportunities to build technical and managerial skills may ease the transition and assure the long-term effectiveness of the unit. Like attribute MT, these considerations will be relatively stable from one day to the next and your answer to this attribute will also be relatively stable. Your answer would only change with: (1) an effort on your part to change your overall managerial style, or (2) changing organizational needs for technical and manage-rial talent.

It is important to remember, however, that the importance of developing subordinates (attribute MD) and the importance of saving time (attribute MT) work at cross purposes in some problems. A manager having both motivations (such as, an answer of 5 to both questions) will achieve neither outcome to the maximum. Instead, a compromise balance between these two motivations is reached (as is also the case with MT = MD = 3).

**Note:** *Group problems* are those that affect the organizational lives of more than one of your subordinates, typically all of them (for example, which person to send to Chicago on a special assignment). *Individual problems* are those that affect only a single subordinate (such as, a client's dissatisfaction with the performance of one of your people).

# APPENDIX B

# A NORMATIVE MODEL OF PARTICIPATION IN DECISION MAKING

The application of the model to a decision problem requires three steps: (1) diagnosis of the situation, (2) rescaling of the problem attributes, and (3) solving the prescriptive equations. The first step requires that each question in Appendix A be answered on the five-point scales that are provided. The second step is to rescale these responses according to the following scheme:

## Rescaled Problem Attributes

| | IMPORTANCE | | | | |
|---|---|---|---|---|---|
| | 1 | 2 | 3 | 4 | 5 |
| Quality Requirement (QR) | 0 | 1 | 2 | 3 | 4 |
| Commitment Requirement (CR) | 0 | 1 | 2 | 3 | 4 |
| Motivation–Time (MT) | 0 | 1 | 2 | 3 | 4 |
| Motivation–Development (MD) | 0 | 1 | 2 | 3 | 4 |

| | No | | MAYBE | | YES |
|---|---|---|---|---|---|
| | 1 | 2 | 3 | 4 | 5 |
| Leader Information (LI) | −1 | −.75 | −.5 | −.25 | 0 |
| Problem Structure (ST) | −1 | −.75 | −.5 | −.25 | 0 |
| Commitment Probability (CP) | −1 | −.75 | −.5 | −.25 | 0 |
| Goal Congruence (GC) | −1 | −.75 | −.5 | −.25 | 0 |
| Conflict (CO) | 0 | .25 | .5 | .75 | 1 |
| Subordinate Information (SI) | −1 | −.75 | −.5 | −.25 | 0 |
| Time Constraints (TC) | 0 | — | — | — | 1 |
| Geographical Dispersion (GD) | 0 | — | — | — | 1 |

For QR, CR, MT, and MD, the above translation amounts to subtracting one from the original scale. For the remaining attributes, the linear transformation results in scales of either −1 to 0 or from 0 to 1.

The third step is to apply the model equations. In these equations, the following additional symbols are employed:

$$
\begin{array}{ll}
D_{Qual} & \text{Decision Quality} \\
D_{Comm} & \text{Decision Commitment} \\
D_{TP} & \text{Decision Time Penalty} \\
Cost & \text{Decision Costs} \\
Devpt & \text{Developmental Benefits} \\
D_{Eff} & \text{Decision Effectiveness} \\
O_{Eff} & \text{Overall Effectiveness}
\end{array}
$$

Additionally, the equations employ a set of coefficients or "functions" that vary with the decision process:

## Functions

| | GROUP | | | | | INDIVIDUAL | | | | | |
|---|---|---|---|---|---|---|---|---|---|---|---|
| | $f_1$ | $f_2$ | $f_3$ | $f_4$ | | $f_1$ | $f_2$ | $f_3$ | $f_4$ | $f_5$ | $f_6$ |
| AI | −1.0 | −1 | 0 | 1 | AI | −1.0 | −1 | 0 | 1 | 0 | −1.0 |
| AII | −0.9 | 0 | 0 | 1 | AII | −0.9 | 0 | 0 | 1 | 0 | −0.5 |
| CI | −0.5 | 0 | 0 | 1 | CI | −0.5 | 0 | 0 | 0 | 0 | −0.2 |
| CII | −0.2 | 0 | 0 | 0 | GI | −0.2 | 0 | 0 | 0 | −1 | 0 |
| GII | 0 | 0 | −1 | 0 | DI | 0 | 0 | −1 | 0 | 0 | −0.9 |

Separate sets of equations are employed depending on whether the situation is a group problem (that is, affecting more than one subordinate) or an individual problem (that is, affecting a single subordinate):

## Group Model

$$D_{Eff} = D_{Qual} + D_{Comm} - D_{TP}$$
$$O_{Eff} = D_{Eff} - Cost + Devpt$$
$$D_{Qual} = QR - QR/2\,[(f_2)(LI) + (f_4)(LI)(ST) + (f_3)(GC) + (f_1)(LI)(1 + GC)(CO)/2 + (f_3)(SI)/2]$$
$$D_{Comm} = CR - CR/2\,[(f_1)(CP) - (f_3 + f_4 + 1)(CO)(CP)/2]$$
$$D_{TP} = (D_{Qual} + D_{Comm})(1 + f_1)(TC)$$
$$Cost = (MT/6)\,[(1 + f_1)(1 - ST) - (f_3 + f_4 - 1)(CO)/2] - 5(f_4 - 1)(GD)$$
$$Devpt = (MD/24)(QR)\,[(1 + f_1) - (f_3 + f_4 - 1)(GC + 0.5)(CO)]$$

## Individual Model

$$D_{Eff} = D_{Qual} + D_{Comm} - D_{TP}$$
$$O_{Eff} = D_{Eff} - Cost + Devpt$$
$$D_{Qual} = QR - QR/2\,[(f_2)(LI) + (f_4)(LI)(ST) + 2(f_3)(GC) + 2(f_3)(SI) + (f_6)(LI)(1 + GC)(CO)/2 + (f_5)(GC)\,(1 + (CR)(CP)/4)]$$
$$D_{Comm} = CR - CR\,[(f_1)(CP)]$$
$$D_{TP} = [(D_{Qual} + D_{Comm})(1 + f_6) + (f_3)(QR)(SI + GC)]\,(TC)$$
$$Cost = (MT/6)\,[(1 + f_6)(1 - ST) - (f_5)(CO)]$$
$$Devpt = (MD/24)(QR)\,[(1 + f_1) - 2(f_5)(GC + 0.5)(CO)]$$

The preceding equations are applied five times in any given situation, once for each vector of functions (that is, coefficients) representing a decision process. The model's choice of decision process is that which produces the largest predicted overall effectiveness (that is, largest $O_{Eff}$). In the case of tied values, the model's preference is (from highest to lowest) AI, AII, CI, CII, and GII for group problems and AI, DI, AII, CI, and GI for individual problems.

$O_{Eff}$ is a prediction of the overall effectiveness of a decision process and includes its consequences on the "human capital" of the organization, specifically decision costs and subordinate development. A prediction that isolates the impact of different processes for the decision only, without their expected consequences on human capital, is *decision effectiveness* ($D_{Eff}$).

**Available Decision-Making Methods
(Group Problems)**

| SYMBOL | DEFINITION |
|---|---|
| AI | You solve the problem or make the decision yourself using the information available to you at the present time. |
| AII | You obtain any necessary information from subordinates, then decide on a solution to the problem yourself. You may or may not tell subordinates the purpose of your questions or give information about the problem or decision on which you are working. The input provided by them is clearly in response to your request for specific information. They do not play a role in the definition of the problem or in generating or evaluating alternative solutions. |
| CI | You share the problem with the relevant subordinates individually, getting their ideas and suggestions without bringing them together as a group. Then *you* make the decision. This decision may or may not reflect your subordinates' influence. |
| CII | You share the problem with your subordinates in a group meeting. In this meeting you obtain their ideas and suggestions. Then *you* make the decision, which may or may not reflect your subordinates' influence. |
| GII | You share the problem with your subordinates as a group. Together you generate and evaluate alternatives and attempt to reach agreement (consensus) on a solution. Your role is much like that of chairperson, coordinating the discussion, keeping it focused on the problem, and making sure that the critical issues are discussed. You can provide the group with information or ideas that you have, but you do not try to "press" them to adopt "your" solution, and you are willing to accept and implement any solution that has the support of the entire group. |

**Available Decision-Making Methods
(Individual Problems)**

| SYMBOL | DEFINITION |
|---|---|
| AI | You solve the problem or make the decision yourself using the information available to you at the present time. |
| AII | You obtain any necessary information from the subordinate, then decide on a solution to the problem yourself. You may or may not tell the subordinate the purpose of your questions or give information about the problem or decision on which you are working. The person's input is clearly in response to your request for specific information. He or she does not play a role in the definition of the problem or in generating or evaluating alternative solutions. |
| CI | You share the problem with the relevant subordinate, getting the person's ideas and suggestions. Then *you* make the decision. This decision may or may not reflect your subordinate's influence. |
| GI | You share the problem with one of your subordinates, and together you analyze the problem and arrive at a mutually satisfactory solution in an atmosphere of free and open exchange of information and ideas. You both contribute to the resolution of the problem with the relative contribution of each being dependent on knowledge rather than on formal authority. |
| DI | You delegate the problem to one of your subordinates, providing the person with any relevant information that you possess, but giving the person full responsibility for solving the problem alone. Any solution that the person reaches will receive your support. |

# REFERENCES

Allport, G. W. (1937). *Personality: A psychological interpretation.* New York: Holt.

Ashour, A. S. (1973). The contingency model of leader effectiveness: An evaluation. *Organizational Behavior and Human Performance, 9,* 339–355.

Bassan, D. M. (1979). *On the descriptive validity of the Vroom-Yetton normative model of leadership.* Unpublished master's thesis, Georgia Institute of Technology.

Blake, R. R., & Mouton, J. S. (1964). *The managerial grid.* Houston: Gulf.

Böhnisch, W. (1987). *Führung und Führungskräftetraining nach dem Vroom/Yetton-Modell.* Unpublished Habilitationsschrift, Johannes-Kepler-Universität, Linz, Austria.

Böhnisch, W., Jago, A. G., & Reber, G. (1987). Zur interkulturellen Validität des Vroom/Yetton-Modells. *Die Betriebswirtschaft, 47,* 85–93.

Böhnisch, W., Ragan, J. W., Reber, G., & Jago, A. G. (1986). *Predicting Austrian leader behavior from a U.S. measure of behavioral intent: A cross-cultural replication.* Manuscript submitted for publication.

Braverman, H. (1974). *Labor and monopoly capital: The degradation of work in the twentieth century.* New York: Monthly Review Press.

Clawson, D. (1980). *Bureaucracy and the labor process.* New York: Monthly Review Press.

Coch, L., & French, J. R. P., Jr. (1948). Overcoming resistance to change. *Human Relations, 1,* 512–532.

Cosier, R. A. (1981). Dialectical inquiry in strategic planning: A case of premature acceptance? *Academy of Management Review, 6,* 643–648.

Davis, J. H. (1969). *Group performance.* Reading, MA: Addison-Wesley.

Drucker, P. (1971). What we can learn from Japanese management. *Harvard Business Review, 49*(2), 110–122.

Drucker, P. (1973). *Management: Tasks, responsibilities, practices.* New York: Harper & Row.

Drucker, P. (1980). *Managing in turbulent times.* New York: Harper & Row.

Dunnette, M. D., Campbell, J. P., & Justaad, K. (1963). The effect of group participation on brainstorming effectiveness for two industrial samples. *Journal of Applied Psychology*, 47, 30–37.

Ettling, J. T., & Jago, A. G. (in press). Participation under conditions of conflict: More on the validity of the Vroom-Yetton model. *Journal of Management Studies*.

Evans, M. G. (1970). The effects of supervisory behavior on the path-goal relationship. *Organizational Behavior and Human Performance*, 5, 277–298.

Fiedler, F. E. (1967). *A theory of leadership effectiveness*. New York: McGraw-Hill.

Fiedler, F. E., & Chemers, M. M. (1984). *Improving leadership effectiveness: The LEADER MATCH concept*. New York: Wiley.

Field, R. H. G. (1979). A critique of the Vroom-Yetton contingency model of leadership behavior. *Academy of Management Review*, 4, 249–257.

Field, R. H. G. (1982). A test of the Vroom-Yetton normative model of leadership. *Journal of Applied Psychology*, 67, 523–532.

Filley, A. C., House, R. J., & Kerr, S. (1976). *Managerial process and organizational behavior* (2nd ed.). Glenview, IL: Scott, Foresman.

Follett, M. P. (1941). *Dynamic administration*. New York: Harper's.

French, J. R. P., Jr., Israel, J., & Ås, D. (1960). An experimental study on participation in a Norwegian factory. *Human Relations*, 13, 3–19.

French, J. R. P., Jr., & Raven, B. (1959). The bases of social power. In D. Cartwright (Ed.), *Studies in social power*. Ann Arbor, MI: Institute for Social Research.

Hersey, P., & Blanchard, K. (1982). *Management of organizational behavior: Utilizing human resources* (4th ed.). Englewood Cliffs, NJ: Prentice-Hall.

House, R. J. (1971). A path-goal theory of leader effectiveness. *Administrative Science Quarterly*, 16, 321–338.

House, R. J., & Dessler, G. (1974). The path-goal theory of leadership: Some *post hoc* and *a priori* tests. In J. G. Hunt & L. L. Larson (Eds.), *Contingency approaches to leadership*. Carbondale, IL: Southern Illinois University Press.

House, R. J., & Mitchell, T. R. (1974). Path-goal theory of leadership. *Journal of Contemporary Business*, 3, 81–97.

Iaffaldano, M. T., & Muchinsky, P. M. (1985). Job satisfaction and job performance: A meta-analysis. *Psychological Bulletin*, 97, 251–273.

Indvik, J. (1986). Path-goal theory of leadership: A meta-analysis. *Proceedings of the 46th Annual Meeting of the Academy of Management*, 189–192.

Jago, A. G. (1977). Hierarchical level determinants of participative leader behavior. *Dissertation Abstracts International*, 38, 2921B. (University Microfilms No. 77-27, 083).

Jago, A. G. (1978). Configural cue utilization in implicit models of leader behavior. *Organizational Behavior and Human Performance*, 22, 474–496.

Jago, A. G. (1979). Leadership skills and leadership styles: The influence of self-confidence on choices of participative decision making methods. *Proceedings of the 21st Annual Meeting of the Southwest Division of the Academy of Management*, 26–30.

Jago, A. G. (1980). Organizational characteristics and participative decision making. *Proceedings of the 12th Annual Conference of the American Institute of Decision Sciences*, 334–336.

Jago, A. G. (1981). An assessment of the deemed appropriateness of participative decision making for high and low hierarchical levels. *Human Relations*, 34, 379–396.

Jago, A. G., Ettling, J. T., & Vroom, V. H. (1985). Validating a revision to the Vroom/Yetton model: First evidence. *Proceedings of the 45th Annual Meeting of the Academy of Management, 220–223.*

Jago, A. G., & Vroom, V. H. (1975). Perceptions of leadership style: Superior and subordinate descriptions of decision making behavior. In J. G. Hunt & L. L. Larson (Eds.), *Leadership frontiers.* Kent, OH: Kent State University Press.

Jago, A. G., & Vroom V. H. (1977). Hierarchical level and leadership style. *Organizational Behavior and Human Performance, 18,* 131–145.

Jago, A. G., & Vroom, V. H. (1978). Predicting leader behavior from a measure of behavioral intent. *Academy of Management Journal, 21,* 715–721.

Jago, A. G., & Vroom, V. H. (1982). Sex differences in the incidence and evaluation of participative leader behavior. *Journal of Applied Psychology, 67,* 776–783.

Janis, I. L. (1982). *Victims of groupthink* (2nd ed.). Boston: Houghton Mifflin.

Kelley, H. H., & Thibaut, J. W. (1969). Group problem solving. In G. Lindzey & E. Aronson (Eds.), *The handbook of social psychology* (2nd ed.) (Vol. 4). Reading, MA: Addison-Wesley.

Kolb, D. A., Rubin, I. M., & McIntyre, J. M. (Eds.). (1984). *Organizational psychology: An experiential approach to organizational behavior* (4th ed.). Englewood Cliffs, NJ: Prentice-Hall.

Lafferty, J. C., & Eady, P. M. (1974). *The desert survival situation* (7th ed.). Plymouth, MI: Experiential Learning Methods.

Lawler, E. E. (1986). *High-involvement management.* San Francisco: Jossey-Bass.

Lawler, E. E., Renwick, P. A., & Bullock, R. J. (1981). Employee influence on decisions: An analysis. *Journal of Occupational Behavior, 2,* 115–123.

Leavitt, H. J. (1958). *Managerial psychology.* Chicago: University of Chicago Press.

Lewin, K. (1938). The conceptional representation and measurement of psychological forces. *Contributions to psychological theory* (Vol. 1, No. 4). Durham, NC: Duke University Press.

Lewin, K., Lippitt, R., & White, R. K. (1939). Patterns of aggressive behavior in experimentally created social climates. *Journal of Social Psychology, 10,* 271–301.

Liddell, W. W., Elsea, S. W., Parkinson, A. E., & Hackett, A. M. (1986). *A replication and refinement of "A test of the Vroom-Yetton normative model of leadership."* Manuscript submitted for publication.

Lieberman, S. (1956). The effects of changes in roles on the attitudes of role occupants. *Human Relations, 9,* 385–402.

Likert, R. (1961). *New Patterns of management.* New York: McGraw-Hill.

Locke, E. A., & Schweiger, D. M. (1979). Participation in decision making: One more look. In B. Staw (Ed.), *Research in organizational behavior* (Vol. 1). Greenwich, CT: JAI Press.

Machiavelli, N. (1964). *The prince* (M. Musa, Trans.). New York: St. Martin's Press.

Maier, N. R. F. (1963). *Problem solving discussions and conferences.* New York: McGraw-Hill.

Maier, N. R. F. (1967). Assets and liabilities in group problem solving: The need for an integrative function. *Psychological Review, 74,* 239–249.

Maier, N. R. F. (1970). *Problem solving and creativity in individuals and groups.* Belmont, CA: Brooks-Cole.

*Managing participation in organizations—MPO* [Computer program] (1987). Houston: Leadership Software, Inc.

Margerison, C., & Glube, R. (1979). Leadership decision-making: An empirical test of the Vroom and Yetton model. *Journal of Management Studies, 16*, 45–55.

Marrow, A. J. (1964). Risk and uncertainties in action research. *Journal of Social Issues, 20*, 5–20.

Mayo, E. (1933). *The human problems of an industrial civilization.* New York: Macmillan.

Mayo, E. (1945). *The social problems of an industrial civilization.* Cambridge: Harvard University Press.

McGregor, D. (1960). *The human side of enterprise.* New York: McGraw-Hill.

McMahon, J. T. (1972). The contingency model: Logic and method revisited. *Personnel Psychology, 25*, 697–710.

Miles, R. E. (1965). Human relations or human resources? *Harvard Business Review, 43*, 148–163.

Miner, J. B. (1984). The validity and usefulness of theories in an emerging organizational science. *Academy of Management Review, 9*, 296–306.

Mintzberg, H. (1973). *The nature of managerial work.* New York: Harper and Row.

Mitroff, I. I. (1982). Dialectic squared: A fundamental difference in perception of the meanings of some key concepts in social science. *Decision Science, 13*, 222–224.

Mitroff, I. I., & Mason, R. O. (1981). The metaphysics of policy and planning: A reply to Cosier. *Academy of Management Review, 6*, 649–651.

Montgomery, D. (1979). *Workers' control in America: Studies in the history of work, technology and labor struggles.* New York: Cambridge University Press.

Ouchi, W. G. (1981). *Theory Z.* Reading, MA: Addison-Wesley.

Osborn, A. F. (1963). *Applied imagination* (3rd ed.). New York: Charles Scribner's Sons.

St. Benedict. (1952). *The rule of St. Benedict* (Abbot J. McCann, Trans.). Westminster, MD: Newman Press.

Servan-Schreiber, J. J. (1968). *The American challenge.* New York: Atheneum.

Schriesheim, C., & Kerr, S. (1977). Theories and measures of leadership: A critical appraisal of current and future directions. In J. G. Hunt & L. L. Larson (Eds.), *Leadership: The cutting edge.* Carbondale, IL: Southern Illinois University Press.

Schweiger, D. M., & Leana, C. R. (1986). Participation in decision making. In E. Locke (Ed.), *Generalizing from the laboratory to field settings: Findings from research in industrial/ organizational psychology, organizational behavior, and human resource management.* Lexington, MA: Lexington Books.

Schweiger, D. M., Sandberg, W. R., & Ragan, J. W. (1986). Group approaches for improving strategic decision making: A comparative analysis of dialectical inquiry, devil's advocacy, and consensus. *Academy of Management Journal, 29*, 51–71.

Shaw, M. E. (1964). Communication networks. In L. Berkowitz (Ed.), *Advances in experimental psychology* (Vol. 1). New York: Academic Press.

Sherif, M. (1958). Superordinate goals in the reduction of intergroup conflict. *American Journal of Sociology, 63*, 349–358.

Smith, B. B. (1979). The TELOS program and the Vroom-Yetton model. In J. G. Hunt & L. L. Larson (Eds.), *Crosscurrents in leadership.* Carbondale, IL: Southern Illinois University Press.

Steers, R. M. (1977). Individual differences in participative decision-making. *Human Relations, 30*, 837–847.

Steiner, I. D. (1972). *Group process and productivity.* New York: Academic Press.

Taylor, D. W., Berry, P. C., & Block, C. H. (1958). Does group participation when using brainstorming facilitate or inhibit creative thinking? *Administrative Science Quarterly, 3,* 23–47.

Taylor, F. W. (1911). *Principles of scientific management.* New York: Harper's

Thorndike, R. (1938). On what types of tasks will groups do well? *Journal of Abnormal and Social Psychology, 33,* 409–413.

Tjosvold, D., Wedley, W. C., & Field, R. H. G. (1986). Constructive controversy, the Vroom-Yetton model, and managerial decision-making. *Journal of Occupational Behaviour, 7,* 125–138.

Van Fleet, D. D., & Yukl, G. A. (1986). A century of leadership research. In D. A. Wren & J. A. Pearce (Eds.), *Papers dedicated to the development of modern management.* Norman, OK: Academy of Management.

Vecchio, R. P. (1983). Assessing the validity of Fiedler's contingency model of leadership effectiveness: A closer look at Strube and Garcia. *Psychological Bulletin, 93,* 404–408.

Vroom, V. H. (1960). *Some personality determinants of the effects of participation.* Englewood Cliffs, NJ: Prentice-Hall.

Vroom, V. H. (1964). *Work and motivation.* New York: Wiley.

Vroom, V. H. (1970). Industrial social psychology. In G. Lindzey & E. Aronson (Eds.), *Handbook of social psychology* (Vol. 5). Reading, MA: Addison-Wesley.

Vroom, V. H. (1984). Reflections on leadership and decision-making. *Journal of General Management, 9*(3), 18–36.

Vroom, V. H., Grant, L. D., & Cotton, T. S. (1969). The consequences of social interaction in group problem solving. *Organizational Behavior and Human Performance, 4,* 77–95.

Vroom, V. H., & Jago, A. G. (1974). Decision making as a social process: Normative and descriptive models of leader behavior. *Decision Sciences, 5,* 743–769.

Vroom, V. H., & Jago, A. G. (1978). On the validity of the Vroom/Yetton model. *Journal of Applied Psychology, 63,* 151–162.

Vroom, V. H., & Jago, A. G. (1987). *The new leadership: Cases and manuals for use in leadership training.* New Haven, CT: Authors.

Vroom, V. H., & Yetton, P. W. (1973). *Leadership and decision-making.* Pittsburgh: University of Pittsburgh Press.

Vroom, V. H., Yetton, P. W., & Jago, A. G. (1976). *Leadership and decision making cases and manuals for use in leadership training* (3rd ed.). New Haven, CT: Authors.

Weiss, A. (1976). Leadership styles: Which are best when? *Supervisory Management, 21*(1), 2–8.

Williamson, H. F. (1952). *Winchester: The gun that won the West.* New York: Barnes.

Yetton, P. W., & Bottger, P. (1983). The relationships among group size, member ability, social decision schemes and performance. *Organizational Behavior and Human Performance, 32,* 145–159.

Yukl, G. A. (1981). *Leadership in organizations.* Englewood Cliffs, NJ: Prentice-Hall.

Zimmer, R. J. (1978). *Validating the Vroom-Yetton normative model of leader behavior in field sales force management and measuring the training effects of* TELOS *on the leader behavior of district managers.* Unpublished doctoral dissertation, Virginia Polytechnic Institute and State University.

# CREDITS

Tables 4–1 and 4–3 (and their reproductions in Appendix B), Tables 5–1, 5–2, 5–3 and Figures 5–1, 5–2, 5–3, and 5–4 are copyright 1974, 1976 by V. H. Vroom, P. H. Yetton, and A. G. Jago. Table 4–2 is copyright 1973 by Kepner-Tregoe, Inc. Figure 12–9 is copyright 1987 by Leadership Software, Inc. Figures 12–10, 12–11, 12–12, and 12–13 are copyright 1987 by V. H. Vroom and A. G. Jago. All are used with permission.

Preliminary versions of Appendices A and B were the basis of presentations made by the authors at the 44th Annual Meeting of the Academy of Management (copyright 1984 by V. H. Vroom and A. G. Jago).

# INDEX

## SUBJECT INDEX

*INTRODUCING—*

**MPO: Managing Participation in Organizations**™
**Software to Accompany Vroom and Jago's** *The New Leadership*

MPO is an "expert system" that brings Vroom and Jago's model alive. Whether used for training or as an on-line managerial decision aid, MPO takes the complexity out of decision analysis. Theoretically sound yet uniquely practical, MPO does more than recommend a course of managerial behavior, it stimulates your thinking about your behavior, the assumptions guiding it, and the organizational consequences. Some of MPO's features:

* ★ Over forty "Help" screens giving you as little or as much information as you need.
* ★ Menu driven. Fast and simple to use. Helpful User's Manual.
* ★ Displayed output can be printed or stored to disk.
* ★ Can be applied to over 1.5 million unique decision-making situations.

**Introductory Offer**

With this card, readers of **The New Leadership** can obtain MPO at the special rate of $39.00.*
(The not copy-protected version of MPO is available for $59.00.) Specify which version you wish and enclose a check or money order for the amount (please add $2.00 per unit for shipping/handling). Texas residents add applicable state and local taxes (Houston area residents add MTA tax). P.O.'s are accepted from Fortune 2000 companies, government agencies, and schools and universities.

*The copy-protected version of MPO requires that the original MPO disk remain in Drive A throughout execution of the program. The not copy-protected version has no such requirement and is therefore fully hard-disk compatible. MPO will operate on an IBM PC, AT, or true compatible. It requires a minimum of 256K of memory, DOS 2.0 or greater operating system, a minimum of one 5¼" disk drive, and either a monochrome or color monitor. A printer is optional. *MPO: Managing Participation in Organizations* is a trademark of Leadership Software, Inc. IBM PC and IBM AT are trademarks of International Business Machines Corporation.

---

Tear out this card and fill in all the necessary information. Then enclose this card in an envelope with your check or money order made out to Leadership Software, Inc. and mail to:

**LEADERSHIP
SOFTWARE, INC.
P.O. Box 271848
Houston, Texas 77277-1848**

Please send me: _____ copies of (circle one) copy-protected/ not copy-protected MPO. Enclosed is a check or money order for _____.

Name _____
(please print)

Address _____

_____

City _____ State _____ Zip _____